Georgia Real Estate License Exam Prep

All-in-One Review and Testing to Pass Georgia's AMP/PSI Real Estate Exam

2nd Edition

Stephen Mettling
David Cusic
Ryan Mettling
Joy Stanfill

Performance Programs Company
502 S. Fremont Ave., Ste. # 724
Tampa, FL, 33606
www.performanceprogramscompany.com

Material in this book is not intended to represent legal advice and should not be so construed. Readers should consult legal counsel for advice regarding points of law.

© 2020 by Performance Programs Company
502 S. Fremont Ave. Suite #724, Tampa, FL 33606
info@performanceprogramscompany.com
www.performanceprogramscompany.com

ISBN: 978-0915777389

Contents

Introduction

Welcome licensee candidates and future real estate professionals!

We know you have worked hard just to get here – you've completed or nearly completed your prelicense curricula, and now all you have to do is pass the state license exam. But easier said than done – and that's where we come in. We know the exam can be tough, and very nerve-wracking to prepare for. That's why we created the Georgia Real Estate License Exam Prep (GA-RELEP) the way we did. Since we have been managing real estate schools and developing curriculum for forty years, we know how all this works – or fails to work. Let us assure you – you made the right decision buying this publication to prepare for your Georgia exam. Here's why.

First, GA-RELEP is comprehensive in that it contains both key content review and testing practice. And the text review is Georgia-specific – not just simplistic national content, but terse, relevant and accurate state laws and regulations presented as a well-organized set of state 'key point reviews' ideal for pre-test memorization. But let's not dismiss the importance of the national content either. GA-RELEP's national key point reviews are a succinct compression of tested national principles and practices that comprise the national portion of state license exams from coast to coast. Our content is drawn from our own national textbook, Principles of Real Estate Practice – one of the most widely used principles textbooks in the country. Finally, our national content, as well as our question selection, is further tailored to the state testing outline promulgated by AMP/PSI for Georgia. Thus the breadth and depth of the key point reviews and test questions reflect the topic emphasis of your Georgia license exam.

A word about the test questions… GA-RELEP's testing practice section consists of ten national practice tests, three state practice tests, and one state exam sample test. The practice tests are roughly 50 questions in length and the simulation test is 100 questions. The test questions are designed to cover the content covered by the law reviews – which reinforces your learning of the total body of information tested by your state exam. The questions are direct, to the point, and designed to test your understanding. When you have completed a given test, you can check your answers against the answer key in Section VII. You may also note that each question's answer is accompanied by a brief explanation, or "rationale" to further reinforce your understanding.

Your particular study and testing practice strategy using GA-RELEP is up to you. But to fully exploit its comprehensive content coverage, you should try to review and memorize the key point reviews as much as possible. Then you should make every effort to take each exam, review your mistakes, and re-read the key point reviews that cover your weaker areas.

In the end, as you know, it's all up to you. Unlike other publications, we are not going to tell you that using this book will guarantee that you pass your state exam. It still takes hard work and study to pass. But we have done our best here to get you ready. Following that, the most we can do is wish you the best of success in taking and passing your state exam. So good luck!!

About the authors

For over forty five years, Stephen Mettling and David Cusic, PhD, have operated Performance Programs Company, one of the nation's most successful training organizations specializing in real estate program development. Mr. Mettling and Dr. Cusic have jointly written over 100 books, courses, and custom programs in all facets of real estate for some of the country's largest real estate schools, associations and organizations.

Mr. Mettling has also served as vice president and author for the country's largest real estate training and publishing organization. Under various capacities, he has managed the acquisition, development, and sale of national real estate textbooks and publications, as well as directed the country's largest affiliated group of real estate schools.

Dr. Cusic, an author and educator with international real estate training experience, has been engaged in vocation-oriented education since 1966. Specializing in real estate training since 1983, he has developed numerous real estate training programs for corporate and institutional clients around the country.

Ryan Mettling, partner and currently publisher of Performance Programs, is an accomplished online curriculum designer, author and course developer. He is responsible for the company's strategic planning, general management, printing and production, e-pub and retail platforms, and multi-channel marketing. Mr. Mettling is a member of the Real Estate Educators Association (REEA), and graduated Valedictorian from the University of Central Florida's College of Business Administration.

Joy Stanfill has had a far-reaching career in real estate that includes over 25 years of teaching experience. She has served as Managing Broker, Director of Education, and Real Estate School Administrator for schools in three states. Joy has authored, marketed and delivered courses in various markets. She has held numerous real estate designations. Most recently, she has served as Faculty Director for a large online real estate school.

Section I: National Principles & Law
Key Point Review

Rights

Land / Real Estate / Real Property

Land: surface, all *natural things* attached to it, subsurface, and air above the surface.

Real estate: land + **manmade** permanent attachments

Real property: real estate + bundle of rights

Constitution guarantees private ownership of real property.

Physical Characteristics of Real Estate

Immobility

- land cannot be moved from one site to another; its location is forever fixed

Indestructibility

- land is permanent and cannot be destroyed since by definition it extends below ground and into the sky
- since land is permanent, it does not depreciate
- only improvements depreciate and are insurable

Non-homogeneity

- land is non-homogeneous; no two parcels of land are exactly the same since they have a different location

---

Land versus Real Estate

Real Estate as Property

    The bundle of rights

        "PUTEE":

        P ossession

        U se

        T ransfer

        E xclusion

        E ncumberable

Legal Title v. Equitable title

Legal title

- full legal ownership of property and the bundle of rights as they apply to it
- contrasts with equitable title

Equitable title

- an interest that gives a lienholder or buyer the right to acquire legal title to a property if certain contractual conditions occur

Property characteristics:

- **property is** either real or personal
- property is either tangible or intangible

Real Property Rights

Airspace = air rights

Surface (of the earth) = surface rights

Subsurface = subsurface or mineral rights

Water rights:

- **Doctrine of Prior Appropriation**

    - state controls water usage
    - state grants usage permits

- **riparian rights (rivers and streams)**

    - applies to rivers and streams
    - if waterway is navigable: owners own land to water's edge
    - if waterway is not navigable: owners own land to midpoint of waterway

- **littoral rights (lakes and seas)**

    - applies to **seas and lakes**
    - abutting property owners own to **high water mark**
    - state owns underlying land

    Memory Tip: **R** : River Riparian   **L**: Lake Littoral

Real Property vs. Personal Property

Real property

- land
- fixtures
- attachments

Personal property

- chattels
- trade fixtures
- emblements

Differentiation criteria: item is real or personal property depending on why, how item is attached to the real estate. Depends on the owners'

- intention; adaptation; functionality; relationship of parties; contract provisions

Trade fixtures

- personal property items temporarily attached to real estate in order to conduct business

Emblements

- plants or crops that are considered personal property despite being attached to land

Conversion

- real to personal property referred to as severance
- personal to real property referred to as affixing

Factory-built housing – mobile homes and manufactured homes

- units are real or personal property: real if permanently affixed to ground; otherwise personal

Regulation Of Real Property Interests

Federal regulation
- grants rights of ownership
- controls broad land usage standards
- regulates anti-discrimination laws
  - examples: land grants; federal flood zones; fair housing laws; FHA; EPA

State regulation
- governs real estate business
- sets regional usage standards
  - examples: license laws; water rights; development regulation

Local regulation
- levies real estate taxes
- controls specific usage
  - examples: property assessing; zoning; building permits; tax levies

Judicial regulation
- applies case law and common law to disputes
- **contrasts with statutory law**

Interests & Estates

Interests and Estates in Land

Interests

Possession / Possessory

- estate in land

Non-possession / Non-possessory:

- private: encumbrance
- public: public interest

Estates In Land

- include right of possession
- leasehold = limited duration
- freehold: duration is not limited

Freehold (own)

- fee simple
  - absolute
  - defeasible
- life estates
  - conventional
  - legal

Leasehold (lease)

- estate for years
- periodic
- estate at will
- estate at sufferance

Freeholds

Fee simple	- *not limited* by one's lifetime - absolute: *highest* form of ownership interest - defeasible: *reverts* to previous owner per conditions
Life estate	- passes *to another* on death of named party - remainder: *named party* to receive estate - reversion: *previous owner* to receive estate
Conventional life estate	- *limited* to lifetime of life tenant/ named party - **ordinary**: estate passes to remainderman or previous owner when life tenant dies - **pur autre vie**: limited to lifetime of another, passes to remainderman or previous owner

Legal life estate	• created by operation of state law as opposed to a property owner's agreement
	• designed to protect family survivors
	• **Homestead:** rights to one's *principal residence*
	- laws protect homestead from creditors
	- family must occupy the homestead
	- cannot be conveyed by one spouse
	- endures over life of head of household
	- interests extinguished if property destroyed

Leaseholds

Estate for years	• specific, *stated duration*, per lease; expires at end of term
Periodic	• lease term *renews automatically* upon acceptance of rent; renews indefinitely if landlord accepts rent
Estate at will	• for *indefinite period* subject to rent payment; cancelable with notice
Estate at sufferance	• tenancy *against landlord's will* and without an agreement

Ownership

Forms of Ownership

Tenancy in severalty	• *sole* ownership of a freehold estate; passes to heirs
Tenancy in common	• co-tenants individually own undivided interests
	• *any ownership share possible*
	• no survivorship
	• can convey to outside parties
Joint tenancy	• equal undivided interest jointly owned
	• survivorship (may require express provision)
	• requires *four unities* to create: time, title, interest, possession
Tenancy by the entireties	• *husband and wife* own equal undivided interest
	• Now applies to same-sex couples in some states
Community property	• *joint property ownership* by spouses as opposed to separate property

Joint Tenancy & Four Unities

Unity of ownership	• owners hold single title jointly
Equal ownership	• owners always hold equal shares
Transfer	• may transfer to new owner as a tenancy in common interest with remaining joint tenants
Survivorship	• on death, interests and rights pass to other joint tenants
Creation	• requires "four unities," *PITT*:

1. *P*ossession: acquire same possessory rights
2. *I*nterest: acquire equal, undivided interests
3. *T*ime: acquire interests at same time
4. *T*itle: acquire interests with same deed

Community Property

Separate	**Community**
• acquired *before marriage*	• all other property earned or acquired during the marriage
• acquired by *gift or inheritance*	
• acquired with *separate-property funds*	
• *income* derived from *separate property*	

Estates in Trust

- *trustor* gives title, deed, trust agreement to trustee
- *trustee* renders fiduciary duties to trustor and beneficiary
- *beneficiary* receives ownership benefits
- **living / testamentary trust** – conveyance of real, personal property during one's lifetime
- **land trust** – grantor and beneficiary are same party; beneficiary uses, controls property but does not appear on public records

Condominiums

- ownership of a *unit of airspace* plus an *undivided interest* in the *common elements* as tenant in common with other owners
- may be sold, encumbered or foreclosed *without affecting other unit owners*
- creation: by developer's declaration
- individually taxed
- managed by condo association
- owners share common area expenses

Cooperatives

- ownership of
  - *shares in owning corporation*
  - *proprietary lease* in a unit
- corporation has sole, undivided ownership
- owners potentially liable for expenses of entire co-op; creditors may foreclose on entire property

Time Shares

- lease or ownership interest in property for periodic use on a scheduled basis
- **lease**: tenant leases property per the lease's schedule
- **freehold**: tenants in common own undivided interests, pay expenses per separate agreement

Encumbrances & Liens

Encumbrances

- non-possessory interests limiting legal owner's rights
- do not include possession
- two types:
  - encumbrances that affect use
  - encumbrances that affect ownership, value, transfer

Encumbrances affecting use: easements, encroachments, licenses, deed restrictions

Encumbrances affecting ownership, value, transfer: liens, deed conditions

Easements

Characteristics	- rights to use portions of another's property - affirmative easement: allows a use - negative easement: prohibits a use
Appurtenant	- *attaches* to the estate - *dominant* tenement's *right to use* or restrict adjacent *servient* tenement - *by necessity*, to *landlocked* owners - party wall easement in a shared structure: to not damage or destroy
In gross	- *does not attach* to the estate - **personal**-- not transferrable, ends upon death of easement holder - **commercial**-- transferrable, granted to a business

14

By prescription	• property used without permission; can come to exist regardless of owner's consent
	• obtainable through *continuous, open, adverse use* over a period of time which varies by state
License	• *personal* right to use a property
	• does not attach
	• non-transferrable
	• revocable
	• ceases upon death of owner

Encroachments

- unauthorized intrusions of one owner's real property onto another's
- may require survey to detect
- may become prescriptive easements if not remedied over prescription period

Deed restrictions

- conditions, covenants imposed on property by deed or subdivision plat
- goes with the property upon transfer
- established to control quality, standards of a subdivision
- apply to land use, type of structure, setbacks, minimum house size, etc.

Deed conditions

- created upon property transfer
- if violated, ownership may revert to previous owner

Deed covenants

- created by mutual agreement
- enforceable by injunction

Liens

- claims attaching to real and personal property as security for debt
- recorded on title effectively reducing equity in the amount of the lien
- does not convey ownership unless a mortgage in a title theory state
- lien attaches to the property
- property can be encumbered by multiple liens
- lien terminates upon payment, recording satisfaction

Lien types and characteristics

Voluntary / involuntary	• mortgage lien / tax lien
General / specific	• against any & all assets / against car or house
Superior / junior	• paid before juniors / paid after superiors by date of recording

15

Lien Priority

- order in which liens against a property are satisfied
- determined by superior v junior class and by date of recordation
- the highest priority lien is paid by foreclosure proceeds before any other lien

Superior Liens by rank (not by date of recordation; paid before junior liens)	Junior Liens (by date of recording)
<ul><li>real estate tax liens</li><li>special assessment liens</li><li>federal estate tax liens</li><li>state inheritance tax liens</li></ul>	<ul><li>federal income tax liens</li><li>judgment liens</li><li>mortgage liens</li><li>vendors' liens</li><li>mechanics' liens (priority by date work performed)</li></ul>

Foreclosure

- Liquidation or transfer of collateral property by judicial, non-judicial, or strict foreclosure

Mortgage lien foreclosure	<ul><li>liquidation of collateral property by *judicial, non-judicial,* or *strict* foreclosure</li></ul>
Judicial foreclosure	<ul><li>lawsuit by creditor followed by court-ordered public sale to enforce lien; may entail *deficiency judgments, redemption rights*</li><li>**deficiency judgment** -- judgment by court on borrower to forfeit other property to pay off any shortfalls from foreclosure</li><li>**redemption right** -- borrower's right to reclaim property before or after foreclosure sale</li></ul>
Non-judicial foreclosure	<ul><li>*"power of sale"* granted to lender; no suit; *no deficiency*</li></ul>
Strict foreclosure	<ul><li>court orders *legal transfer of title directly to lender* without public sale</li></ul>
Deed in lieu of foreclosure	<ul><li>*"power of sale"* granted to lender; no suit; *no deficiency* judgment; *no redemption* period after sale</li></ul>

Lien vs. Title Theory State

- **lien theory state** -- lender of mortgaged property holds equitable title rather than legal title; borrower holds legal title.

- **title theory state** – lender holds legal title to the mortgaged property until the mortgagor satisfies the terms and obligations of the loan.

Legal vs. Equitable Title

- **Legal title:** owner enjoys full bundle of rights
- **Equitable title:** party can obtain legal title subject to agreements with creditors

Notice

Notice:

- how ownership is evidenced to the public

Actual notice:

- *knowledge acquired directly* through demonstrable evidence, e.g., presenting or inspecting a deed, visiting a party in possession

Constructive notice:

- *knowledge one could have obtained*, as presumed by law; imparted by recording in public records "for all to see"

Voluntary / Involuntary Title Transfer

Voluntary transfer	Involuntary transfer
- deed - will - public grant	- descent (without will, with heirs) - escheat (without will nor heirs) - foreclosure (loan default) - eminent domain (public good) - adverse possession (hostile, open use)

Deeds of Conveyance

Key characteristics:

- grantor grants deed to grantee
- legal title transfers upon intentional delivery and grantee's acceptance

Deed Validity

Requirements:

1. grantor
2. grantee
3. in writing
4. legal description
5. granting clause
6. consideration
7. grantor's signature
8. acknowledgement
9. delivery and acceptance

Deed Clauses

Premises	• granting
Habendum	• type of estate
Reddendum	• restrictions
Tenendum	• other property included

Deed Types

Bargain and sale	"I own but won't defend"
General warranty	"I own and will defend"
Special warranty	"I own and warrant myself only"
Quitclaim	"I may or may not own, and won't defend"
Special purpose deeds	used for different purposes, interests conveyed, or by different parties

Transfer Tax

- **Documentary stamp tax:** tax on conveyance of real property based on price of property conveyed
- Facilitates ad valorem assessment
- Payment evidenced on deed

Wills

Key characteristics

- will transfers estate to heirs upon death
- maker = owner; devisor or testator
- heir = beneficiary or devisee

Types of wills

- witnessed: in writing and two witnesses
- holographic: will in testator's handwriting
- nuncupative: oral will written by witnesses; generally not valid for property transfer

Validity of will

- legal age; mentally competent; entitled "last will & testament;" signed, witnessed, voluntary

Testate / Intestate

Order of Title Transfer

Dies testate with heirs:	• first to creditors
	• then to homestead
	• then **to heirs by will**

18

Dies intestate with heirs:	• first to creditors
	• then to homestead
	• then *to heirs by laws of descent*
Dies intestate, no heirs:	• first to creditors
	• then **to state by escheat**

Involuntary Title Transfer

Adverse possession

- "unwanted owner" may claim ownership to a property
- must show "claim of right" as reason
- must be notorious possession (unconcealed)
- must be hostile (possessor claims ownership)
- must be continuous for a statutory period of time

Title Records

Features

- Instruments affecting title must be recorded
- Gives public notice of ownership, condition of title
- Determines property marketability
- Protects lienholders; establishes chronology for lien priority

Key terms
- chain of title – successive property owners from original grant to present
- cloud on title – unrecorded claims
- suit to quiet title – lawsuit to settle claims
- abstract of title: written chronology of recorded owners, transfers, encumbrances

Forms Of Title Evidence

- title insurance (best form of evidence)
- attorney's opinion of abstract
- title certificates
- Torrens registration

Leases

Key characteristics

- lease is both an instrument of conveyance and contract of covenants between tenant and landlord
- lease conveys **temporary, exclusive** use of premises in exchange for rent and right of reversion

Tenant rights and obligations

- rights: use, possession, quiet enjoyment, profits
- tenant obligations: pay rent; maintain premises; follow rules

Landlord rights and obligations

- rights: receive rent; repossess upon expiration; monitor tenant compliance
- obligations: property condition, habitability, support services

Estate Types

Gross lease	• landlord pays expenses; tenant pays higher rent than net
Net lease	• tenant pays some or all expenses; rent is less than gross
Percentage lease	• landlord receives rent minimum plus percentage of retailer's sales
Residential lease	• gross lease hybrid; short term; uniform terms reflect landlord-tenant standards
Ground lease	• landlord owns and leases ground but does not own improvements
Proprietary lease	• for cooperative unit owners; indefinite term; assigned to new unit owner on sale
Leasing of rights	• leasehold transfer of rights for limited use; examples: air, mineral, water rights

Lease Termination

Causes	- default	- term expiration
	- notice	- voluntary agreement
	- property destruction	- condemnation
	- death	- abandonment under certain conditions

Uniform Residential Landlord and Tenant Act

Purposes	• balance landlord and tenant rights • standardize leases • have uniform eviction procedures • protect tenants • serve as model for state legislation
Leases	• clear lease terms • fair market rent • cannot waive rights
Deposits	• limits on amounts • tenant's right to interest • rules and deadlines for returning
Landlord Obligations	• bargain in good faith • provide maintenance and repairs • comply with building codes • provide safety and access • procedure for delivery of notices
Tenant Obligations	• maintain condition • abide by rules and regulations • no damage or abuse • abide by approved uses • no disturbance of other tenants

Land Use

Planning and Zoning Definitions

Building code:	A standard of construction of an improved property established by local government officials
Certificate of occupancy:	A document confirming that a newly constructed or renovated property has fully complied with all building codes and is ready for occupancy
Concurrency:	A planning policy that requires developers to correct foreseen negative impacts of a development during the construction period of the project itself rather than afterward
Condemnation:	1. A decree that a parcel of private property is to be taken for public use under the power of eminent domain. 2. A government order that a is no longer fit for use and must be demolished.
Deed restriction:	A provision in a deed that limits or places rules on how the deeded property may be used or improved
Eminent domain:	A power of a government entity to force the sale of private property for subsequent public use
Land use control:	Regulation of how individual owners use property in a municipality or planning district. Control patterns are in accordance with a master plan

Master plan:	An amalgamated land use plan for a municipality, county, or region which incorporates community opinion, the results of intensive research, and the various land use guidelines and regulations of the state. Acts as a blueprint for subsequent zoning ordinances and rulings
Non-conforming use :	A legal or illegal land use that is not consistent with the current zoning ordinance
Police power:	A government's legal authority to create, regulate, tax, and condemn real property in the interest of the public's health, safety, and welfare
Restriction:	A limitation on the use of a property imposed by deed, zoning, state statute, or public regulation
Special exception:	A land use in conflict with current zoning that is authorized because of its perceived benefit to the public welfare
Variance:	A land use that conflicts with current zoning but is authorized for certain reasons, including undue hardship to comply and minimal negative impact to leave it alone
Zoning ordinance:	A municipal land use regulation

Land Use Planning

Goals of land use control

- preserve property values; promote highest and best use; safeguard public health, safety and welfare; control growth; incorporate community consensus
- process: develop plan; create administration; authorize controls

The master plan

- long term growth and usage strategies; often required by state law
- local plans fuse municipal goals and needs with state and regional laws

Planning objectives

- control growth rates: how much growth will occur and at what rate
- control growth patterns: type of growth desired, where it should be located
- accommodate demand for services and infrastructure

Plan development

- research trends and conditions; blend local and state objectives into master plan

Planning management

- commission makes rules, approves permits, codes, and development plans

Public Land Use Controls

Zoning

- "police power" granted by state-level enabling acts; zoning ordinance: creates zones, usage restrictions, regulations, requirements
- enables urban land managers to create separate land uses that do not conflict with one another nor create incompatible adjacencies

Types of zone

- residential, commercial, industrial, agricultural, public, PUD
- residential zoning regulates *density*, or number of dwellings in an area
- commercial zoning regulates *intensity*, or how much commercial activity is permitted in relation to size of the site

Zoning administration

- Zoning Board of Adjustment oversees rule administration and appeals

Zoning Appeals

- **Nonconforming use:** legal if use existed prior to zone creation, illegal otherwise
- **Variance:** use exception granted based on hardship
- **Special exception:** based on public interest
- **Amendment:** change of zones; rezoning

Eminent Domain

- allows a government entity to purchase a fee or easement interest in privately owned real property for the **public good** and for **public use** in exchange for "just compensation"

Planned Unit Development (PUD)

- PUD zoning designed to regulate use of whole tracts of land with a singular design
- Design purposes are to achieve optimum space efficiency and open space

Subdivision Regulation

- plat of subdivision and relevant requirements must be met and approved; must meet FHA requirements for insured financing
- location, grading, alignment, surfacing, street width, highways
- sewers and water mains
- lot and block dimensions
- building and setback lines
- public use dedications
- utility easements
- ground percolation

Building Codes

- comprehensive onsite and offsite construction and materials standards; must be met to receive certificate of occupancy

Environmental Restrictions

- flood control; solid waste disposal; air quality; water quality; marine protection; noise control; toxic substances controls; lead paint; CERCLA; Superfund

---

Zoning Appeals

Zoning Board of Adjustment:	oversees rule administration and appeals
Nonconforming use:	legal if use existed prior to zone creation, illegal otherwise
Variance:	use exception granted based on hardship
Special exception:	based on public interest
Amendment:	change of zones; rezoning

Environmental Laws

Legislation	Date	Regulated
Solid Waste Disposal Act (later part of RCRA)	1965 (1976, 1999, 2002)	landfills
Air Quality Act, Clean Air Act	1967 (1970)	air quality standards
National Environmental Policy Act (NEPA)	1969 (1970)	created EPA
Flood Control Act	amended 1969	building in flood zones; flood insurance
Resource Recovery Act	1970	solid waste disposal
Water Quality Improvement Act	1970	dumping in navigable waters; wetlands
Water Pollution Control Act amendment	1972	dumping in navigable waters; wetlands
Clean Water Act	1972 (1977)	dumping in navigable waters; wetlands
Lead-based paint ban (US Consumer Product Safety Commission rule)	1978	lead-based paint in residences
PCB ban (EPA rule)	1979	polychlorinated biphenyls
RCRA amendment	1984	underground storage tanks
Comprehensive Environmental Response, Compensation and Liability Act (CERCLA)	1980	hazardous waste disposal
Superfund Amendment and Reauthorization Act	1986	hazardous waste cleanup costs
Asbestos ban (EPA rule)	1989	asbestos in building materials
Residential Lead-based Paint Hazard Reduction Act (EPA and HUD rule)	1992 (1996)	lead-based paint disclosure and treatment
Flood Insurance Reform Act	1994	flood insurance in flood zones
Brownfields legislation	2002	industrial site cleanup

Legal Descriptions

Purpose

- to accurately locate and identify the boundaries of a parcel of real property to a degree acceptable by courts of law in the state where the property is located
- general criterion is that it alone provides sufficient data for a surveyor to locate the parcel

Metes and Bounds Method

- describes perimeter by landmarks, monuments, distances, angles
- usable within rectangular survey system
- starting at point of beginning (POB), follow perimeter, **return to POB**

Lot and Block System (Recorded Plat Method)

- used to describe properties in residential, commercial, industrial subdivisions
- tracts of land divided into lots, then grouped into blocks

Rectangular Survey System

Key points:	• simplify and standardize property descriptions • all land in system surveyed using longitude and latitude lines • lines created uniform grids of squares called townships
Meridians:	• north-south lines six miles apart
Parallels:	• east-west lines six miles apart
Range:	• north-south strip between meridians
Tier:	• east-west strip of area between parallels; also called township strip
Township:	• the six-mile by six-mile square at the intersection of a range and a tier
Section of a township:	• a 1 mile x 1 mile square; 1 section = 640 acres; 36 sections per township
Fractions of a section:	• going from the smallest to largest unit, indicate size and location within successively larger quarters or halves of the section: E 1/2 of the NE 1/4 of the NE 1/4 of Section 8

Contract Law

Contract Defined

- An agreement between two or more parties who have a "meeting of the minds," and have pledged to perform (or refrain from performing) some act
- A *valid* contract is *legally enforceable* by meeting certain requirements of contract law.
- If a contract does not meet requirements, it is not valid and the parties to it cannot resort to a court of law to enforce its provisions

Contract Status

Valid

- meets all requirements

Valid but unenforceable

- certain oral contracts; if performed, cannot change outcome

Void

- not valid; unenforceable

Voidable

- may be rescinded due to subsequent discoveries: if performed, cannot change outcome

Contract Validity

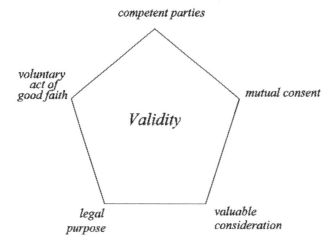

Competent parties

- legal age
- mental competency
- legitimate authority

Mutual consent

clear and unequivocal **offer and acceptance** with an underlying **meeting of the minds**

Valuable consideration

- exchange of valuable consideration for performance by the other party; not "love and affe

Legal purpose

- promise, intent and content must be lawful; if illegal, contract is void – cannot contract to the law

Voluntary, good faith

- no duress, coercion, fraud or misrepresentation

Conveyance Contract Requirements

- must be in writing
- must contain legal description
- must be signed by one or more parties
- **exception: per Statute of Frauds,** leases for one year or less may be verbal and still be enforceable

---

Offer / Counteroffer / Acceptance

Offer

- intention to enter into contract
- must contain all intended terms
- must be in writing
- expires in "reasonable time" or date and time specified

Acceptance

- unequivocal and manifest agreement to offer
- no changes to offer whatsoever
- signed, preferably dated

Completed contract

- communication of acceptance to offeror
- if by mail, offer is communicated upon mailing

Counteroffer

- new or amended terms of a received offer
- original offer is void

Revoking an offer

- may be done at any time prior to offeree's communication of acceptance

Termination of an offer

- acceptance; rejection; revocation; expiration; counteroffer; death or insanity of either party

---

Contract Assignment

- assignable unless expressly prohibited or contract is a personal service contract (listings)

Contract Preparation

- restricted unless licensed as attorney or a party to the contract
- licensees must be aware of contract preparation restrictions in the states where they operate

---

Contract Classifications

Oral vs. written

- oral, or parol, contract may not be enforceable

Express vs. implied

- express: all terms expressly agreed to
- implied: unintentional agreement deemed to exist due to terms implied by actions

Bilateral vs. unilateral

- bilateral: both parties promise to perform
- unilateral: one party performs only if other party performs

Executed vs. executory

- executed: fully performed
- executory: performance yet to be completed

Termination

Causes

- performance
- infeasibility
- mutual agreement
- cooling-period rescission
- revocation
- abandonment
- lapse of time
- invalidity of contract
- breach of contract

Breach & Remedies

Rescission	• cancel contract; return deposits
Forfeiture	• defaulting party gives up something according to contract terms
Liquidated damages	• damages due a damaged party as stated in contract
Suit for damages	• civil suit for money damages not covered by contract
Specific performance	• suit to force party to fulfill contract promises

Agency

The Agency Relationship In Real Estate

- principal (client) hires agent (broker) to find ready, willing, and able customer (buyer, seller, tenant, landlord)
- client – agent relationship governed by fiduciary duties of trust, confidence, good faith

Universal / General / Special

Universal	• represent in all matters • can contract for principal
General	• represent in business matters • agent can contract for principal
Special	• represent in single business transaction • normally agent cannot contract for principal • characterizes the brokerage relationship

Agency Creation

- Express written **or oral** agreement (listing)

  - established for a specified transaction
  - contains an express expiration

- **Implied** agreement by actions of either party

  - can be intentional or unintentional
  - can obligate the agent to fiduciary duties and professional standards of care
  - not allowed to exist in some states

Termination

- **Voluntary**
    - fulfillment
    - expiration
    - mutual agreement

- **Involuntary**
    - incapacity
    - abandonment or destruction of property
    - renunciation
    - breach
    - bankruptcy
    - revocation of license

Duties & Obligations

Agent's Fiduciary Duties to Client

- **Skill, care and diligence:**   proactive; competent; act within bounds of expertise

- **Loyalty:**   place client interest above customer and self

- **Obedience:**   provided actions, instructions are legal

- **Confidentiality:**   extends beyond listing term indefinitely

- **Full disclosure;**   property condition; customers; material facts

- **Accounting;**   proper handling of monies and documents

Obligations Owed Customers

- honesty and fair dealing
- reasonable care and skill
- proper disclosure

Breach of duty: potential consequences

- loss of listing; compensation; license suspension, suit for damages

Misrepresentation and Fraud

Puffing – licensee boasting about property's benefits

Fraud

- misstatement or failure to disclose material fact
- knowledge that statement was false or fact should have been disclosed

30

- party relied on misstatement
- party was damaged by misstatement

Misrepresentation – misstatement or concealment of fact

- intentional misrepresentation: **purposeful misstatement** of material fact
- intentional omission: **purposeful concealment** of material fact
- negligent misrepresentation: **unintended misstatement** that agent should have known
- negligent omission: **unintended concealment** that agent should have known

---

Single / Dual / Sub / No Agency

Single agency
- seller or buyer agency
- tenant or landlord representation

Subagency
- outside brokers and agents who help listing agent
- listing broker's own agents
- (disallowed in some states)

Dual agency
- representing both sides
- potentially illegal or conflict of interest
- must disclose & obtain written consent

- **Types of dual agency**
  - voluntary by consent
  - involuntary by actions of parties (implied agency)
  - duties: all but full disclosure and loyalty

- **Dual agency duties**
  - disclose to both parties; obtain written consent
  - owes duties of skill, care, diligence, obedience, confidentialit accounting
  - does not owe duties of full disclosure and loyalty; exclusive representation of client's interest

No agency
- "facilitator" or "transaction broker"
- representing neither party in the transaction
- duties to both parties: accounting; skill, care and diligence; honesty ar fair dealing; disclosures affecting property value

---

Disclosure Rules

(Note: Agency disclosure rules vary by state – see State section for laws in your state.)

Objectives of disclosure
- declare
- explain
- offer choice
- obtain documented consent

Seller agent disclosures to client

- in writing
- on or before listing is executed

Seller agent disclosures to customer

- in writing
- upon first face-to-face contact, or upon substantive communication, depending on state law
- oral disclosure permitted but must have written follow-up

Buyer agent disclosures to seller

- in writing
- upon first contact with listing agent or seller
- substantive contact is assumed

Dual agent disclosures

- "informed, written consent"
- may not disclose price or financing positions or motivations unless authorized

Facilitator disclosures

- on becoming transaction broker or on substantive contact, whichever is first

Listing Agreements

Key characteristics	• broker's **enforceable contract** of employment • establishes **special agency** relationship • defines **roles** of parties • creates **fiduciary duties** for the agent • describes agent's **scope of authority**
Parties	• listing broker-- fiduciary of buyer client or seller client • subagent-- fiduciary of listing broker's client • customer-- non-fiduciary principal in transaction
Fiduciary duties	• to client: loyalty; obedience; disclosure; care; diligence; accounting • to customer: honesty, care and disclosure
Authority	• limited agency agreement • broker may not contract for client unless specifically authorized • clients liable only for broker's acts within scope of authority
Contract law	• unilateral contract • oral listing is valid and enforceable • exclusive listing in some states must be written to be enforceable • personal service contract-- not assignable

Types

Exclusive right-to-sell

- given to one broker
- usually must be written
- must expire
- broker gets commission if property transfers during period

Exclusive agency

- exclusive excepting owner
- oral or written
- must expire
- broker gets commission unless owner sells

Open listing

- non-exclusive
- oral or written
- no stated expiration
- procuring cause gets commission
- no commission if client procures customer

Net listing

- all sale proceeds above a seller's minimum price go to the broker
- discouraged, if not illegal

Multiple listing

- listing placed in MLS
- owners consent to rules and provisions of MLS

Buyer agency agreements

- create a fiduciary relationship with the buyer
- if exclusive, buyer agrees to only work with the buyer representative in procuring a property
- must have an expiration date along with other requirements of a valid listing

---

Compensation / Termination

Compensation
- negotiated between agent and principal
- where disputed among agents, agent with procuring cause is owed commission
- based on results: find ready willing and able customer

Causes for termination
- performance
- infeasibility
- mutual agreement
- revocation
- abandonment
- breach
- expiration
- invalidity
- incapacitation or death
- involuntary transfer
- destruction of property

33

Agent's performance	• may perform only authorized tasks
	• must verify owner and property data
	• may delegate duties to salespeople and other brokers
Revoking a listing	• clients always have power to revoke during period
	• may incur liability for commission or damages

Brokerage

Who May Broker

(Varies from state to state)

Yes

1. sole proprietorship
2. for-profit corporation
3. general or limited partnership
4. joint venture

No

1. non-profit corporation
2. business trust
3. cooperative association

Broker-Agent Relationship

Legal relationship

- salesperson
  - is agent & fiduciary of broker
  - acts in broker's name
  - is subagent of client

- salesperson may not
  - have two employers
  - be paid by other parties
  - bind clients contractually

Salesperson's employment status

- employee or independent contractor
- defined by agreement

Obligations and responsibilities

- agent to broker:
  - obtain & sell listings
  - follow policies and employment provisions
  - promote ethics and broker's reputation
- broker to agent:
  - provide data, office support, compensation, training
  - uphold ethics, policies, and employment agreement

Agent compensation

- commissions per schedule after splits with cooperating brokers

---

Commingling & Conversion

Not allowed !!

Commingling
- mixing broker's personal or business funds with trust funds
- includes failure to deposit funds in a timely manner

Conversion
- using trust funds for personal or business purposes

Advertising Requirements

- no misleading ads
- ads must contain broker's ID
- broker is responsible for content
- no blind ads (concealed identity)
- must disclose if agent owns property

Telephone Consumer Protection Act

- regulates unsolicited telemarketing calls
- solicitors must identify themselves, how they can be contacted
- must comply with any do-not-call request
- consumers can place phone numbers on Do-Not-Call list

CAN-SPAM Act
- bans sending unwanted email 'commercial messages' to wireless devices
- requires express prior authorization
- requires an 'opt out' choice to terminate the sender's messages

---

Anti-Trust Laws

Sherman, Clayton anti-trust laws
- NO restraint of trade; monopolies;
- predatory pricing; exclusive dealing

no collusion:
- two or more businesses conspiring to disadvantage a competitor

no price fixing:
- two or more brokers agreeing to fix prices

no market allocation:
- colluding to restrict competition in a market segment in exchange for a competitor's reciprocal agreement

Sale Contracts

Key characteristics

- binding, bilateral contract for purchase and sale
- the enforceable "blueprint" for closing
- contract is executory, or to be fulfilled
- expires upon closing
- must be in writing
- for validity, must
  - contain valuable consideration
  - identify property
  - be signed by all

Creation / Deposit / Contingencies

Creation
- created by unqualified acceptance of an offer
- gives buyer equitable title, and power to force specific performance

Deposit, or earnest money escrow
- secures contract validity and buyer's equitable interest
- varies in amount
- deposit controlled by disinterested party who must act according to escrow instructions

Contingencies
- conditions that must be met for the contract to be enforceable
- must be clear
- have expiration date
- require diligence to satisfy

Buyer default
- seller can cancel, claim liquidated damages or sue for specific performance (i.e., buyer's deposit)

Seller default
- buyer can cancel or sue for damages or specific performance

Primary Clauses

- parties
- consideration
- legal description
- price and terms
- loan approval provisions
- earnest money
- escrow
- closing and possession dates
- conveyed interest

- type of deed
- title evidence
- property condition warranty/disclosures
- closing costs
- damage and destruction
- default
- broker's agency disclosure and who pays commission
- seller's representations: property condition, marketable title

Options

Essentials	<ul><li>optionor gives option to optionee to buy at a given time and price; optionee must pay for option right</li><li>unilateral contract: seller must perform, buyer need not</li><li>if option is exercised, option becomes bilateral sale contract</li><li>options are assignable</li></ul>
Contract requirements	<ul><li>non-refundable consideration for the option right</li><li>price and terms of the sale</li><li>option period expiration date</li><li>legal description</li><li>must be in writing</li><li>must meet contract validity requirements</li><li>option should be recorded</li></ul>
Common clause provisions	<ul><li>how to exercise option</li><li>terms of option money forfeiture</li><li>how option money will be applied to purchase price</li></ul>

Contract for Deed

Essentials	<ul><li>purchase price is paid over time in installments</li><li>seller retains title, buyer takes possession, equitable title</li><li>at end of period, buyer pays balance, gets legal title</li></ul>
Interests and rights	<ul><li>seller may encumber or assign interest</li><li>seller remains liable for underlying mortgage</li><li>buyer may use, possess, or profit</li><li>buyer must make periodic payments, maintain the property, and purchase at the end of the term</li></ul>
Default and recourse	<ul><li>buyer may sue for cancellation and damages or specific performance</li><li>seller may sue for specific performance or damages, or may need to foreclose</li></ul>

Economics

Supply

- the quantity of a product or service available for sale, lease, or trade at any given time

Demand

- the quantity of a product or service that is desired for purchase, lease, or trade at any given time

Supply / Demand / Price

Real Estate Supply	- property available for sale or lease; measured in dwelling units, square feet, acres
Real Estate Demand	- property buyers and tenants wishing to acquire; measured in households, square feet, acres
Interaction	- if supply increases relative to demand, price decreases - if demand increases relative to supply, price increases

Supply-Demand Cycle

unmet demand →
    construction adds supply →
        market equilibrium →
            construction adds more supply →
                oversupply →
                    construction stops →
                        market equilibrium →
                            demand absorbs supply →
                                unmet demand →
                                    cycle repeats

Real Estate Supply-Demand Cycle

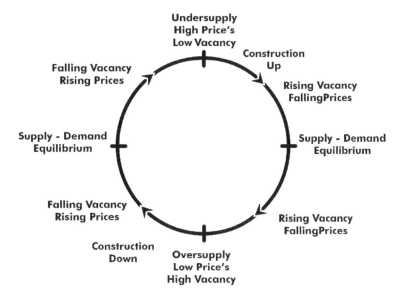

Factors Influencing Supply and Demand
- cost, availability of financing
- availability of developable land
- construction costs
- capacity of infrastructure
- governmental regulation and police powers
- changes in the economic base
- in- and out-migrations of major employers
- labor availability
- land availability

Government Influences on the Real Estate Market
- local zoning power
- local control and permitting of new development
- local taxing power
- federal influence on interest rates
- environmental legislation and regulations

Market Indicators
- **vacancy rates**
  - o increases indicate buyer / tenant market & falling prices / rents
  - o decreases indicate seller / landlord market & rising prices / rents
- building **permits** – increases indicate declining vacancy; increasing prices & construction
- prices
  - o increases indicate rising demand or declining supply or both
  - o decreases indicate falling demand or rising supply or both

Appraisal

Concepts and Principles of Value

Supply and demand	• When demand exceeds supply, scarcity exists, values rise. • When supply exceeds demand, surplus exists, values decline. • When supply and demand are equal, the market is in balance, values stabilize.
Utility	• A property's use in the marketplace contributes to the demand for it.
Transferability	• How readily or easily title or rights to real estate can be transferred affects the property's value.
Anticipation	• The benefits a buyer expects to derive from a property over a holding period influence what the buyer is willing to pay for it.
Substitution	• A buyer will pay no more for a property than the buyer would have to pay for an equally desirable and available substitute property.
Contribution	• The contribution to value of an improvement is equal to the change in market value that the addition of the improvement causes.
Change	• Market conditions affect the benefits that can arise from the property.
Highest and best use	• A property achieves its maximum value when it is put to whichever use generates the greatest income and return. The highest and best use must be legally permissible, physically possible, financially feasible, and maximally productive.
Conformity	• A property's maximal value is attained when its form and use are consonant with surrounding properties and uses
Progression and regression	• The value of a property is influenced by the values of neighboring properties.
Assemblage	• Conjoining adjacent properties can create a combined value in excess of the values of the unassembled properties. This excess value is called **plottage value.**
Subdivision	• The division of a single property into smaller properties can result in a higher total value.

40

Types of Value

Market value	• an estimate of the price at which a property will sell at a particular time; this type of value is the one generally sought in appraisals and used in brokers' estimates of value
Insured value	• the face amount a casualty or hazard insurance policy will pay in case a property is rendered unusable
Reproduction value	• the value based on the cost of constructing a precise duplicate of the subject property's improvements, assuming current construction costs
Replacement value	• the value based on the cost of constructing a functional equivalent of the subject property's improvements, assuming current construction costs
Salvage value	• the nominal value of a property that has reached the end of its economic life; also an estimate of the price at which a structure will sell if it is dismantled and moved
Assessed value	• the value of a property as estimated by a taxing authority as the basis for ad valorem taxation
Depreciated value	• a value established by subtracting accumulated depreciation from the purchase price of a property
Book value	• the value of the property as carried on the accounts of the owner; the value is generally equal to the acquisition price plus capital improvements minus accumulated depreciation
Investment value	• the value of an income property as indicated by the capitalized value of the cash flow the property generates

Market Value Requirements

The price willing buyer and seller would agree on given:

- a cash transaction
- reasonable market exposure
- parties have market and property use information
- there is no pressure to complete the transaction
- transaction is arm's length: parties are not related
- marketable title
- no hidden influences

41

Appraisal Process

1. Identify the purpose
2. Assimilate the relevant data
3. Assess the highest and best use
4. Estimate the value of the land
5. Apply the three approaches to value
6. Reconcile the values from the approaches
7. Compile the report

Sales Comparison Approach

1. Identify comparable sales
2. Compare comps to the subject and make adjustments to the comparables
3. Weight values indicated by adjusted comparables for the final value estimate of the subject

Adjusting Comparables

Rules for selecting comparables
- must be physically similar
- in subject's vicinity
- recently sold in arm's length sale

Rules for adjusting comparables
- never adjust the subject!
- deduct from comparable if better than subject
- add to comp if worse than subject
- Remember: ("Subtract if Superior !")

Weighting adjustments
- best indicator has fewest and smallest adjustments and smallest net adjustment from the sale price

Cost Approach

Types of cost appraised
- reproduction – cost of making a precise replica
- replacement – cost of making a functional equivalent

Steps in the approach

1. Estimate land value
2. Estimate replacement cost of improvements
3. Estimate total depreciation
4. Subtract: (cost of improvements - depreciation) = depreciated improvements cost
5. Add land back in: (land value + depreciated improvements) = value estimate of property

Key Aspects of Depreciation

Depreciation	• **loss of value** from deterioration, functional obsolescence, or economic obsolescence
Deterioration	• **wear and tear** from use and aging
Functional Obsolescence	• **outmoded** physical or design **features**: curable or incurable
Economic Obsolescence	• loss of value due to adverse **changes in surroundings**: incurable
Curability	• curable: cost to cure is less than resulting contribution to value
	• incurable: cost to cure exceeds contribution to value

Income Approach

- Based on the principle of anticipation: the expected future income stream of a property underlies what an investor will pay for the property
- Also based on the principle of substitution: that an investor will pay no more for a subject property with a certain income stream than the investor would have to pay for another property with a similar income stream.

Steps in the Income Approach

1. Estimate potential gross income
2. Estimate effective gross income (total potential income - vacancy)
3. Estimate net operating income (NOI) (effective income - expenses)
4. Select and apply capitalization rate (NOI ÷ cap rate)

Gross rent multipliers (GRMs)

- Simplified income-based methods to estimate value
- Method consists of applying a multiplier to the estimated gross rent of the subject
- Multiplier is derived from market data on sale prices and gross rent
- Does not necessarily produce accurate value estimates

GRM Formula

- GRM = price divided by monthly rent
- Value = GRM times monthly rent

Preparing a Comparative Market Analysis

Steps

1. Identify comparables sold, for sale properties, and expired listings
2. Compile comparison data for each comparable: price, sale date, location, age, lot size, site aspects, living area, bedrooms, etc.
3. Complete adjustments for differences; rules:
   a. Never adjust the subject
   b. Add value to the comparable if a feature is inferior to the subject
   c. Subtract value from the comp if a feature is superior to the subject
4. Derive total adjustments for each comparable
5. Reconcile all value-adjusted comps to the subject to identify a value estimate

Regulation of Appraisal Practice

FIRREA

- Financial Institutions Reform, Recovery and Enforcement Act (**FIRREA**) enacted in 1989 to regulate appraisal practices
- requires that competent individuals whose professional conduct is properly supervised perform all appraisals used in federally-related transactions
- As of January 1, 1993, federally-related appraisals must be performed only by state-certified appraisers
- **USPAP** - Uniform Standards of Professional Appraisal Practice – competency standards established by the **Appraiser Qualifications Board** of the Appraisal Foundation

USPAP

- Uniform Standards of Professional Appraisal Practice
- requires recognized appraisal methods
- must exercise a defined level of due diligence
- must properly report results
- must make proper disclosures and assumptions

Finance

Mortgage Transaction

Elements
- promissory note: promise to repay loan
- mortgage: pledge of property as collateral for loan

Mechanics
- borrower gives lender promissory note and mortgage
- lender gives borrower funds and records a lien

Hypothecation
- use of real property as collateral for a mortgage loan

Financial components
- original principal: capital amount borrowed on which interest payments are calculated
- loan balance: remaining unpaid principal at any point in the life of the loan
- interest: charge for the use of money; rate fixed or variable
- Annual Percentage Rate (APR) includes interest and all other finance charges; lender must disclose on residential properties
- point: one percent of the loan amount
- loan origination fee: charged by lender at origination to obtain required return
- term: period of time for repayment of interest and principal
- payment: the periodic payment of interest and/or principal
- down payment: borrower's cash payment applied to the purchase price
- loan-to-value ratio: the loan's share of the total value of the property
- equity: at closing, the borrower's cash invested in the property; thereafter, the difference between the market value and the loan balance

---

Trust Deed Transaction

Elements
- promissory note: trustor's promise to repay loan
- deed of trust: title to property as collateral for loan

Mechanics
- trust deed conveys title from the borrower/trustor to a third-party trustee
- trustee holds title on behalf of the lender/beneficiary until the debt is repaid

Promissory note
- legal instrument executed by borrower stating debt amount, loan term, method and timing of repayment, interest rate, promise to pay; may repeat other provisions from mortgage document or deed of trust; negotiable instrument assignable to a third party

---

Mortgage Clauses

Payment of principal and interest: prepayment and late charges
- borrower must make timely payments according to the terms of the note
- late payments or early payoffs may trigger penalties

Funds for taxes and insurance
- borrower must make monthly payments to cover taxes and hazard insurance
- borrower may also have to pay flood insurance and mortgage insurance premiums
- **escrow account:** reserve account for periodic payments of taxes and insurance.
- Real Estate Settlement Procedures Act (RESPA) limits funds the lender can require for this purpose.

PITI
- borrower's monthly payment for principal and interest is called the p&i payment (principal and interest)
- the amount which includes the escrow payment is called PITI (principal, interest, taxes, insurance).

Charges and liens
- borrower is liable for paying any charges, liens, or other expenses that may have priority over the mortgage or trust instrument.

Hazard or property insurance
- borrower must keep property insured as the lender requires.

Occupancy, preservation, maintenance and protection of the property
- borrower must take and maintain occupancy as the borrower's principal residence according to requirements
- borrower must not abuse or neglect the including use for illegal purposes, creating hazardous waste on the property, or destroying the improvements

Protection of lender's rights in the property
- lender may take actions to protect its rights in the property if the borrower jeopardizes the property's value. The costs of these actions would be charged to the borrower

Mortgage insurance
- Lender may require private mortgage insurance, or PMI which protects the lender against loss from borrower default
- applies to loans that are not backed by the Federal Housing Administration (FHA) or Veterans Administration (VA) and that have a down payment of less than 20% of the property value

Inspection
- lender may inspect the property with reasonable cause to fear damage to the collateral

Condemnation
- if the property is condemned or taken by eminent domain, lender reserves a claim on any resulting proceeds

Transfer of the property or a beneficial interest in borrower
- if borrower sells the property without the lender's approval, the lender may demand immediate repayment of the loan balance. this alienation clause, aka a due-on-sale clause, allows lender to prevent unapproved loan assumptions
- the requirement to repay the loan before the scheduled due date is called **acceleration**.

Borrower's right to reinstate
- if lender holds borrower in default, borrower has the right to reinstatement by performing certain actions, usually paying overdue payments plus expenses the lender
- clause is called a redemption clause
- gives the borrower time to satisfy obligations and prevent a forced sale

Release
- agreement to release the lien obligation when borrower has paid off the loan
- release clause, aka **defeasance** clause, may require lender to execute a **satisfaction of mortgage,** aka **release of mortgage**
- if deed of trust, lender directs trustee to execute a **release deed** or **deed of reconveyance** to the borrower as trustor.
- release deed or satisfaction should be recorded as necessary

Escalation clause
- allows lender to increase the loan's interest rate

Loan Qualification

Equal Credit Opportunity Act
- lender must evaluate applicant according to applicant's own income and credit information
- lender cannot deny credit based on
  - discounted income from part-time work
  - future plans to have family
  - locational factors
  - protected classes

Income qualification
- income ratio and debt ratio qualify borrower's income; income ratio applied to gross income determines housing expense maximum; debt ratio takes revolving debt into account
- income ratios: 25-28% conventional; 31% FHA-insured
- debt ratios: 36% conventional; 43% FHA and 41% VA

Cash qualification
- lender verifies applicant's sources of cash for down payment; extra cash enhances income qualification evaluation

Net worth
- extent to which applicant's assets exceed liabilities as a further source of reserves

Credit evaluation
- lender obtains credit reports to evaluate applicant's payment behavior

Loan commitment
- written pledge by lender to grant loan under specific terms; firm, lock-in, conditional, take-out

Loan-to-value ratio (LTV)
- relationship of loan amount to property value
- expressed as a percentage
- 80% LTV = loan is 80% of property value

Laws Affecting Mortgage Lending

Truth-in-Lending and Regulation Z
- **Reg Z** implements **Truth-in-Lending Simplification and Reform Act** and **Consumer Credit Protection Act**
  - Lender must **disclose finance charges** and APR prior to closing;
  - Borrower has limited right of rescission, but excludes primary residence
  - Lender must follow **advertising requirements** for full disclosure of costs, loan mechanics

Equal Credit Opportunity Act (ECOA)
- prohibits discrimination in lending based on
  - race or color
  - religion
  - national origin
  - sex

47

- marital status
- age
- dependency upon public assistance
- licensees assisting in qualifying must also comply
- denied applicants must get notice within 30 days

Real Estate Settlement Procedures Act (RESPA)
- standardizes settlement practices & ensures buyers understand settlement costs
- lender must:
  - provide CFPB booklet explaining loans, settlement costs and procedures
  - provide CFPB Loan Estimate of settlement costs within three days of application
  - provide CFPB Closing Disclosure three days before loan consummation

National Flood Insurance Act
- borrowers of "federally-related loans" must obtain flood insurance if property is in designated flood-hazard area
- flood-zone maps indicate where homeowners must obtain insurance

---

The Mortgage Market

Supply and demand for money
- relationship between supply and demand for money affects interest rates, consumer prices, availability of mortgage money; regulated by Federal Reserve

Federal Reserve control of money supply among banks
- sells T-bills to reduce money supply and increase interest rates; buys T-bills to increase supply and decrease rates
- sets the reserve requirement for member banks
- increase reserves to tighten money and raise interest rates
- decrease reserves to loosen money and lower interest rates
- sets the discount rate for member banks
- increase rate to tighten money
- decrease rate to increase money supply

Federal Home Loan Bank System (FHLBS)
- counterpart to the Fed for savings and loan associations

Federal Deposit Insurance Corporation (FDIC)
- insures deposits up to $250,000 per depositor, per insured bank, for each account ownership category

The primary mortgage market
- originates mortgage loans directly to borrowers;
- includes savings and loans, commercial banks, mutual savings banks, life insurance companies, mortgage bankers, credit unions

The secondary mortgage market
- buys existing loans to provide liquidity to primary lenders; Fannie Mae, Ginnie Mae, Freddie Mac, investment firms, life insurance companies, pension funds

Role of FNMA, GNMA, and FHLMC
- FNMA buys conventional, FHA- and VA-backed loans and pooled mortgages; guarantees payment on mortgage-backed securities
- GNMA guarantees payment on certain types of loans
- FHLMC buys and pools mortgages; sells mortgage-backed securities

Mortgage loan originator v. lender/banker v. broker
- mortgage loan originator: solicits, negotiates mortgage loans; requires MLO license
- mortgage broker: an intermediary who brings mortgage borrowers and mortgage lenders together, but does not use its own funds to originate mortgages
- mortgage banker: person or entity who funds or services loans for others and/or who sells mortgages to the secondary market

Types of Mortgages

Conventional mortgages
- Originated by banks and private financial institutions
- No government-related insurance or guarantees as with FHA or VA
- Typically require 20% down payments; smaller down payments may require PMI
- Assumptions require approval

Government loan programs
- **FHA** – federally insured loan programs (see following)
- VA – federally guaranteed loan programs (see following)

Amortized fixed-rate v adjustable loans
- **Amortized:** payments include increasing increments of principal which retire loan balance over loan term
- Fixed rate: interest rate does not change – can have for amortized or interest-only loans

Adjustable loans: interest rate fluctuates up or down with an index; payments may also vary

Adjustable Loan Characteristics

- **mechanics**: rate adjusts up or down with index; payments may or may not change;
- negative amortization: loan balance increases if payments are less than what is owed given the balance and rate, i.e., unpaid monthly amounts are added to the principal balance
- rate and payment caps: maximum amounts the interest rate or payments can increase in a given adjustment period or over the life of the loan; protects borrower from unaffordable increases
- index and margin: interest rate tied to any number of financial indices; margin equals a fixed point spread between the index and the interest rate
- **teaser rates:** to attract borrowers, adjustable loans may have low initial rates which increase over subsequent adjustment periods to a more permanent market level.

Custom Mortgages

- **partially amortized with a balloon:** payments will not retire principal balance over life of the loan, thus requiring a lump-sum payment, or "balloon" payment at end of term
- **interest-only loans:** loans where payments are interest only, and the principal balance is retired in full at maturity using a balloon payment
- **biweekly mortgage:** loan payments are every-two weeks, a device that reduces total interest paid, but also shortens risk period for the lender
- **package mortgage:** mortgage loans which also finance articles of personal property as part of the purchase transaction
- **home equity loans:** funds borrowed using the homeowners equity for collateral; funds can be used for any purpose

- **purchase money mortgage:** a seller-financed loan to the buyer of portions of the purchase price using the property as collateral; usually accompanied by a senior underlying first mortgage
- **reverse annuity mortgage:** a financial arrangement where the homeowner pledges equity to a lender in exchange for periodic payments of the pledged equity; in essence it is the periodic receipt of equity liquidation in exchange for an increase of debt owed on the property.

FHA Loans

Insured loans granted by approved lenders to qualified borrowers.

Loan term:	• 15, 30 years
Qualifying ratios:	• income: 31% • debt: 43%
Minimum downpayment:	• 3%
Mortgage insurance:	• required at 78% LTV or above • premium = one-time 1.75-2.25% of loan amount, plus annual premium
Points:	• None
Maximum loan amount:	• varies by Metropolitan Statistical Area

---

VA Loans

Guaranteed loans:	• granted by approved lenders to qualified veterans
Qualifying ratios:	• depends on lender
Minimum downpayment:	• None
Points:	• 1.25 - 3.3, depending on downpayment, type of loan, type of veteran

Investment

Investment Terminology

Appreciation: an increase in the value of a property owing to economic forces beyond the control of the investor

Asset: a tangible or intangible item of **value**

Basis;   a measurement of how much is invested in the property for tax purposes; adjusted basis is the **original** cost of the asset plus capital improvements minus depreciation

Capital gain (or loss):   the difference between the net **sales** proceeds of an asset and its adjusted basis

Cash flow: the remaining positive or negative amount of income an investment produces after subtracting all operating expenses and debt service from gross income

Equity: that portion of a property's value owned by the legal owner, expressed as the difference between the property's market value and all loan balances outstanding **on** the property

Leverage;   the relationship between the yield rate of an investment and the interest rate of funds borrowed to finance the investment; if the yield rate is greater than the loan rate, positive leverage results; if the yield rate is less than the **loan** rate, negative leverage results

Liquidity;   the degree to which an investment is readily marketable, or convertible to another form of asset; if immediately salable, an investment is liquid; the longer it takes to sell, the more illiquid the investment; real property is relatively illiquid in comparison with other types of investment

Tax shelter: an investment that produces depreciation or other non-cash losses that a taxpayer can deduct **from** other income to reduce tax liability

Investment Characteristics

Ownership benefits
- income
- appreciation
- tax shelter: depreciation and interest deductions

Ownership risks
- relatively illiquid
- management intensive
- negative leverage and price movements

Investment Entities

Direct	• investor buys directly and manages personally
Syndicate	• group of investors who combine funds to buy, develop, and/or operate a property
General partnership	• all members own and manage
Limited partnership	• general partner manages; limited partners own but do not manage
Real Estate Investment Trust	• investors buy trust certificates; trust invests in real estate assets • investors share returns per ownership percent

Taxation of Real Estate Investments

Income-producing investments are taxed on
- the annual income they make, plus
- on any gain realized when sold

Taxable income
- gross income minus allowed expenses and deductions
- net income from the investment is added to the investor's other ordinary taxable income

Cost recovery, or depreciation
- deduction of a portion of property's value from gross income each year over the depreciable life of asset
- depreciable life defined by tax laws

Depreciable basis
- the non-land, or improvement portion of an income-producing property
- cannot depreciate land value

Depreciation schedules / terms
- 27.5 years to 39 years

Capital gain and loss
- the taxable gain (profit) or loss incurred when the income property is sold
- if sales proceeds exceed the current adjusted basis there is a gain; if less, then it is a loss

Adjusted basis
- the **cost** of the investment plus **capital improvements** less **depreciation**

Interest
- deductible from income for tax purposes
- cannot deduct principal

Tax liability On Sale Of Residence

- seller of a principal residence owes tax on capital gain that results from sale unless excluded
- capital gain is the amount realized minus the adjusted basis
- gains tax exclusion: up to $250,000 for a single seller and $500,000 for a married couple can be excluded from gains tax every two years

Gain on Sale

selling price of old home	$350,000
- selling costs	35,000
= amount realized	315,000
beginning basis of old home	200,000
+ capital improvements	10,000
= adjusted basis of old home	210,000
amount realized	315,000
- adjusted basis	210,000
= gain on sale	105,000

Investment Analysis of an Income Property (See also Math Section, "Investment")

Pre-tax Cash Flow

potential rental income	$70,000
- vacancy and collection loss	4,200
= effective rental income	65,800
+ other income	2,000
= gross operating income	67,800
- operating expenses	35,000
- reserves	3,500
= net operating income (NOI)	29,300
- debt service	20,000
= pre-tax cash flow	$9,300

After-tax cash flow

pre-tax cash flow
- tax liability
= after tax cash flow

Taxable Income	**Tax Liability**
NOI	taxable income
+ reserves	x tax bracket
– interest	= tax liability
– depreciation)	
= taxable income	

53

Taxation

Taxing Authorities

Taxing entities
- property tax, or ad valorem taxation -- not to be confused with an income-property's annual tax on taxable income
- no federal ad valorem taxation
  - can impose a tax lien, but not annual property tax
- states may levy property taxes
  - typically delegated to **county and local jurisdictions**
  - states may also impose tax liens

Tax districts which levy property tax
- counties
- cities
- municipalities
- townships
- special tax districts
- established to collect funds for schools, fire protection, parks, community colleges, libraries, road maintenance, other public services

Property Tax Calculation

Property tax
- **ad valorem** tax levied annually on the taxable value of a property in order to help fund government and public services
- taxable value is based on assessed value

Tax base and tax rate
- **tax base**
  - the total of all assessed values in a jurisdiction excluding exemptions
- **tax rate**
  - also, the **millage** rate
  - rate applied to taxable value of each property to determine its tax levy
- **assessed value**
  - the valuation of properties for tax purposes, completed by **assessors**
- **equalization factors**
  - value-adjusting factors applied to assessed value to increase fairness, evenness of tax levies

Homestead exemption
- a tax exemption of a portion of the assessed value of a principal residence
- granted to the homeowner, provided
  - he or she is the head of the family
  - has resided at the property for the required length of time

Other exemptions
- properties immune from ad valorem tax
  - government-owned properties
- exempt from taxes
  - properties owned by non-profit-organizations

Tax rate derivation
- (1) taxing entity determines **budget requirements** to be met by ad valorem tax
- (2) divide **tax requirement** by the **tax base**

Tax rate mills
- tax rate stated as mills ($.001), or
- dollars per $100 of assessed value, or
- dollars per $1,000 of assessed value, or
- as a percentage of assessed value

Tax billing and collection
- individual tax bill
  - (rate x taxable value)
- taxable value
  - (assessed value minus exemptions and adjustments)

Special assessments
- levied against specific properties that will benefit from the planned improvement
- assessment amount based on pro rata share of benefitting properties
- creates voluntary or involuntary tax lien

Tax Lien Enforcement

Tax lien enforcement process
- tax lien enforcement & collection occurs via
  - tax certificate issuance
  - certificate buyer pays taxes due
  - application for a tax deed
  - tax sale and foreclosure initiation

Sale of tax certificates
- tax certificate buyer pays taxes due
- after a period of time may apply for a tax deed

Tax deed conveyance
- conveys title in the tax sale

Tax sale
- buyer must pay taxes due
- defaulted taxpayer may be able to redeem property
- if not redeemed, state issues tax deed to convey title to buyer

Fair Housing Laws

Anti-discrimination
- federal and state laws prohibit discrimination in housing
- citizens entitled to live wherever they wish without discrimination
- **state fair housing laws** reflect national laws with certain differences
- **fair housing and local zoning**
  - fair housing does not preempt local zoning, but zoning cannot be discriminatory against protected classes

Civil Rights Act of 1866
- no discrimination in selling or leasing housing **based on race**
- **Executive Order 11063:** no **race discrimination** involving FHA- or VA-backed loans

Civil Rights Act of 1968
- Title VIII (Fair Housing Act)
- no housing discrimination based on **race, color, religion, national origin**
- certain exceptions permitted

Forms of illegal discrimination
- discriminatory misrepresentation
- advertising
- unequal services
- steering
- blockbusting
- restricting access to market
- redlining

Title VIII exemptions
- selling, leasing single family home without broker or discriminatory advertising, with conditions
- 1-4 unit rental building where owner is occupant
- leasing facilities owned by private clubs
- facilities owned by religious organizations and leased to members

Jones v. Mayer
- discrimination in selling/renting residential housing based on race is prohibited without exception or exemption

Equal Opportunity in Housing poster
- brokers must display
- affirms compliance with fair housing laws
- failure to display can be construed as discrimination
- see example on following slide

Fair Housing Amendments Act of 1988
- no discrimination based on
  - sex
  - against the handicapped
  - families with children
- **exemptions**
  - government-designated retirement housing

- retirement community (62+ years of age)
- retirement community if 80 % of dwellings have one person who is 55+
- 1-4 unit dwellings where owners have no more than three houses

Discrimination by the client
- laws apply to owners as well as agents
- agent liable if goes along with client discrimination
- agent should withdraw from relationship with discriminatory client

Violations and enforcement
- file HUD complaint
- file suit in court
- may obtain injunction, damages
- violators subject to prosecution

Fair financing laws (See also Finance Section)
- Equal Credit Opportunity Act (ECOA)
  - lenders must be fair, impartial in loan qualifying
  - may not discriminate based on race, color, religion, national origin, sex, marital status, age
  - must state reasons for credit denial
- Home Mortgage Disclosure Act
  - prohibits redlining
  - lenders must report location of loans

Americans with Disabilities Act (ADA)
- purpose is to prohibit discrimination against persons with disabilities
- applies to accessing public, employment, education, transportation facilities
- applies to private employers with 15+ employees and public employees
- Title **I: Employment**
  - must have equal opportunity, enforced by ECOA
- **Title II: State, local government**
  - cannot discriminate in state and local services
- **Title III:** Public **accommodations**
  - cannot discriminate in public accommodations, commercial facilities
- **Title IV:** Telecommunication
  - concerns accommodations in telecommunications, public service messaging
- **Title V:** miscellaneous
  - general provisions as to how ADA affects other laws, insurance, lawyers
- licensees should clearly understand provisions of Title I and III
- ADA requirements
  - landlords must modify housing to be accessible without hindrance
  - access must be equivalent to that provided for non-disabled persons
- penalties
  - violations can result in citations, license restrictions, fines, injunctions

---

Property Disclosures

Residential property condition
- Seller's Disclosure Form
  - sellers (not agents) must complete form in many states for prospective buyers
  - describes property condition at time of sale on state-approved forms
- owner's role
  - seller must affirm whether or not problems exist with property or it's systems
  - if unknown, seller must so state; if a defect is known, seller must disclose

- o if seller is unaware of a problem, s/he can state "no representation" which removes liability for not disclosing
- o seller must sign, deliver to buyer and buyer must acknowledge receipt
- licensee's role
  - o must disclose any material facts that are known or reasonably should have known
- right of rescission
  - o if seller does not complete and deliver form, buyer receives a right to rescind contract and reclaim deposit
  - o right to cancel continues until closing or occupancy
- property condition and material facts
  - o material fact = a fact affecting the property's value or the prospect's decision to contract
  - o property stigmas are not material facts (previous crime, suicide, disease, etc.)
  - o no requirement to disclose non-material facts
  - o material facts can include the surrounding area in addition to the immediate premises

Environmental issues

- licensees and principals are responsible for disclosing, remediating hazards
  - o lead-based paint
    - if property built before 1978, must disclose possible lead hazard
    - use form "Protect Your Family from Lead in Your Home"
  - o mold
    - must be disclosed if present in home
  - o asbestos
    - can cause lung cancer; must be removed by experts to prevent contamination
  - o air quality
    - can/should test for carbon monoxide, radon, formaldehyde, other toxic chemicals prior to sale
  - o carbon monoxide
    - emitted by gas space heaters, chimneys, furnaces, stoves, etc.
    - detectors should be in every home
  - o septic systems
    - can release contaminants into soil
    - should inspect periodically and prior to any conveyance
  - o radon
    - detectable radioactive ground gas that can cause cancer;
  - o urea formaldehyde
    - hazard in foam insulation and pressed wood products, eg, particle board
  - o underground storage tanks (UST)
    - commercial hazard if leaking; should disclose presence of any UST
- Clean Air Act
  - o controls air pollution, air quality on national scale
  - o creates pollutant- emission standards
- Clean Water Act
  - o governs, sets standards for controlling water pollution
  - o applies to all waters connected to navigable waterways
- Safe Drinking Water Act
  - o regulates, protects public supply of drinking water
  - o sets protection standards, requires water suppliers to report discovered health risks
  - o sellers must disclose property's source of drinking water, proximity to septic systems
  - o should test any well system
- Brownfields Law
  - o brownfields = abandoned commercial sites likely to contain toxic material
  - o law provides funds, liability protections and tax exemptions for reclamation
- Environmental Protection Agency (EPA)
  - o integrates federal environmental research, funding, monitoring, standard-setting, and enforcement into one agency
- licensee disclosure obligations, liabilities

- o licensees should have general awareness and know where to get expert help
- o not expected to have expert knowledge of law or physical condition
- o critical role is to
    - be aware of potential hazards
    - disclose material facts, have attorney draft disclosures
    - know where to find expert help

Warranties

- purpose and scope
    - o aka, home service contracts, to cover service, repair of systems, appliances
    - o typically annual contracts with costs depending on property size, location, type, degree of coverage
    - o may be included in purchase price of a home
- limitations – warranties may exclude
    - o pre-existing conditions, accidental breakages, poor installations, outdoor systems, certain appliances, etc.
    - o homeowner must use warranty company to have services performed

Inspections

- process
    - o inspections detect oversights or need for repairs
    - o identify need for maintenance procedures
    - o inspections uncover system, pest infestation, environmental issues
- termite inspections
    - o not easily detectable by non-experts; should do annual inspections
- environmental inspections, audits
    - o home inspections should include environmental issues / hazards
    - o can also conduct site assessments which examine possible impairments
- environmental impact statements (EIS)
    - o performed for federally, some privately funded development projects
    - o addresses air, water quality, noise, health, safety, wildlife, traffic, sewer impacts of project
    - o culminates in permit or permit denial
- licensee disclosure duties
    - o in most states, licensees must disclose known, material facts on residential properties
    - o must also disclose known results of any residential inspection
    - o when not required, licensees should suggest professional inspections / audits

Homeowners' Associations

- property disclosures include homeowners' associations
    - o must disclose if subject to common interest plan
    - o must disclose association's membership obligation, dues, restrictions
    - o association must provide required disclosure documents, forms, timing requirements
    - o seller responsible for disclosures, agent must ensure seller complies

---

Codes Of Ethics

Sources of practitioner ethics

- federal, state legislation
- state license regulation
- industry self-regulation via trade associations, institutes
- predominant influence in practitioner ethics is the Code of Ethics of the National Association of Realtors®
    - o covers all aspects of practice and transactions

Duties to clients
- most codes of ethics uphold commitment to fulfilling fiduciary duties, including
  - honesty in representing values, property condition
  - respecting other broker-client relationships
  - submitting all offers
  - avoiding commingling, conversion
  - maintaining transaction files
  - maintaining confidentialities
  - managing client property competently

Other Professional Practices

Duties to customers
- honesty and fair dealing
- disclosing sources of compensation
- conducting honest advertising that is not misleading

Disclosures
- comply with federal, state, and ethical disclosure requirements, including
  - disclosure in ads

Professional relationships
- avoid disparagement of competitors
- do not exploit unfair advantages
- arbitrate differences, disputes rather than litigate
- respect agency relationships of others
- conform to accepted standards of co-brokerage practices

Closings

Settlement Process	• identify selling terms & costs
	• determine non-prorated debits and credits
	• complete prorated debits and credits
	• complete closing statement
	• disburse funds

Key Points On Closings	• seller must prove marketability of title (via title insurance)
	• must remove all encumbrances before title transfer
	• escrow officer disburses buyer's funds, loan monies once conditions are met
	• conditions include survey, inspections, title insurance, reserves, PMI

RESPA

Purpose	• clarify, disclose costs; eliminate kickbacks, undisclosed fees

Applicability	• for residential property • federally-related mortgage, including VA, FHA • Regulated by Consumer Financial Protection Bureau (CFPB)
Information booklet	• lender must provide CFPB booklet, "Your Home Loan Toolkit"
Loan estimate	• lender must provide CFPB's H-24 Loan Estimate of settlement costs within three days of application
Closing disclosure	• lender must use CFPB's H-25 Closing Disclosure
Referral fees and kickbacks	• RESPA prohibits payment of referral fees and kickbacks • business relationships between firms involved in the transaction must be disclosed

---

Truth-in-Lending Integrated Disclosures Rule (TRID)

Key points	• combines financial disclosure requirements of RESPA & Truth-in-Lending Act (TILA) • replaces "Good Faith Estimate" and HUD-1 forms • uses new "Loan Estimate" form" and "Closing Disclosure" form
Forms and procedures	• lender must provide mandatory: "Your Home Loan Toolkit" booklet at loan application • Loan Estimate form: 3 business days after loan application • Closing Disclosure: 3 business days before consummation • Terms in both forms must generally be the same
Good faith	• Loan Estimate costs based on best information available • Closing Disclosure costs equal estimate costs within certain tolerances
Types of charges	• no limitation on increase over estimate • 10% tolerance charges • 0 tolerance charges
Applicable transactions	• most closed-end consumer mortgages, including: construction loans, loans secured by vacant land, loans to trusts • not covered: home equity loans, reverse mortgages, loans on mobile homes, loans by small lenders (no more than 5 loans per year)
The H-25 form	• 5 pages, variable by loan type

61

Debits & Credits

Amount buyer must produce:	excess of ***buyer's debits*** over credits
Amount seller must receive:	excess of ***seller's credits*** over debits

Buyer's credits
- earnest money
- loan amount
- seller's share of prorations buyer will pay

Buyer's debits
- purchase price
- expenses (per agreement or custom)
- buyer's share of prorations prepaid by seller
-

Seller's credits
- purchase price
- buyer's share of prorated items prepaid by seller

Seller's debits
- expenses (per agreement or custom)
- seller's share of prorated items the buyer will pay
- loan balance and other liens to be paid off

30-Day 12-Month Proration

Formula:

Monthly Amount = (Annual amount ÷ 12)
Daily Amount = (Monthly amount ÷ 30)
Proration = (Monthly amount x no. of months) + (Daily amount x no. of days)

Example:

An annual tax bill is $1,800. Closing is on April 10. What is the seller's share of the taxes?

1. ($1,800 ÷ 12) = $150 monthly amount
2. ($150 ÷ 30) = $5.00 daily amount
3. ($150 x 3 months) = $450 Jan - Mar; ($5 x 10) = $50 Apr 1 - Apr 10; ($450 + 50) = $500 seller's share

365-Day Method

Formula:

Daily amount = Annual amount ÷ 365 days; or
Daily amount = Monthly amount ÷ no. of days in month
Proration = (Daily amount x no. of days)

Example:

An annual tax bill is $1,800. Closing is on April 10. What is the seller's share of the taxes?

1. ($1,800 ÷ 365) = $4.93 daily amount
2. Jan 1 thru April 10 = (31 + 28 + 31 + 10) days, or 100 days
3. ($4.93 x 100 days) = $493 seller's share

Risk Management

Four Risk Management Strategies

1) **Avoidance**
   - refrain from risky activity
     - ❑ e. g., assuring buyers a property will appreciate

2) **Reduction**
   - reduce probability of loss
   - reduce severity of loss
   - share responsibility for a decision

3) **Transference**
   - pass risk to another party
   - get E & O insurance
   - by contract; insurance

4) **Retention**
   - accept risk
   - take responsibility for consequences
   - eg, pricing strategy on a listing

Risk Management Procedures

- **education**
  - o knowledge and skill reduce risk
  - o understand forms and contracts
- **disclosure**
  - o provide information to reduce misunderstanding & lawsuits
- **disclosure areas**
  - o agency
  - o property condition
  - o fiduciary / statutory duties
  - o personal interest in selling a property
  - o documentation and record keeping
  - o maintain evidence of compliance, transaction recordkeeping

Insurance Types–To Manage Risk

- general liability
- errors and omissions (E & O, to cover negligence in discharging service duties)
- fire and hazard
- flood
- casualty
- workers'
- personal property
- consequential loss
- surety bond

Primary Areas of Risk

Agency
- fulfill agency disclosure requirements
- discharge fiduciary duties and duties to customers
- avoid conflicts of interest
- uphold legal confidentialities

Property disclosures
- seller's property condition disclosure
- material facts disclosure
- lead paint, infestations, mold, radon

Listing and selling
- listing agreement accuracy
- comparative market analysis results
- closing cost estimates
- advertising
- authorizations and permissions
- exceeding expertise

Contracting process
- contracts for real estate must be in writing
- inaccuracy endangers contract
- avoid unauthorized practice of law
  - may fill in blanks on standard contract forms
  - do not give legal advice to public

Fair housing
- advertising may not state preference, limitation or discrimination based on race, color, religion, national origin, sex, handicap, familial status
- licensee must not be involved with discriminatory actions of a client or customer
- advertising may not state preference, limitation or discrimination based on race, color, religion, national origin, sex, handicap, familial status
- licensee must not be involved with discriminatory actions of a client or customer
- make sure listing and purchase contracts are in compliance

Antitrust
- cannot collude on prices; fix prices
- cannot conspire with other companies to restrict trade or unjustly impair a competitor
- cannot create monopolies
- cannot allocate markets among competitors

Rules and regulations
- prime causes of discipline
  - commission of prohibited acts
  - practicing with an expired license
  - disclosure failures
  - earnest money mishandling

Misrepresentation
- **unintentional**
  - inaccurate information conveyed unknowingly

- occurs most often in measurements, property characterizations
  - **intentional**
    - fraud
    - knowingly conveying false information

- ways to reduce risks in misrepresentation
  - measure and calculate areas accurately
  - do not over-rely on measurements by others
  - refrain from exaggeration
  - avoid stating opinions a consumer might take for expertise

Recommending providers

- risks include
  - consumer dissatisfaction
  - possible liability for undisclosed business relationship
- best practices
  - do not recommend vendors
  - provide a list of trusted vendors with a disclaimer and no recommendation

Trust fund handling

- mishandling of earnest money deposits
- commingling trust funds
- conversion of trust funds
- errors in use of trust accounts

Property Management

Management Functions

Types of manager

- individual, managing properties for multiple owners; building manager, employed to manage a single property; resident, employed to live and manage on site.
- may specialize in a property type
- manager is a fiduciary of the principal
- specific functions determined by management agreement

Reporting

- monthly, quarterly, annually
- annual operating budget, cash flow reports, profit and loss statements, budget comparison statements

Budgeting

- operating budget: rental rates, capital expenditures, reserves, salaries and wages; projects income based on past performance and current market
- expenses, variable and fixed; capital expenditures: outlays for major renovations and construction; cash reserves set aside for variable expenses

Renting

- keep property rented and tenanted;
- select compatible tenants and collect scheduled rents
- legal issues: compliance with fair housing laws, Americans with Disabilities Act, and ECOA

65

Property maintenance	• balance costs of services, owner financial objectives, and tenant needs • routine, preventive, or corrective; staffed in-house or contracted out
Construction	• tenant alterations, renovations, expansion, environmental remediation • legal concerns: Americans with Disabilities Act

The Management Agreement

Components	• names; description; lease term; owner's purpose; responsibilities; authority; budget; allocation of costs; reporting; compensation; Equal Opportunity statement
Rights, duties and liabilities	• landlord: receive rent; receive premises in specified condition; enter and inspect; examine books; contract, hire vendors, set rents; pay management fee; comply with laws • manager: hire and fire; contract; perform management tasks without interference; maintain financial records, make reports, budget, collect rent, find tenants, maintain property, meet owner goals; liability for trust funds; comply with laws

Leasing Considerations

Landlord rights and responsibilities	• rights: enter premises, receive payment, retake on termination, pursue remedies • responsibilities: provide habitable conditions; maintain heating, cooling, electrical, plumbing; keep clean and in repair
Tenant rights and responsibilities	• rights: quiet enjoyment, habitable conditions, right to sue for default • responsibilities: pay rent, obey rules, give proper notice, return property in prescribed condition, use only for intended purpose
Evictions	• actual: legal procedure; notice, suit, judgment, taking • constructive: tenant vacates on account of landlord failure to maintain premises
Termination of a lease	• expiration, performance, agreement, abandonment, breach, notice, destruction of premises, condemnation, foreclosure, death of either party (tenancy at will), death of landlord (life estate)
Security deposit procedures	determined by law, rules, and agreement

Section II: Real Estate Math Review

Basic Math

Fractions

Adding and subtracting same denominator:

      Formula: $a / c + b / c = (a + b) \div c$

      Example: $1/2 + 1/2 = (1 + 1) / 2 = 2/2 = 1$

Adding and subtracting different denominators:

      Formula: $a / c + b / d = (ad + bc) / cd$

      Example: $1/2 + 1/3 = (3 + 2) / 6 = 5/6$

Multiplying:

      Formula: $(a / c) \times (b / d) = ab / cd$

      Example: $(2/5) \times (4/6) = 8/30 = 4/15$

Decimals and Percents

Converting decimals to percentages

      Formula: *Decimal number x 100 = Percentage number*

      Example: $.022 \times 100 = 2.2\%$

Converting percentages to decimals

      Formula: *Percent number ÷ 100 = Decimal number*

      Example: $2.2 \div 100 = .022$

Multiplying percents

      Formula: *1. Percent number ÷ 100 = Decimal number*

                        2. Beginning number x Decimal number = Product

      Example: 75% of 256 (75% x 256) = ?

                   1. $75 \div 100 = .75$

                   2. $256 \times .75 = 192$

Dividing by percents

Formula: *1. Percent number ÷ 100 = Decimal number*

                      2. Beginning number ÷ Decimal = Dividend

Example: 240 ÷ 75% = ?

                    1. 75% ÷ 100 = .75

                    2. 240 ÷ .75 = 320

Decimals, Fractions, and Percentages

Converting fractions to percents

Formula: (1)   a / b or a ÷ b = a divided by b = decimal number

                (2)   decimal number x 100 = percent number

Example: (1)   2 / 5 = 2 divided by 5 = 0.4

                (2)   .4 x 100 = 40%

Converting a percent to fraction and reducing it

Formula: (1)   X% = X ÷ 100 or X / 100

                (2) $\frac{X \div a}{100 \div a}$ where a is the largest number that divides evenly into both numerator and denominator

Example: (1)   40% = 40 ÷ 100, or 40 / 100

                (2) $\frac{40 \div 20}{100 \div 20} = \frac{2}{5}$

Converting fractions to decimals and percentages

Formula: *Decimal x 100 = Percent number*

Example: .75 x 100 = 75%

Equations

Additions and Subtractions

Formula: *if*   *a = b + c*

                then   *b = a - c (subtracting c from both sides)*

                and   *c = a - b (subtracting b from both sides)*

Example: 10   = 6 + 4

6   = 10 - 4

4   = 10 - 6

Multiplications and Divisions

Formula: *if* $a = b \times c$

     then $b = a / c$ *(dividing both sides by c)*

     and $c = a / b$ *(dividing both sides by b)*

Example: $10 = 2 \times 5$

     $2 = 10 \div 5$

     $5 = 10 \div 2$

Linear and Perimeter Measurement

Linear measure of rectangles

Formula: *Side A = Area ÷ Side B*

Example: A rectangular house has one side 40' side long and area of 1,200 SF. What is the length of the other side?

     Side A = (1,200' ÷ 40') = 30'

Perimeter measurement

Formula: *Perimeter = Sum of all sides of an object*

Example: A five-sided lot has the following dimensions:

     Side A = 50' Side B = 60'
     Side C= 70' Side D = 100'
     Side E = 30'

     What is the perimeter of the lot?

     P = 50' + 60' + 70' + 100' + 30' = 310'

Area Measurement

Square and rectangle

Formula: *Area = Width x Depth (Horizontal) or Width x Height (Vertical)*

     Width= Depth (Height) ÷ Area

     Depth (Height)= Width ÷ Area

Example: A house is 40' deep and 30' wide. What is its area?

Area = 40' x 30' = 1,200 SF

Triangle

Formula: *Area = (Height x Base) ÷ 2*

Note: Base is also sometimes referred to as "width"

Example: An A-frame house has a front facade measuring 30' across and 20' in height. What is the area of the facade?

Area = (30' x 20') ÷ 2 = 300 Square feet (SF)

Square foot-to-acre conversion

Formula: *Acres = Area SF ÷ 43,560 SF*

Example: How many acres is 196,020 SF?

196,020 SF ÷ 43,560 SF = 4.5 acres

Acre-to-square foot conversion

Formula: *SF = Number of acres x 43,560 SF*

Example: How many square feet is .75 acres?

.75 acres x 43,560 SF = 32,670 SF

Linear and Area Conversion Chart

Linear measures

(cm = centimeter; m = meter; km = kilometer)

1 inch	=	1/12 foot	=	1/36 yard		
1 foot	=	12 inches	=	1/3 yard		
1 yard	=	36 inches	=	3 feet		
1 rod	=	16.5 feet	=	1/320 mile		
1 mile	=	5280 feet	=	1760 yards	=	320 rods
1 centimeter	=	1/100 m				
1 meter	=	100 cm	=	1/1000 km		
1 kilometer	=	1,000 m				

Area measures

1 square inch	=	1/144 sq. foot				
1 square foot	=	1/9 sq. yard	=	144 sq. inches		
1 square yard	=	9 sq. feet	=	1,296 sq. inches		
1 acre	=	1/640 sq. mi	=	43,560 SF	=	208.71 ft x 208.71 ft
1 square mile	=	640 acres	=	1 section	=	1/36 township
1 section	=	1 mi x 1 mi	=	640 acres	=	1/36 township
1 township	=	6 mi x 6 mi	=	36 sq. mi	=	36 sections

70

Metric conversions

(cm = centimeter; m = meter; km = kilometer)

1 inch	=	2.54 cm				
1 foot	=	30.48 cm	=	.3048 m		
1 yard	=	91.44 cm	=	.9144 m		
1 mile	=	1609.3 m	=	1.60 km		
1 centimeter	=	.3937 inch				
1 meter	=	39.37 inches	=	3.28 feet	=	1.094 yards
1 kilometer	=	3,281.5 feet	=	.621 mile		

Fractions of sections, acres, and linear dimensions

Fraction		# Acres
1 section	=	640 acres
1/2 section	=	320 acres
1/4 section	=	160 acres
1/8 section	=	80 acres
1/16 section	=	40 acres
1/32 section	=	20 acres
1/64 section	=	10 acres

Calculating Area from the Legal Description

Formula:

(1) *First multiply all the denominators of the fractions in the legal description together.*

(2) *Then divide 640 by the resulting product.*

Examples:

How many acres are in the Northern 1/2 of the Southwestern 1/4 of Section 6?

640 / (2 x 4) = 640 / 8 = 80 acres

How many acres are in the Western 1/2 of the Northwestern 1/4 of the Northeastern 1/4 of Section 8?

640 / (2 x 4 x 4) = 640 / 32 = 20 acres

Volume Measurement

Formula:

Volume = Width x Height x Depth   (assume objects with 90 degree angles)

Base = (Height x Depth) ÷ Volume

Height = (Base x Depth) ÷ Volume

Depth = (Base x Height) ÷ Volume

Example:

What is the volume of a 40' x 30' x 20' house?

40' x 30' x 20' = 24,000 cubic feet

71

Leases

Percentage Lease Rent Calculation

Formula: *Monthly percentage rent = Sales x percent of sales charged*

Example: A store generates $50,000 per month. The lease calls for 1.5% percentage rent. Monthly rent amount?

($50,000 x .015) = $750 / month

Contracts for the Sale of Real Estate

Percentage of Listing Price Calculation

Formula: *Percentage of listing price = Offer ÷ Listing price*

Example: A property listed for $150,000 receives an offer for $120,000. The offer's percentage of listing price is:

$120,000 ÷ $150,000 = 80%

Earnest Money Deposit Calculation

Formula: *Deposit = Offering price x required or market-accepted percentage*

Example: A seller requires a 2% deposit on a property listed for $320,000. The required deposit (assuming a full price offer) is:

$320,000 x 2% = $6,400

Appraisal & Value

Adjusting Comparables

Rules:
1. Never adjust the subject!

2. If the comparable is superior to the subject, subtract value from the comparable.

3. If the comparable is inferior to the subject, add value to the comparable.

Example: The subject has a $10,000 pool and no porch. A comparable that sold for $250,000 has a porch ($5,000), an extra bathroom ($6,000), and no pool.

Adjustments to comp: $250,000 (+10,000 - 5,000 - 6,000) = $249,000 indicated value of subject

72

Gross Rent Multiplier

Formulas: *Sales price = Monthly rental income x GRM*

Monthly rental income = Sales price / Gross Rent Multiplier

Note: Gross rent multiplier is often abbreviated as GRM.

Examples:
1. What is the value of a fourplex with monthly rent of $2,800 and a GRM of 112?

    $2,800 rent x 112 GRM = $313,600

2. What is the GRM of a fourplex with monthly rent of $2,800 and a value of $313,600?

    313,600 price ÷ $2,800 rent = 112 GRM

Gross Income Multiplier

Formulas   *Gross Income Multiplier = Sales price ÷ Annual income*

Sales price = Annual income x Gross Income Multiplier

Annual income = Sales price ÷ Gross Income Multiplier

Note: Gross income multiplier is often abbreviated as GIM.

Examples:
1. What is the value of a commercial property with an annual income of $33,600 and a GIM of 9.3?

    $33,600 income x 9.3 GIM = $312,480

2. What is the GIM of a commercial property with annual income of $33,600 and a value of $312,480?

    $313,600 price ÷ $33,600 = 9.3 GIM

Cost Approach Formula

Formula: *Value = Land value + (Improvements + Capital additions - Depreciation)*

Example: Land value = $50,000; home replacement cost = $150,000; new garage added @ $30,000; total depreciation = $10,000

Value = $50,000 + (150,000 + 30,000 - 10,000) = $220,000

Depreciation

Formulas: *Annual depreciation = Beginning depreciable basis ÷ Depreciation term*

Depreciable basis = (Initial property value + Any capital improvements - Land value)

Note: The depreciation term is in number of years.

Example: Property value = $500,000; land value = $110,000; depreciation term = 39 years

Step 1: ($500,000 - $110,000) = $390,000 depreciable basis

Step 2: ($390,000 ÷ 39 years) = $10,000 annual depreciation

Income Capitalization Formula

Formulas: *Value = Annual Net Operating Income ÷ Capitalization rate*

Capitalization rate = Annual Net Operating Income ÷ Value

Annual Net Operating Income = Value x Capitalization rate

Examples:
1. A property generates $490,000 net income and sells at a 7% cap rate. What is its value?

   $490,000 ÷ 7% = $7,000,000 value

2. A property has a net income of $490,000 and sells for $7,000,000. What is its cap rate?

   $490,000 ÷ 7,000,000 = .07, or 7%

3. A property's value is $7,000,000 and the cap rate is 7%. What is the property's net operating income?

   $7,000,000 x .07 = $490,000

Net Operating Income (NOI, Net Income)

Formula: *NOI = Potential rent - Vacancy loss + Other income - Operating expenses*

Note: NOI does not include debt payments!

Example: A building has 10 office suites generating annual potential rent of $10,000 each. Vacancy = 10% and annual expenses are $35,000. Vending machines yield $5,000. What is the NOI?

$100,000 rent - 10,000 vacancy + 5,000 other income - 35,000 expenses = $60,000 NOI

74

Finance

Points

Definition: 1 point = 1% of the loan amount or .01 x loan amount

Formulas: *Points = Fee paid ÷ Loan amount*

                     Fee paid = Loan amount x Points

                     Loan amount = Fee paid ÷ Points

Examples:
1. A borrower pays $500 for a $10,000 loan. How many points are paid?

   $500 ÷ 10,000 = .05 = 5 points

2. A borrower pays 5 points on a $10,000 loan. What is the fee paid?

   $10,000 x .05 = $500

3. A borrower pays $500 as 5 points on a loan. What is the loan amount?

   $500 ÷ .05 = $10,000

Rules of
Thumb: 1 point charged raises lender's yield by .125%

                   8 points charged raises lender's yield by 1%

Example: A lender wants to yield 7% on a 6.5% loan. How many points must he or she charge?

                   (7% - 6.5%) = .5%

                   .5% ÷ .125% = 4 points

Interest Rate, Principal and Payment

Caveat!

       Interest rates in mortgage financing apply to the <u>annual</u> interest payment and <u>exclude</u> principal payment. Remember to convert annual payments to monthly or vice versa as the question requires, and to exclude principal payments from your calculations!

Formulas: *Payment = Principal x Rate*

                   Principal = Payment ÷ Rate

                   Rate = Payment ÷ Principal

Examples:
1. A borrower has a $100,000 loan @ 6% interest. What are the annual and monthly payments?

   Annual payment = $100,000 x .06 = $6,000
   Monthly payment = $6,000 ÷ 12 = $500

2. A borrower has a $500 monthly payment on a 6% loan. What is the loan principal?

    Principal = ($500 x 12) ÷ 6% = ($6,000 ÷ .06) = $100,000

3. A borrower has a $500 monthly payment on a $100,000 loan. What is the loan rate?

    Rate = ($500 x 12) ÷ $100,000 = ($6,000 ÷ 100,000) = .06 = 6%

Total Interest, Interest Rate, and Loan Term

Formulas: *Interest-only loan:*   *Total interest = Loan amount x Rate x Term in years*

             Amortized loan: *Total interest = (Monthly PI payment x 12 x term) - Loan amount*

Examples: 1. A borrower obtains a 10-year interest only loan of $50,000 @ 6%. How much interest will he or she pay?

             ($50,000 x .06 x 10) = $30,000

             2. A borrower obtains a 10-year amortized loan of $50,000 @ 6% with monthly payments of $555.10. How much interest will he or she pay?

             ($555.10 x 12 x 10) - $50,000 = $16,612

Amortization Calculation

Formulas: *Month 1:*   *Principal paid = Monthly payment - (Loan amount x Rate ÷ 12)*

             Month 2:   *New loan amount = (Previous month principal - Principal paid)*

                           Principal paid = Monthly payment - (New loan amount x Rate ÷ 12)

Example: A borrower obtains a 30-year $100,000 amortized loan @ 7% with a $665.31 monthly payment. What is the principal paid in the second month?

             Month 1:   Principal paid = $665.31 - ($100,000 x 7% ÷ 12) = $665.31 - (583.33 interest paid) = $81.98

             Month 2:   New loan amount = $100,000 previous month beginning loan amount - $81.98 principal paid = $99,918.02

                         Principal paid = $665.31 - ($99,918.02 x 7% ÷ 12) = $665.31 - (582.86 interest paid) = $82.45

Loan Constants

Formulas: *Monthly payment = (Loan amount x Loan constant) / 1000*

             Loan amount = (Monthly payment ÷ Loan constant) x 1000

Loan constant = (Monthly payment ÷ Loan amount) x 1000

Examples:
1. A borrower obtains a loan for $100,000 with a 6.3207 constant. What is the monthly payment?

   Monthly payment = ($100,000 ÷ 1,000) x 6.3207 = $632.07

2. A borrower has a monthly payment of $632.07 on a loan with a monthly constant of 6.3207. What is the loan amount?

   Loan amount = ($632.07 ÷ 6.3207) x 1000 = $100,000

3. A borrower obtains a loan for $100,000 with a monthly payment of $632.07. What is the loan constant?

   Loan constant = ($632.07 ÷ $100,000) x 1,000 = 6.3207

Loan - to - Value Ratio (LTV)

Formulas:
LTV ratio = Loan ÷ Price (Value)

Loan = LTV ratio x Price (Value)

Price (Value) = Loan ÷ LTV ratio

Examples:
1. A borrower can get a $265,600 loan on a $332,000 home. What is her LTV ratio?

   LTV Ratio = $265,600 ÷ 332,000 = 80%

2. A borrower can get an 80% loan on a $332,000 home. What is the loan amount?

   Loan = $332,000 x .80 = $265,600

3. A borrower obtained an 80% loan for $265,600. What was the price of the home?

   Price (value) = $265,600 ÷ .80 = $332,000

Financial Qualification

Income ratio qualification

Formula:
Monthly Principal & Interest (PI) payment = Income ratio x Monthly gross income

Example:
A lender uses a 28% income ratio for the PI payment. A borrower grosses $30,000 per year. What monthly PI payment can the borrower afford?

Monthly PI payment = ($30,000 ÷ 12) x .28 = $700

77

How much can the borrower borrow if the loan constant is 6.3207? (See also-loan constants)

Loan amount = ($700 ÷ 6.3207) x 1,000 = $110,747.22

Debt ratio qualification

Formulas:

Debt ratio = (Housing expense + Other debt payments) ÷ Monthly gross income

Housing expense = (Monthly gross income x Debt ratio) - Other debt payments

Example:

A lender uses a 36% debt ratio. A borrower earns $30,000 / year and has monthly non-housing debt payments of $500. What housing payment can she afford?

Housing expense = ($30,000 ÷ 12 x .36) - 500 = ($900 - 500) = $400

Investment

Appreciation Calculations

Simple appreciation

Formulas:

Total appreciation = Current value - Original price

Total appreciation rate = Total appreciation ÷ Original price

Average annual appreciation rate = Total appreciation rate ÷ number of years

One year appreciation rate = (Annual appreciation amount) ÷ (Value at beginning of year)

Examples:

1. A home purchased for $200,000 five years ago is now worth $300,000. What are the total appreciation amount, total appreciation rate, and average appreciation rate?

    Total appreciation = ($300,000 - 200,000), or $100,000

    Total appreciation rate = ($100,000 ÷ 200,000), or 50%

    Average annual appreciation rate = 50% ÷ 5 years = 10%

2. A home costing $250,000 is worth $268,000 one year later. What is the one-year appreciation rate?

    One-year appreciation rate = ($18,000 ÷ 250,000) = 7.2%

Compounded appreciation

Formula:

Appreciated value = Beginning value x (1+ annual rate) x (1+ annual rate) ...... for the number of years in question

Example:

A $100,000 property is expected to appreciate 5% each year for the next 3 years. What will be its appreciated value at the end of this period?

Appreciated value = $100,000 x 1.05 x 1.05 x 1.05 = $115,762.50

Rate of Return, Investment Value, Income

Formulas: Where Income = net operating income (NOI); Rate = rate of return, cap rate, or percent yield; and Value = value, price or investment amount:

Rate = Income ÷ Value

Value = Income ÷ Rate

Income = Value x Rate

Examples:

1. An office building has $200,000 net income and sold for $3,200,000. What was the rate of return?

   Rate = ($200,000 NOI ÷ 3,200,000 price) = 6.25%

2. An office building has $200,000 net income and a cap rate of 6.25%. What is its value?

   Value = ($200,000 ÷ 6.25%) = $3,200,000

3. An office building sells for $3,200,000 at a cap rate of 6.25%. What is its NOI?

   Income = $3,200,000 x 6.25% = $200,000

Basis, Adjusted Basis, and Capital Gain

Formulas: *Capital gain = Amount realized - Adjusted basis, where*

Amount realized = Sale price - Selling costs

Adjusted basis = Beginning basis + Capital improvements - Total depreciation

Total depreciation = (Beginning depreciable basis ÷ Depreciation term in years) x Years depreciated

Depreciable basis = Initial property value + Capital improvements - Land value

Example: Tip: work example backwards from last formula to first formula.

An apartment building was purchased for $500,000, with the land value estimated to be $100,000. The owner added a $100,000 parking lot. The property was depreciated on a 40-year schedule (for present purposes!). Three years later the property sold for $700,000, and selling costs were $50,000. What was the capital gain?

1. depreciable basis = $500,000 purchase price + 100,000 parking lot - 100,000 land = $500,000

2. total depreciation = ($500,000 ÷ 40 years) x 3 years = $37,500

79

3. adjusted basis = $500,000 purchase price + 100,000 parking lot - 37,500 total depreciation = $562,500

4. amount realized = $700,000 sale price - 50,000 selling costs = $650,000

5. capital gain = $650,000 amount realized - 562,500 adjusted basis = $87,500

Depreciation

Formulas: *Annual depreciation = (Beginning depreciable basis) ÷ (Depreciation term in number of years)*

Depreciable basis = (Initial property value + Capital improvements - Land value)

Example: Property value = $500,000; land value = $110,000; depreciation term = 39 years

1. ($500,000 - 110,000) = $390,000 depreciable basis

2. ($390,000 ÷ 39 years) = $10,000 annual depreciation

Equity

Formula: *Equity = Current market value - Current loan balance(s)*

Example: A home that was purchased for $150,000 with a $100,000 loan is now worth $300,000. The current loan balance is $80,000. What is the homeowner's equity?

Equity = $300,000 value - $80,000 debt = $220,000

Net Income

Formula: *NOI = Potential rent - Vacancy loss + Other income - Operating expenses*

Note: NOI does not include debt payments!

Example: A building has 10 office suites generating annual potential rent of $10,000 each. Vacancy = 10% and annual expenses are $35,000. Vending machines yield $5,000. What is the NOI?

$100,000 rent - 10,000 vacancy + 5,000 other income - 35,000 expenses = $60,000 NOI

Cash Flow

Formula: *Cash flow = (Net Operating Income - Debt service) where debt service is PI payment*

Example: A building generates $100,000 NOI after expenses and has a debt payment of $40,000. What is its cash flow?

Cash flow = $100,000 - 40,000 = $60,000

Investment Property Income Tax Liability

Formula: *Tax liability = (NOI + Reserves - Interest expense - Depreciation) x Tax bracket*

Example: An office building has NOI of $200,000, an annual reserve expense of $20,000, interest expense of $130,000 and annual depreciation of $50,000. Assuming a 28% tax bracket, what is its income tax liability?

Tax liability = ($200,000 + 20,000 - 130,000 - 50,000) x 28% = $11,200

Return on Investment

Formula: *ROI = NOI ÷ Price*

Example: An investment property generates a cash flow of $100,000 and appraises for $1,500,000. What is the owner's return on investment?

ROI = $100,000 ÷ 1,500,000 = 6.67%

Return on Equity

Formula: *ROE = Cash flow ÷ Equity*

Example: An investment property generates a cash flow of $100,000. The owner has $500,000 equity in the property. What is the owner's return on equity?

ROE= $100,000 ÷ 500,000 = 20%

Real Estate Taxation

Converting Mill Rates

Definition: 1 mill = $.001; a mill rate of 1 mill per $1,000 = .1%; a 1% tax rate = 10 mills

Formula: *Tax = (Taxable value ÷ 1000) x Mill rate*

Example: A tax rate on a house with a $200,000 taxable value is 7 mills per thousand dollars of assessed valuation. What is the tax?

Tax = ($200,000 ÷ 1,000) x 7 mills = $1,400

81

Tax Base

Formula: *Tax base = Assessed valuations – Exemptions*

Example: A town has a total assessed valuation of $20,000,000 and exemptions of $4,000,000. What is the tax base?

$20,000,000 - 4,000,000 = $16,000,000

Tax Rate, Base, and Requirement

Formulas: *Tax rate = Tax requirement ÷ Tax base*

Tax base = Tax requirement ÷ Tax rate

Tax requirement = Tax base x Rate

Example: A town has a tax base of $160,000,000 and a budget of $8,000,000. What is the tax rate?

Tax rate = ($8,000,000 ÷ 160,000,000) = .05, or 5%, or 50 mills

Special Assessments

Formula: *Special assessment = Total special assessment cost x Homeowner's share*

Example: A homeowner owns 100' of an 800' seawall that must be repaired. The total assessment will be $80,000. What is the homeowner's assessment?

1. Homeowner's share = 100' ÷ 800' = .125, or 12.5%

2. Special assessment = $80,000 x 12.5% = $10,000

Commissions

Commission Splits

Formulas: *Total commission = Sale price x Commission rate*

Co-brokerage split = Total commission x Co-brokerage percent

Agent split = Co-brokerage split x Agent percent

Broker split = Co-brokerage split - Agent split

Example: A $300,000 property sells at a 7% commission with a 50-50 co-brokerage split and a 60% agent split with her broker. What are total, co-brokerage, agent's, and broker's commissions?

Total commission = $300,000 x .07 = $21,000

Co-brokerage splits = $300,000 x .07 x .50 = $10,500

Agent split = $10,500 x .60 = $6,300

Agent's broker's split = $10.500 - 6,300 = $4,200

Seller's Net

Formula: *Seller's net = Sale Price - (sale price x commission) - Other closing costs - Loan balance*

Example: A home sells for $260,000 and has a loan balance of $200,000 at closing. The commission is 7% and other closing costs are $2,000. What is the seller's net?

Seller's net = ($260,000 - (260,000 x .07) - 2,000 - 200,000) = $39,800

Price to Net an Amount

Formula: *Sale Price = (Desired net + Closing costs + Loan payoff)) (1 - Commission rate)*

Example: A homeseller wants to net $50,000. The commission is 7%, the loan payoff is $150,000, and closing costs are $4,000. What must the price be?

Sale price = ($50,000 + 4,000 + 150,000) ÷ .93 = $219,355

Closing Costs, Prorations

30-Day 12-Month Method

Formulas: *Monthly amount = Annual amount / 12*

Daily amount = Monthly amount / 30

Proration = (Monthly amount multiplied by the # months) + (Daily amount multiplied by the # days)

Example: An annual tax bill is $1,800. Closing is on April 10. What is the seller's share of the taxes?

1. Monthly amount = ($1,800 ÷ 12) = $150; no. of months = 3

2. Daily amount = ($150 ÷ 30) = $5.00; no. of days = 10

3. Proration = ($150 x 3) + ($5 x 10) = ($450 + 50) = $500 seller's share

---

365-Day Method

Formula: *Daily amount = (Annual amount ÷ 365) or (Monthly amount ÷ Length of month)*

                      Proration = Daily amount multiplied by the # days

Example: An annual tax bill is $1,800. Closing is on April 10. What is the seller's share of the taxes?

     1.   Daily amount = ($1,800 ÷ 365) = $4.93

     2.   Jan 1 thru April 10 = (31 + 28 + 31 + 10) days, or 100 days

     3.   Proration = $4.93 x 100 days = $493 seller's share

Income Received in Advance (Rent)

Logic: *Credit buyer and debit seller for buyer's share*

Example: Seller receives $1,000 rent. The month is ¾ over.

     1.   Buyer's share is ($1,000 x 25%) = $250

     2.   Credit buyer / debit seller $250.

Expenses paid in Arrears (Tax)

Logic: *Credit buyer and debit seller for seller's share*

Example: Buyer will pay $1,000 taxes. The year is ¾ over.

     1.   Buyer's share is ($1,000 x 25%) = $250

     2.   Credit buyer / debit seller $750.

Insurance Coverage

Recovery with Co-Insurance Clauses

Formula: Recovery = (Damage claim) x (Percent replacement cost covered ÷ Minimum coverage requirement)

Example: An owner insures a home for $100,000. Replacement cost is $150,000. A co-insurance clause requires coverage of 80% of replacement cost to avoid penalty. Fire destroys the house. What can the owner recover from the insurer?

     Claim recovery = $150,000 x (67% cost covered ÷ 80% required) = $125,625

Section III: Georgia Laws & Practices

The following section is a condensation of GA Real Estate License Law as codified in the Georgia Real Estate License Law (Title 43, Ch. 40), GREC Rules and Regulations, and BRRETA. Additional statutes summarized include Title 10 and Title 16. Use the following link to access these statutes:

https://www.grec.state.ga.us/about/relaw.html

Other Georgia laws summarized are cited in the respective subsection.

Table of Contents

Part I. Definitions

Associate broker: acts on behalf of real estate broker in performing real estate acts.

Agency: relationship in which broker acts on behalf of real estate client with express authority.

Applicant: has completed requirements for license or approval.

Bank: financial institution regulated by financial institutions regulations council and authorized to provide federally insured checking accounts.

Broker: performs one of the following for another and receives or expects to receive compensation:
- **Negotiates** or assists in prospecting for listings, sales, purchases, exchanges, rental, leases or options of real estate, or serves as referral agent for same;
- **Collects rents**, assessments or other trust funds;
- **Selling timeshare intervals** or other parcels for compensation
- **Collects advance fees** other than advertising fees, when promoting the sale in listing publications, or for referral information to brokers;
- **Auctions** real estate;
- Performs **property management** or **community association** services;
- Provides **real estate consulting** services;
- Advertises that s/he is engaged in real estate.

Brokerage agreement
- express written contract
- client promises to pay broker valuable consideration for producing a seller, buyer, tenant, or landlord who is ready, able and willing to sell, buy, or rent the property or in consideration of broker's performing property management or community association management services.

Brokerage engagement: written contract wherein seller, buyer, landlord or tenant becomes the client of broker and promises to pay broker a valuable consideration or agrees broker may receive valuable consideration from another in consideration of broker producing a seller, buyer, tenant, or landlord ready, able and willing to sell, buy, or rent property or in consideration of broker's performing property management or community association management services.
- Examples of brokerage engagements: exclusive listing contract, open listing contract, buyer broker agreement, property management agreement, community association management agreement, and exclusive tenant representation contracts.

Brokerage relationship: agency and non-agency relationship between broker and consumer that results in brokerage engagement.

Buyer: acquired or attempted to acquire real estate interest.

Candidate for licensure: in process of completing licensing requirements or approval.

Client: consumer who has entered into brokerage agreement with broker.

Customer: consumer who has not entered into brokerage agreement but for whom broker performs ministerial acts.

Dual agent: broker who simultaneously has brokerage relationship with both parties in same transaction.

Firm: corporation, partnership, limited liability company, sole proprietorship, or other business entity licensed as broker.

Franchise: name use of which requires permission from another with right in trade name by state or federal law.

Franchisor: business entity owning and controlling trade name used by others

Licensee: Licensed as community association manager, salesperson, associate broker, or broker.

Ministerial acts: acts performed by broker or affiliated licensees for person who does not require discretion or exercise of licensee's judgment.

Person: individuals and firms.

Property management services: Acts on behalf of broker to manage community associations and performs no other real estate activity.

Purchaser: attempts or succeeds in acquiring interest in land.

Real estate: condo, leasehold or other interest in land whether corporeal, incorporeal, freehold, non-freehold, in Georgia or elsewhere. Includes mobile homes affixed to land.

Salesperson: Someone other than associate broker who performs real estate activity on behalf of broker.

Statutory overnight delivery: delivery through Unites States Postal Service or commercial firm regularly engaged in document delivery in which sender has directed delivery be no later than next business day and received acknowledgement of receipt by addressee or agent of addressee.

Timely: reasonable time under the particular circumstances.

Part II. The Real Estate Commission

Purpose, Structure and Authority

Purpose of Georgia Real Estate Commission (GREC) and License Law
- To protect public interest by regulating real estate brokerage industry through licensing of practitioners

Members
- Six members appointed by Governor, confirmed by Senate
- Five licensees must have been Georgia residents minimum five years; sixth no connection with real estate industry and must have recognized interest in consumer concerns
- Serve five-year terms until successor is appointed
- Must recuse themselves from voting if conflict of interest
- May be removed by Governor for inability to perform duties, incompetence, dishonesty, or disciplinary sanction
- Meet at least monthly

Commissioner
- Full-time employee and chief executive officer
- Appointed by GREC
- Must have good moral character and qualifications as required by GREC
- No interest in real estate or related business
- Hires staff including investigators
- Commissioner and staff, if licensed, must be on inactive status during GREC employment

Scope of authority and powers
- Hire and evaluate staff
- Enter into contracts as needed to fulfill duties
- Provide a licensing process; issue, revoke or suspend licenses: censure licensees
- Promulgate rules and regulations pertaining to professional conduct of licensees
- Administer license law by enforcing the rules and regulations
- Ensure that consumers and licensees receive due process rights

Quorum
- Four members comprise a quorum

Fees
- GREC establishes fees; must be reasonable and determined by cost of operations
- All fees deposited into state treasury to cover administration and enforcement of license law

Seal, records
- GREC must have seal to authenticate acts

Part III. Licensing Regulation

License Requirements

Ethics qualification
- Licenses granted only to persons with good reputation for honesty, trustworthiness, integrity, and competence to transact business in manner to safeguard interest of public
- Failing to meet license requirements for any license is grounds for denial of license without a hearing

Broker or associate broker licensing requirements
- 21 years of age
- Georgia resident, unless applying for reciprocity
- High school graduate or equivalency certificate
- Criminal History Report completed
- Maintain active license status three or more of past five years
- Evidence of completing approved 60-hour broker course
- If licensed as community association manager, evidence of completion of additional 75 hours of coursework approved by GREC
- After course work, pass state exam approved by GREC

Salesperson licensing requirements
- 18 years of age
- Georgia resident unless applying for reciprocity
- High school graduate or equivalency certificate
- Criminal History Report
- Evidence of completing approved 75-hour salesperson's course
- After completing course, pass state exam approved by GREC.
  - if final exam is failed, applicant may retake as soon as scheduling permits
- **Post-license requirement**: within one year of license issuance, complete 25-hour post-license course and course exam approved by GREC.
  - if not completed within one year, license will lapse and salesperson required to surrender wall license and pocket card.
  - if lapsed, can be reinstated
    - if enrolled in course within one year of licensure, paid required course fees, but has not completed all course sessions or exams, may reinstate by completing course within six months of lapsing
    - if not reinstated within six months, must complete 25-hour course and pay penalties required by GREC to reinstate

Firm licensing requirements
- Designate qualifying broker responsible for assuring that firm and affiliated licensees comply with license law rules and regulations
- Authorize qualifying broker to bind the firm to any settlement of contested cases before GREC when necessary
- Violations of license law by the firm subject qualifying broker to disciplinary measures
- License granted only if every person acting as licensee holds a real estate license
- Specific requirements for types of firms
  - sole proprietorship must be solely owned by licensed broker
  - corporation must have corporation officer as qualifying broker
  - partnership must include copy of partnership agreement and certificate of trade name. limited partnership must have general partner as qualifying broker. general partnership must have corporation officer whose actions are binding as qualifying broker.

- limited liability company must have member, or manager as qualifying broker, must have certificate of authority to do business in Georgia, and if applicable, copy of certified copy of trade name
- trade name of any franchise must include franchise name and either firm's name or firm's trade name

- **License denial**: GREC may deny firm license if stockholder, member, or partner does not bear good reputation for honesty, trustworthiness, and integrity, has been convicted of certain crimes, or has been disciplined by real estate regulatory agency.

Community association manager licensing requirements
- 18 years of age
- Georgia resident, unless applying for reciprocity
- High school graduate or equivalency certificate
- Criminal History Report
- After completion of course of study, pass exam approved by GREC
- Furnish evidence of completion of at least 25 hours in community association manager's course approved by GREC no earlier than one year before and no later than one year after issuance of original salesperson's license, or 18 months after if salesperson qualifies for six-month extension.

Fidelity bond requirement
- Broker providing community management services must have fidelity bond or insurance to protect community associations against loss of any funds being held or controlled by broker
    - waived if broker collects, maintains, controls, or disburses funds totaling less than $60,000

College course alternatives for meeting prelicense education requirements
- Applicants may qualify to sit for exam by presenting college transcripts for real estate courses as follows:
    - salesperson applicant: at least 10 quarter hours or six semester hours
    - broker applicant: 15 quarter hours or 9 semester hours
    - community association manager: 4 quarter hours or 2 semester hours with concentration in community associations and management
    - courses must deal with principles, fundamentals, or essentials of real estate. College correspondence courses or continuing education courses do not satisfy these requirements

All licensees must be licensed under active Georgia broker
- Cannot be licensed under more than one Georgia broker
- May also affiliate with another state's broker if
    - that state's laws allow affiliations in both states
    - Georgia licensee has written permission of Georgia broker holding license citing duties that licensee may undertake for each broker and that licensee may not undertake brokerage activity for Georgia property except on behalf of Georgia broker

Residents of disaster areas
- If licensee resides in county designated as disaster area by state or federal authorities and suffers uninsured major damage or loss to residence or place of business
    - GREC may extend licensee's renewal period for up to two years without further payment of fee upon satisfactory proof of licensee's uninsured major damage or loss
    - GREC may make appropriate adjustments in deadline dates for applications filed by applicants and licensees

Required criminal history report
- Within 60 days prior to applying for licensure, individual must at, his/her expense, attach to application
- the certified criminal history report issued by Georgia Crime Information Center of Georgia Bureau of Investigation
- Non-Georgia resident: equivalent certified criminal history report from resident state
- When report reveals criminal conviction, individual must supply GREC a certified copy of

- o citation, accusation, information or indictment that lead to conviction, and
- o certified copy of sentence

Applicants with prior disciplinary action
- Must provide GREC certified copy of any allegations that preceded final order, and final order of licensing agency
- GREC may deny a license to applicant with prior criminal conviction or disciplinary actions

Request for hearing after denial
- Applicant may request formal hearing in writing to GREC within 60 days of GREC mailing notice of denial
- If GREC affirms denial, applicant may not re-apply without again passing qualifying examination required for that license and paying any required fees
- If applicant does not make written application for formal hearing within 60 days, application will lapse. May not make another application without passing any qualifying examination and paying any required fees

Broker licensed as salesperson
- Broker or associate broker can be licensed as a salesperson by surrendering broker's license and applying for salesperson license
- No exam required
- May later be relicensed as broker with no additional exam required

Any check to GREC returned as unpaid
- May be cause for denial of license or imposing a sanction

Filing applications
- Applications are filed during regular business hours or mailed to GREC in a letter postmarked by United States Postal Service
- Standards for filing applications and fees by electronic means or courier services may be established by GREC

Licensee wishing to be employed by unlicensed person to perform brokerage activity with real estate owned by unlicensed person
- Must surrender license to GREC
- May not reinstate without qualifying as original applicant

Falsifying or misrepresenting on application
- may result in withdrawal of approval

Suspended or revoked licensees
- Licensees with suspended or revoked licenses may not apply for other licenses

Licensing fee
- Must pay fee with application for initial license as broker, associate broker, salesperson, or community association manager.
- If applicants do not apply within three months of passing licensing exam, the application fee
- Must apply within one year.

Child support non-compliance
- Applicants or licensees found to be in non-compliance with order for child support may be refused the initial license, or their active licenses may be suspended

Exemptions from Licensing

Exemptions from Georgia licensure

- Owners, general partners of limited partnership, landlords, prospective purchasers or regular employees of owners performing management or investment acts their employer's property
- Person who manages resident apartment complexes under contract approved by any federal agency for organization exempt from federal taxes, if person was engaged in managing that property prior to January 1, 1989
- Attorney-in-fact under power of attorney to convey real estate for owner or lessor
- Licensed practicing attorney acting solely as incident to practice of law
- Receiver, trustee in bankruptcy, administrator, executor, guardian, or one acting under court order or authority of will or trust instrument
- Employee of government agency conducting official duties
- Employee of public or private utility performing acts on property owned, leased, or to be acquired by utility company
- Person, as owner or through another person engaged by owner full-time, or owner of management company whose principals hold controlling ownership of property, provides property management services or community association management services, buys, sells, leases, manages, auctions or otherwise deals with property
- Person employed full-time by owner of property to provide property management services or community association management services, selling, buying, leasing, managing, auctioning or otherwise dealing with property.
- Person employed full-time by community association to provide community association management services
- Person acting as referral agent not involved in negotiations, execution of documents, collection of rent, management of property and who
  - does not receive fee from party being referred and does not charge advance fee; and
  - does not act as referral agent in more than three transactions per year
- Person employed by broker to assist in property management services on property on which broker has written management agreement if activities authorized in agreement between broker and employee and limited to
  - delivering or receiving lease application, lease, or amendments
  - receiving security deposit, rental payment, or related payment, for delivery to and made payable to broker or owner
  - showing rental unit, provided employee is acting under direct instructions of broker, and executing leases or rental agreements
  - providing information authorized by broker about rental unit, lease application or lease
  - providing information to tenant about status of security deposit or rent payments, or to owner about financial accounts and payments from owner's tenants
  - performing ministerial acts authorized by broker in written agreement between broker and employee
  - broker utilizing services of such employee held responsible for activities of individual
- Person providing property management services on properties available for less than 90 days' occupancy ("innkeepers exemption") if meeting all the following
  - property manager has written agreement with owner specifying terms of property management, reporting of income and expenses, and remitting of income to owner
  - agreement between property manager and owner does not allow manager to rent or lease, and any agreement between manager and guest or occupant is not lease or rental agreement
  - applicable zoning laws do not prohibit short-term occupancy uses
  - guest's or occupant's occupancy is for less than 90 days
  - no deposit except cost of rental required for minimum rental period
  - guest or occupant pays required state or local sales taxes or excise taxes, and property manager has any required state or local business license or permits
  - property manager has authority to specify rooms or units to be occupied
  - no extra charge for basic utilities
  - notice not required for guest or occupant to terminate occupancy (certain exceptions apply)
  - room or unit is not permanent residence of guest or occupant

92

- Member of community association who provides community association management services to only one association of which he/she is member
- Person who performs only physical maintenance on property; or
- Licensed certified public accountant acting solely to practice of accounting

Exceptions DO NOT apply to:
- Any person other than owner or full-time employees of owner who perform acts of broker on property required to be registered
- Real estate licensees
- Persons attempting to use exceptions to evade licensure

License Reciprocity

Applicant moved to Georgia or is applying for non-resident licensure
- may be granted license without exam or education if candidate produces original certification issued within 12 months prior to application. Must show that the applicant
  - passed exam for type of license being applied for in Georgia
  - met prelicense and CE requirements by other state
  - is in good standing
  - has not had disciplinary action imposed by state's licensing body

- If certification does not comply with conditions, must pass qualifying exam for Georgia license candidate is seeking

Expired and Inactive Licenses

Lapsed / expired license
- If not renewed by expiration date, license is lapsed
- If lapse due solely for failure to pay renewal fee, licensee may reinstate
  - within two years of lapsing: pay all fees and charges
  - more than two years and less than five years lapsed: pay all fees and complete CE required
  - more than five years: must meet education and exam requirements for new license
- Lapsed longer than one year, not subject to CE requirements: must meet CE requirements to reinstate
- Nonresident license lapsed for failure to pay renewal fee may reactivate by paying fee of an original applicant if licensee maintained active license in state of residence during license lapse and has met its continuing education requirements
- If license has lapsed over a year and is not subject to continuing education requirements, when reinstating, license subject to continuing education

Inactive status
- Licensees who does not wish to be actively engaged in real estate may continue license by written request within 30 days of ceasing work that he/she be placed on inactive status
  - Prohibited from engaging in the real estate activity except regarding property owned by licensee
- To reinstate inactive license, licensee must have broker signature; a broker must make application to GREC prior to resuming brokerage activity
  - Must first meet CE requirement unless licensee maintained active license in another state that has continuing education requirements while inactive in Georgia
  - Inactive licensee must notify GREC in writing of any address change within 30 days
  - All inactive licensees required to pay renewal fee. If not paid, license will lapse
- Inactive licensee may be employee of unlicensed person to perform non-brokerage activities

License Renewal Requirements

Continuing education requirements for renewal of individual licenses
- Minimum of nine hours of GREC-approved courses per year of four-year renewal period (total 36 hours); no exam required
- Effective July 1, 2016, must complete at least three hours on license law during each renewal period
- Salesperson renewing first time may count 25-hour post-license course as 9 hours of continuing education, requiring additional 27 hours
- Inactive licensees must complete CE requirement prior to reactivating license
- Not required for those on U.S. military duty or on General Assembly while serving. If exemption option is taken for over two years of duty, must complete 25-hour post-license course within six months of conclusion of duty.
- Exemption to continuing education requirement: individuals actively licensed on January 1, 1980
- College courses at accredited college or university of four quarter hours or two semester hours if:
  - counts toward obtaining major in real estate or courses dealing with principles, fundaments, or essentials of real estate
  - counts toward obtaining major in business administration, accounting, finance, or marketing
  - courses are in agency, real property law, and contract law
  - not college correspondence course or college continuing education courses
- If CE is not completed, licensee cannot renew and license will lapse

Renewal dates
- Original license valid four years, expiring on last day of applicant's birth month
- Renewal every four years on last day of applicant's birth month

Broker renewal
- Broker must complete renewal form regarding status of broker's trust account(s) and any trust account(s) broker allows affiliated licensees to maintain

Auctioneer Licensing

Auctioneers licensing
- Must obtain license to auction real property
- No person may hold themselves out as engaging in or conducting auctions without Georgia auctioneer license
- Auctioneers may not sell real property unless also licensed as real estate broker, associate broker, or salesperson

Companies
- Companies may not engage in, advertise, or conduct business of auctioning without first being registered by GREC

Part IV. Disciplinary Actions

Hearings, Revocation, Suspension and Censure of Licenses

GREC may initiate actions on its own
- GREC may on its own motion investigate applicants or licensees if within three years of initiation of investigation
- GREC must investigate upon receipt of written, sworn request by anyone
- Exceptions to three-year rule are investigations of applicants for licensure, allegations of fraudulent conduct or mishandling funds

Investigative report concludes whether a possible violation occurred.
- If no violation, file is closed
- If violation occurred, sanction(s) can be imposed and citation issued

Issuance of subpoenas; hearings
- Commissioner, chairperson, or respondent may issue subpoenas for documents or material pertaining to investigation and apply to superior county court to require compliance
- Results of investigations kept by GREC and cannot be released except for hearing
- If licensee is suspended or surrendered due to contested case, GREC may publish names on GREC website or other official GREC publications
- GREC may have closed meetings for disciplinary proceedings
- Applicants who are refused license must be given opportunity for hearing
  - unless otherwise agreed, hearing held in county of domicile of GREC
  - if aggrieved by final decision, entitled to judicial review in superior court of county of domicile of GREC

GREC sanctions and disciplinary actions
- Refusal to grant or renew a license
- Revocation or suspension of license for indefinite period
- Demote broker license to a salesperson's license
- Censure license
- Administer a reprimand
- Impose monetary assessments to reimburse GREC's expenses
- Impose maximum $1,000 fine for each violation with fines for multiple violations of up to $5,000 in any one disciplinary hearing,
- Require real estate course completion in brokerage
- Require periodic reports by independent accountant of broker's designated trust account
- Limit or restrict licensee or applicant approval as GREC deems necessary to protect the public
- Subpoena records

Failure to comply
- If licensee fails to comply with final order, GREC may suspend or revoke license after opportunity for a hearing

Injunctions
- GREC may obtain court injunction to stop licensee from performing activity in violation of License Law
- Injunction is obtained from superior court of county in which violation occurred

Performing real estate activity without a license
- Is a misdemeanor

- Individual who offers, attempts or agrees to perform real estate activity with intention or promise of receiving valuable consideration is deemed a licensee. Commission of a single 'licensed activity' by unlicensed person constitutes violation
- GREC may have cease and desist order issued prohibiting individual from illegally practicing real estate.
- Fine may be levied for each transaction in violation
- GREC may seek additional remedies

Citations and letters of finding for minor infractions:
- GREC empowered to issue citation to licensee stating alleged violation and informing licensee of opportunity to request contested case hearing
  - citation may include order to
    - complete course in brokerage or instruction
    - file periodic reports by independent accountant on broker's trust account, or
    - pay maximum fine of $1,000 for each violation; multiple violations limited to $5,000 in any one citation
    - perform combination of the above
  - if licensee fails to request hearing within 30 days of service of citation, order contained in citation is final
  - failure to comply with final order may result in imposition of sanction on license, after notice and opportunity for hearing
- GREC issues letter of findings to licensee if alleged violation appears to have done no harm to third party
  - confidential and does not appear on license history of licensee
  - does not constitute public record and is not available for inspection by public
  - findings not disclosed to any person or agency other than GREC or Commissioner

Hearings; judicial review
- GREC may not censure, revoke or suspend a license without first providing an opportunity for a hearing
- If licensee fails to appear at hearing ,GREC may proceed to hear evidence and take action as if licensee or applicant had been present
- Notice of hearing, final decision must be served upon licensee or applicant by personal service or by certified mail
- Any person aggrieved by final decision in contested case is entitled to judicial review
  - initial judicial review of final decision of GREC is available solely in the superior court of the county of domicile of GREC
  - all hearings in contested cases must be conducted by Office of State Administrative Hearings.
- When GREC denies application based on applicant's failure to meet requirements, it notifies applicant of denial and offers applicant opportunity to request hearing before Office of State Administrative Hearings

Post-hearing procedures
- Upon initial decision by Office of State Administrative Hearings, any party may request review of initial decision within 30 days
- A party may move that the matter be remanded to the Office of State Administrative Hearings for purposes of taking additional testimony, but granted only for good cause shown
- All motions, briefs or other documents pertaining to matters pending before GREC must be filed at least seven days prior to scheduled hearing date

Notification of legal action
- Licensee required to notify GREC in writing of final disposition of any action filed in any court or with any administrative agency within ten days of conclusion of proceedings
- Notice of any criminal action must be given to GREC within ten days of conviction and include copy of indictment, accusation, and conviction

Surrendering license or notice of suspension or revocation
- Licensee must forward wall certificate of licensure and pocket card immediately to GREC

- If broker, must forward all affiliated licensee's wall certificates and pocket cards in addition to broker's
- No refund of fee made for surrendered, suspended, or revoked licenses

License reinstatement

- Licensees who surrender license or have license revoked must apply for licensure as original applicant to seek reinstatement
- When broker or associate broker license is revoked or surrendered, individual must wait at least ten years before reapplying for licensure

Education, Research and Recovery Fund

Purpose of Fund

- GREC established the Real Estate Education, Research and Recovery Fund to compensate consumers who suffer losses due to licensees' violations of License Law, Rules or Regulations

Source of funds

- $20 of each license application is paid into fund
- Fund must have minimum $1 million balance. If balance drops, GREC may assess $30 per year for all license renewals to replenish Fund
- Income from invested fund must be used for real estate education and research

Collection from fund

- By anyone except bonding companies who suffer damages resulting from violations of licensee
- Aggrieved must obtain judgment against licensee from court of competent jurisdiction.
- If court feels aggrieved party is unable to collect, court makes an order directing GREC pay from Fund
- Fund may pay actual and/or compensatory damages.
- Maximum amount per transaction regardless of number of persons aggrieved: $25,000
- No person who establishes a claim may ever obtain more than $25,000.00 from Fund.
- Maximum liability for acts of one licensee $75,000
- Statute of limitation: 2 years from cause of action

Effect on licensee

- License automatically revoked upon Fund payment of settlement of judgment
- If judgment against firm, qualifying broker's license automatically revoked
- Licensee may not be relicensed until he/she repays in full, plus interest
- Filing bankruptcy does not relieve licensee of requirement

Part V. Violations & Unfair Trade Practices

Prohibited / unfair trade practices

- Enforced by Fair Housing Division of the Georgia Commission on Equal Opportunity
- Fair housing violations based on **race, color, religion, sex, disability, familial status, or national origin** (**seven** federally protected classes)
    - **refuse to sell**, or rent or deny real estate to any person
    - **discriminate** in terms, conditions, or privileges of sale, rental or in provision of services or facilities
    - make, print, or publish any notice, statement, or ad that indicates any **preference, limitation, or discrimination**
    - **misrepresenting** that real estate is not available for inspection, sale, or rental when it is available
    - misrepresenting that change will or may occur in area to **induce or discourage listing**, purchasing, selling, or renting
    - misrepresenting that change may occur in **composition of area** based on any protected class and that change will result in lowering property values, increase in criminal or antisocial behavior, or decline in quality of schools
- Misleading or **inaccurate advertising** regarding terms, value, policies or services
- **Failing to account** for or remit money in licensee's possession which belongs to others
- **Commingling** money or other property of consumers
- Failing to maintain and deposit in **separate**, federally insured account at financial institution money received unless all parties agree otherwise in writing
- Failing to **disclose in writing**
    - receipt of fee, rebate or other item of value on expenditures made on principal's behalf for which principal is reimbursing licensee
    - payment to another broker commission, fee or something of value for referral of principal
    - receipt of anything of value for referral of any service or product to a principal
- **Representing a broker other than broker** holding license, without knowledge and consent of broker holding license
- **Accepting commission** or other valuable consideration **from anyone other than broker** holding licensee's license without consent of that broker
- Acting as agent and **undisclosed principal** in transaction
- Guaranteeing future profits which may result from resale of real property
- Placing sign offering property for sale or rent without written consent of owner or owner's agent
- Failing to remove sign within ten days after expiration of listing
- Offering real estate for sale or lease without knowledge and consent of owner or owner's agent or on terms other than those authorized by owner or owner's agent
- Inducing any party to break contract or brokerage agreement to substitute any other contract or brokerage agreement with another principal
- Negotiating sale, exchange, or lease directly with party licensee knows has a written exclusive brokerage agreement with another broker regarding that property unless current brokerage agreement stipulates licensee holding agreement will not provide negotiation services to client
- Indicating that price opinion provided by licensee is an appraisal unless licensee holds appraiser classification
- Performing or attempting to perform any licensing acts on property in another state without having been properly licensed or otherwise complying with that state's brokerage laws
- Paying commission or compensation to an unlicensed person for performing licensing activity. Exceptions include
    - estate or heirs of deceased real estate licensee who had valid Georgia real estate license at time commission earned and at time of death
    - citizen of another country as referral agent if that country does not license real estate brokers and Georgia licensee paying compensation obtains and maintains reasonable written evidence that payee is
        - a citizen of other country
        - is not a resident of this country
        - is in real estate brokerage business in other country

- by brokerage firm holding licensee's license to an unlicensed firm in which individual licensee owns more than 20% interest if
  - licensee earned the commission on behalf of the brokerage firm
  - unlicensed firm does not perform real estate brokerage activity
  - licensee and brokerage firm have written agreement authorizing payment to the unlicensed firm
  - brokerage firm obtains and retains written evidence that licensee owns more than 20% interest in unlicensed firm to which the compensation will be paid
- Failing to include expiration date in any written listing agreement and failing to leave copy with principal
- Failing to deliver, within reasonable time, completed copy of purchase agreement or offer to buy or sell to purchaser and seller; failing to provide a copy of any document used in a real estate transaction to any individual signing such document
- Failure of broker to deliver complete closing statement to seller at closing
- Failure of broker to deliver to buyer complete statement of all money received from buyer and how and for what it was disbursed
- Making any substantial misrepresentations
- Acting for more than one party in transaction without written consent of all parties
- Failure to place deposits and other money with his/her broker, as soon after receipt as practicably possible;
- Creating a lien to cast a cloud on title when no valid claim under listing contract exists
- Demonstrating incompetency or dishonest dealings, failing to safeguard interest of the public
- Obtaining a brokerage agreement, sales contract, or lease knowing or having reason to believe that another broker has exclusive brokerage agreement, unless licensee has written permission from that broker
  - licensee is permitted to present proposal or bid for community association management upon written request from community association board of directors
- Broker failing to retain all records pertaining to trust funds and real estate transactions for three years failing to produce documents at request of GREC
- Falsifying or being a party to falsification of contract or other real estate document
- Failing to obtain written agreement of parties regarding payment of interest earned on trust funds
- Failing to disclose agency relationships in timely manner
- Attempting to perform any act authorized to be performed only by broker, associate broker, or salesperson while licensed as community association manager
- Attempting to sell, lease, or exchange property of member of community association to which a licensee is providing community association management services without written consent of association
- Failing to deliver to community association terminating a management contract the following within 30 days of termination or time specified in agreement
  - complete and accurate record of all transactions and funds handled during contract period not previously accounted for
  - all records and documents received from community association or received on association's behalf
  - any funds held on behalf of community association
- Inducing any person to alter, modify, or change another licensee's fee or commission without that licensee's prior written consent
- Failing to obtain written agreement to refer a person to another licensee and to inform person being referred whether licensee will receive valuable consideration for referral
- Failing to include financing terms in sales contract having financing contingency
- Conducting business under name other than that which is registered with GREC
- Failing to notify broker of personal real estate activities
- Failing to include correct amount of earnest money, security deposit, or terms in sales contract or lease
- Paying referral fee to unlicensed party
- Failure to register trust fund account with GREC
- Failure to have bank designate account as trust or escrow account
- Broker continuing to permit affiliated licensee to conduct transactions after licensee's license has been lapsed for more than one month

- Failing to deposit earnest money within three business days of receipt unless contract provides otherwise
- Failing to notify GREC of final disposition of any administrative, civil, or criminal action within ten days of conclusion of court or hearing
- Broker failing to sign release form immediately upon personally receiving request of community association manager, salesperson, or associate broker to be released from broker's firm
- Transferring licensee failing to account for or return to releasing broker all items belonging to broker
- Failing to deposit into trust account trust funds received in transaction in which licensee is a principle;
- Failing to include fixed date of expiration in listing agreement
- Broker failing to obtain agreement of all parties prior to disbursing funds
- Licensee making false statement of material fact on application, or cause false statement to be submitted
- Failing to reconcile trust or escrow account at least monthly. If discrepancy occurs, failing to provide explanation of discrepancy and corrective action taken
- Performing or attempting to perform brokerage acts on property located in another state without being properly licensed in that state or otherwise complying with state law's regarding brokerage

Additional violations
- Failing to:
  - notify GREC in writing within 30 days of address change, of opening or closing of trust account, of transferring to new company, or of leaving firm to go inactive
  - affiliate with new company or apply to go inactive within 30 days of GREC'S receipt of notice that broker holding license no longer will do so and has mailed letter to licensee's last known address indicating broker is returning license to GREC
  - respond within 30 days to written inquiry from GREC requesting further information on any application licensee has filed with the commission
- Submitting to GREC check returned unpaid
- Non-broker license performing broker duty or act, either with proper delegation by the broker or without the broker's authorization
- Acceptance of bonus by affiliated licensee without broker's permission
- Paying fee or commission to licensee representing another party to transaction except with full knowledge and written consent of all parties
- Failing of licensees, schools and instructors to notify GREC in writing within one month of change in mailing address, residence address and email address if email used

Part VI. Brokerage Relationships & Disclosures

Brokerage Relationships in Real Estate Transactions Act (BRRETA)

Brokerage Relationship in Real Estate Transactions Act (BRRETA)
- Governs relationships between consumers, brokers and affiliated licensees
- Act not intended to prescribe or affect contractual relationships between brokers and affiliated licensees
- May serve as basis for private rights of action and defenses by consumers and brokers

Broker's legal relationship to customers or clients
- Broker who performs brokerage services for client or customer owes only duties and obligations in BRRETA unless parties agree otherwise in writing signed by parties
- Broker NOT considered to have fiduciary relationship with any party
- Responsible only for exercising reasonable care in discharge of duties specified in BRRETA, and for client, as specified in brokerage engagement
- When broker with brokerage relationship with customer or client enters into new brokerage relationship with customer or client, broker must timely disclose that fact and new brokerage relationship to all brokers, customers or clients involved in contemplated transaction

Agency disclosure
- Written disclosures must be made in a timely manner, but not later than when any party first makes an offer to purchase, sell, lease, or exchange real property
- A licensee must make written disclosure to both parties in transaction, revealing the party or parties for whom licensee's firm is acting as agent or dual agent, or if firm is not acting as agent of either party, and from whom that licensee's firm will receive any valuable consideration

BRRETA responsibilities to all clients engaged by broker (seller, buyer, tenant, landlord)
- Perform terms of brokerage agreement with client
- Promote interest of client by
  - seeking sale or lease at price and terms in brokerage engagement or at price and terms acceptable to seller or landlord client
  - seeking property at price and terms in buyer or tenant brokerage agreement, or at price and terms acceptable to buyer or tenant client
  - timely presenting all offers to and from client, even when property is subject to contract
  - disclosing to client material facts concerning transaction of which broker has actual knowledge
  - advising client to obtain expert advice regarding material matters beyond expertise of broker
  - timely accounting for money and property received in which client has or may have interest
- Exercise reasonable skill and care in performance of duties set forth in BRRETA, rules and regulations, and other duties agreed to in brokerage engagement
- Comply with all BRRETA and applicable statutes and regulations, including fair housing and civil rights statutes
- Keep confidential all information received during course of engagement which is made confidential by express request or instruction from seller unless seller permits disclosure or disclosure is required by law
  - disclosure between broker and any affiliated licensee assisting broker in representing client is not breach of duty of confidentiality

Material facts disclosure
- Adverse material facts pertaining to physical condition of property
  - material defects
  - environmental contamination

- facts required by statute actually known by broker and not discoverable by reasonably diligent inspection of property
- All material facts pertaining to adverse physical conditions neighborhood within one mile of property which are known to broker and which could not be discovered upon diligent inspection of the neighborhood or through review of reasonably available governmental regulations, documents, records, maps, and statistics
- Broker NOT obligated to seek out adverse material facts pertaining to physical condition of property or existing adverse conditions in immediate neighborhood
- Brokers must not knowingly give prospective tenants or buyers false information
- Broker NOT liable to buyer or tenant for providing false information if broker did not have actual knowledge that information was false and **discloses to buyer source of information**

Client / customer obligations regardless of BRRETA
- Seller must disclose to prospective buyers or tenants all adverse material facts actually known pertaining to physical condition of property
- Buyers and tenants must inspect and familiarize themselves with potentially adverse conditions related to physical condition of property, any improvements, and neighborhood

Cannot sue if in compliance with BRRETA
- Cannot bring action against broker or affiliated licensees for revealing information in compliance with BRRETA
- No broker liability for failure to disclose any matter other than those matters enumerated in BRRETA
- No liability on part of broker without a finding of fraud

Broker performing ministerial acts
- Broker engaged by a seller, buyer, tenant or landlord may provide assistance to other party in transaction by performing ministerial acts without violating brokerage engagement

Duration and termination of relationships between broker and clients
- Brokerage relationships commence when client engages the broker, and continue until
  - completion of performance of engagement, or if no completion, earlier of
    - expiration date agreed upon by parties or in amendment
    - any authorized termination of relationship
    - if no expiration is provided and no termination occurred, one year after initiation of engagement.
- After termination, broker owes no further duties to client except
  - accounting of all moneys and property
  - keeping confidential all information received during engagement, unless
    - client permits the disclosure
    - disclosure is required by law
    - information becomes public from a source other than broker

Disclosure duties prior to entering into brokerage engagement relationships
- types of agency relationships available through broker
- any brokerage relationships held by broker with other parties which would conflict with interests of prospective client actually known to broker
- broker's compensation and whether broker will share compensation
- broker's obligations to keep information confidential

Compensation does not determine form or creation of relationship
- Who pays broker's commission does not determine whether brokerage relationship is created between broker and consumer

Dual agency consent requirements
- Must have written consent of all clients containing
  - description of transactions
  - statement that broker represents two clients whose interests are adverse

- o statement that dual agent will disclose adverse material facts
- o statement that broker disclose any material relationship broker has with other clients in transaction other than that incidental to the transaction
- o statement that client is not required to consent to dual agency and that consent was given voluntarily
- No cause of action allowed against dual agent for making required disclosures
- Broker may without liability withdraw from representing client who has not consented to disclosed dual agency at any time prior to existence of dual agency
  - o Withdrawal must not prejudice ability of broker to continue representing other client in transaction

Must have office policy regarding dual agency
- Every broker must develop and enforce office brokerage relationship policy among affiliated licensees which specifically permits or rejects disclosed dual agency

Dual agency written disclosure requirements
- Must be made to both parties in transaction disclosing
  - o party to whom licensee's firm is acting as dual agent
  - o who will pay the consideration
- Must be made no later than when any party first makes offer to purchase, sell, lease or exchange

Designated agency (exclusive representation)
- Broker may assign different licensees as designated agents to exclusively represent opposing clients in same transaction
- Any company policy must ensure each client is represented in compliance with BRRETA
- If broker appoints different designated agents, neither broker, affiliated licensees, nor brokerage firm will deemed to be dual agents
- Confidential information
  - o Designated agents may not disclose, except to designated agent's broker, information made confidential by request or instruction of client, except information allowed or required to be disclosed by BRRETA or other laws
  - o Broker of designated agent may not reveal confidential information received from either designated agent or client
    - confidential information is any information the disclosure of which has not been consented to by the client that could harm the negotiating position of the client
  - o Designated agents may not permit disclosure by broker or affiliated licensees of any information made confidential by express request or instruction of party prior to creation of the designated agency
  - o Broker must maintain confidential information unless permitted by client or required by law
  - o No liability as result of a broker and affiliated licensee's compliance

Transaction broker and performing ministerial acts
- Transaction broker may provide assistance to consumers by performing ministerial acts
- Ministerial acts include
  - o identifying property for sale, lease, or exchange
  - o providing real estate statistics and information on property
  - o providing any pre-printed real estate form contracts, leases, and related exhibits and addenda
  - o acting as scribe in preparation of real estate contracts, leases, and related exhibits and addenda
  - o locating architects, engineers, surveyors, inspectors, lenders, insurance agents, attorneys, and other professionals
  - o identifying schools, shopping facilities, places of worship, and other similar facilities

Required actions of transaction brokers
- Timely present all offers
- Timely account for all money
- Timely disclose adverse material facts pertaining to property's physical condition including
  - o material defects in property
  - o environmental contamination

- facts required by statute or regulation known by broker which could not be discovered by reasonably diligent inspection by buyer
- material facts pertaining to immediate neighborhood known to broker and not discoverable by diligent inspection of the neighborhood or through the review of reasonably available governmental regulations, documents, records, maps, and statistics
- Transaction brokers may not knowingly give any party false information
  - Broker not liable if broker did not have actual knowledge that information was false and discloses to party source of information
- Seller must disclose to prospective buyers all adverse material facts pertaining to physical condition
- Buyers must inspect and familiarize themselves with potentially adverse conditions related to physical condition of property, improvements, and neighborhood
- Violations do not create broker liability without finding of fraud on part of broker

No agency with MLS
- Broker does not have an agency relationship with common source information company such as multiple listing service.

Business brokerage
- Business brokers must hold appropriate license issued by GREC if sale of business involves the transfer of any interest in real property.

Stigmatized property disclosure not required
- Need not disclose if property was occupied by person infected with virus or other disease highly unlikely to be transmitted through occupancy
- Need not disclose if property was site of homicide or other felony, or suicide or death by accidental or natural causes

Part VII. Management Responsibilities of RE Firms

Brokerage Operations Requirements

Broker or qualifying broker requirement by type of firm
- Sole proprietorship by definition owned entirely by licensed broker
- Qualifying broker for partnership must be a partner
- Qualifying broker for limited partnership must be the general partner
- Qualifying broker for limited liability company must be a member; manager may serve as the qualifying broker
- Qualifying broker for corporation must be an officer
- Broker must have signatory powers on all trust accounts

Death, resignation or termination of qualifying broker
- Company must secure new qualifying broker within 60 days or cease all real estate brokerage activity until new qualifying broker is secured
- While seeking new qualifying broker, firms must designate the following to sign documents and applications required to be filed with GREC, and to disburse trust funds as required
  - partnership - designated partner
  - limited liability company - member
  - corporation – officer

Licensee's employee v. independent contractor status
- License law does not stipulate employee v IC relationship with broker

Change of address
- Broker must notify GREC in writing with 30 days of change of broker's place of business

Name of Firm
- Broker may not conduct business under any name other than name in which broker's license is issued

Broker or Qualifying Broker Responsibilities and Requirements

Broker or qualifying broker held responsible
- For any licensee affiliated with broker or broker's firm who violates license law, rules or Rules and Regulations
- To instruct licensees of provisions of License Law and Rules and Regulations
- To notify GREC of any violations of License Law or Rules and Regulations

Broker or qualifying broker held responsible for affiliated licensee violations unless broker can demonstrate that broker
- Had reasonable procedures in place for supervising affiliate's actions
- Did not participate in violation
- Did not affirm violation

Broker or qualifying broker must establish and manage procedures for:
- Reviewing all advertising to ensure compliance
- Providing programs for study and review of rules and regulations
- Reviewing within 30 days all listing contracts, leases, sales contract, management agreements and offers to buy, sell, lease or exchange real property secured or negotiated by firm's associates
- Systematic review of firm's trust account practices to assure compliance
- Ensuring only licensed personnel perform licensing acts
- Assuring that compensation is paid only to licensees assigned to firm
- Ensuring proper disbursements are made from trust accounts
- Providing continuing and reasonable safekeeping of all real estate transactions records
- Providing all licensed personnel with written policies and procedures
- Ensuring firm and all licensed affiliates have written agreement specifying terms under which licensee is compensated
  - GREC does not regulate or negotiate content of agreement
- Assuring availability of manager to assist licensees and the public in real estate transactions
- Broker may delegate any management duties but remains responsible for the acts of the person to whom duty is delegated

Transferring licensees in and out of firm
- Broker procuring licensee affiliation with firm must enter into written agreement specifying
  - terms for compensation during time of affiliation
  - how licensee will be compensated for work begun but not completed prior to termination of affiliation
- GREC requires that agreements are entered into, but will not regulate content or enforce provisions
- Dispute between over agreement terms are not grounds for broker's refusal to sign release and forward wall certificate to GREC, nor for parties to file complaint with GREC
- When licensee requests release, releasing broker must immediately sign release and forward wall certificate to GREC
  - if licensee assumes responsibility for delivery to new broker, must deliver as soon as possible after receipt
- Transferring licensee prohibited from having or using any written brokerage engagement secured through brokerage, unless authorized by broker
- Names of prospective customers or clients given in writing to departing licensee during affiliation must be accounted for to that broker
- All property plats, keys and other property belonging to broker must be returned in person by departing licensee, including
  - "for sale" signs
  - notebooks
  - listing cards
  - records used in connection with transacting or managing property or community associations
- When terminating affiliation, licensee may not have contact with any of firm's clients that licensee is serving under any brokerage engagement until the expiration of engagement
- Broker wanting licensee affiliate with firm must enter into written agreement expressing terms for transferring from broker
- Licensee failing to meet requirements is not grounds for broker's refusal to sign release and forward wall certificate, but is grounds for filing with GREC a formal written complaint
- When broker returns wall certificate to GREC, must include release signed by and licensee
- Licensee must transfer license to another broker or apply for inactive status within one month of GREC's receipt of wall certificate
- If broker is releasing licensee for reason other than licensee's request and is unable to obtain licensee's signature, broker must send GREC copy of letter mailed to licensee's last known address indicating
  - broker is returning license to GREC, and
  - licensee has one month from GREC'S receipt of licensee's wall certificate to transfer to another broker or place license on inactive status

- Licensee whose license is released by a broker may not engage in real estate activities until licensee
  - personally delivers to GREC approved application to transfer license to new broker or has postmarked letter containing application; or
  - receives from GREC wall certificate of licensure authorizing licensee to serve as broker or qualifying broker of a firm
- Licensee transferring to new broker may continue to act as licensee for former broker with regard to transactions begun prior to transfer, provided both brokers agree in writing
  - to licensee's actions on behalf of former broker
  - to specific transactions on which licensee will act on behalf of former broker
  - that former broker assume full responsibility for licensee's activities in the listed transactions
  - agreement expresses terms under which licensee will be compensated by former broker

Wall certificate of licensure
- Salesperson or community association manager may not commence brokerage activities until broker receives licensee's wall certificate
- To change status to broker, sole proprietorship, or qualifying broker of corporation, limited liability company, or partnership: may not commence brokerage activities until wall certificate received

Qualifying brokers affiliated with multiple firms
- Person licensed as broker or qualifying broker may serve as broker or qualifying broker with more than one licensed firm
- Associate broker affiliated with licensed firm may serve as broker or qualifying broker for more than one licensed firm provided person has notified in writing broker with whom affiliated of intended services with another firm

Support Personnel & Ministerial Activities

Support personnel activity limitations
- Both firm and affiliated licensee responsible for acts of support personnel and compliance with legal requirements
- Support personnel may not perform any real estate brokerage activities; may only perform only ministerial duties
- Individual actively licensed with one firm may work as support personnel for a different firm or for licensee(s) of a different firm
- Inactive licensee may work as support personnel for a firm or any affiliated licensee

Written agreement requirements
- Broker must have written agreement with support personnel specifying duties and prohibited activities

Ministerial activities permitted
- Answer phone and forward calls and emails to a licensee
- Submit data on listings to multiple listing service
- Check on status of loan commitments after contract is negotiated
- Assemble documents for closings
- Secure public information documents from courthouse or other sources available to public
- Have keys made for firm listings and install or remove lock boxes from firm listings
- Write ads and promotional materials for approval of firm and any affiliated licensee
- Place ads in media as directed by firm
- Record and deposit earnest money, security deposits and rents
- Type contract forms as directed by firm or affiliated licensee
- Monitor personnel files and license reports from GREC
- Compute commission checks

- Place and remove signs on real estate
- Order items of routine repair as directed by firm or affiliated licensee
- Act as courier for delivering or obtaining documents and keys
- Schedule appointments with owner or owner's agent for licensee to show listed real estate
- Arrange dates and times for inspections, mortgage application, pre-closing walk-through, or closing
- Schedule an open house
- Accompany licensee to open house or showing for security purposes only
- Perform physical maintenance on real estate

GREC-prohibited activities by support personnel
- make cold calls for securing prospects
- host open houses, kiosks, home show booths or fairs
- prepare promotional material or ads without review and approval
- show real estate
- answer questions on title, financing, or closings (other than time and place)
- answer questions regarding listings except information on price and amenities expressly authorized in writing by licensee
- discuss or explain a contract, listing, lease, agreement, or other real estate document with anyone outside the firm
- negotiate or agree to any commission, commission split, management fee, or referral fee on behalf of licensee
- discuss attributes or amenities of real estate under any circumstances, with a prospective purchaser or lessee
- discuss with real estate owner terms or conditions of real estate offered for sale or lease
- collect or hold deposit monies, rent, other monies or anything of value received from owner, prospective purchaser or lessee
- provide real estate owners or prospective purchasers or lessees with advice, recommendations or suggestions as to sale, purchase, exchange, or leasing of real estate listed, to be listed, or currently available for sale or lease

Cannot create appearance of being licensed
- Unlicensed support personnel or inactive licensed support personnel may not hold themselves as being actively licensed

Part VIII. Managing Trust Accounts

Trust/Escrow Account Regulations

Trust or escrow account regulations
- Broker who accepts trust funds must maintain separate, federally insured trust-designated account at financial institution in Georgia
  - monies must be deposited into trust account within **three** business days
  - account must not be subject to attachment or garnishment
- Broker may have more than one trust account if GREC is advised
- Broker who does not accept trust funds is **not required** to maintain account
  - if broker later receives trust funds, broker must open account within one business day of receipt of trust funds
- If broker maintains account, s/he must notify GREC of bank name and number of account
- Broker must give authorization to GREC to examine account
  - GREC may examine account at any time with reasonable cause
  - GREC will examine each broker's trust account(s) during each renewal period. In lieu of an examination, GREC may
    - accept written report from certified public accountant reporting compliance, or
    - accept with broker's renewal application and fee a summary of data on account(s) on GREC form
  - GREC may require broker supply written reports on status of broker's trust account(s)
- Broker may maintain more than one trust account if GREC is advised
- Broker not entitled to any part of earnest money, security deposit, or other trust funds as broker's commission or fee until transaction has been consummated or terminated

Licensee acting as principal
- Must deposit in trust account in state bank or trust company or any foreign bank which authorizes GREC to examine its records
  - must leave on deposit portions of all payments received on contracts necessary to meet amounts concurrently due and payable on existing mortgages, taxes and insurance reserves
  - deposits must be maintained until disbursement is made under terms of encumbrance and proper accounting is made to parties
  - GREC deems property "owned by a licensee" if deed reflects only name of the licensee
    - If licensee owns interest less than 100% and receives any trust funds on property, must deposit funds into trust account of a licensed real estate firm
- GREC may allow nonresident broker to maintain trust account in state of residence if GREC is authorized to examine account
- Community association managers, salespersons, or associate brokers who receive security deposits or other trust funds on property they own must deposit those funds into broker's trust account

Additional depositing rules
- Licensees must place cash, checks, or other items of value received by licensee into broker's custody as soon after receipt as is practicably possible
- Broker holding trust funds must
  - promptly deposit funds in federally insured checking account designated by the bank as trust account and registered with GREC
  - make appropriate arrangement for safekeeping any items of value received other than cash or checks
  - if interest bearing account, broker must obtain written agreement of parties prior to deposit, indicating to whom broker will pay any interest earned

Broker's own funds in trust account
- Broker may maintain own funds in designated trust account only if they are clearly identified as the broker's deposit in broker's name and only for the following purposes

- minimum balance that must be maintained in order to keep the account open
- if bank requires service charge be paid, broker may maintain in broker's name amount to cover charge
- amount sufficient to cover other bank charges and costs of maintaining account

Broker's commission in trust account
- Broker may allow commissions due held in broker's designated trust account to remain in account if
  - broker's accounting system designates commissions as broker's funds and properly accounts for them
  - each month broker removes broker's funds that exceed minimum necessary to cover bank charges
  - only checks made payable to broker may be used to withdraw monies designated as broker's fund

Accounting requirements
- Broker must maintain accounting system in which each deposit is detailed as follows
  - names of buyer and seller or tenant and landlord or member and community association or broker
  - amount and date of deposit
  - identification of property
  - amount, payee and date of each check drawn on account in connection with that deposit
- Accounting requirements can be met with manual or electronic accounting system, but must:
  - include all components required by law and sound business practices
  - be readily accessible
  - be in readily understandable format, and
  - be reasonably available for authorized GREC representative

Trust fund disbursements
- Broker may disburses trust funds under the following circumstances
  - upon rejection of offer
  - upon withdrawal of offer not yet accepted
  - at closing of transaction
  - upon securing written agreement signed by all parties
  - upon filing of interpleader action or upon order of a court of competent jurisdiction
  - upon reasonable interpretation of contract which directed broker to deposit funds
  - prior to disbursing, broker has reasonable assurance that bank has credited funds to account
- When broker makes a disputed disbursal, broker must immediately notify all parties in writing of disbursal
- Broker who claims part of earnest money as broker's commission is in compliance if
  - in sales or lease/purchase transaction, transaction closed
  - in lease or rental transaction, possession has been delivered to tenant
  - broker has written agreement, separate from sales contract or lease agreement, signed by all parties agreeing that broker is entitled to any commission
- All refunds of earnest money must be paid by check or credited at the closing of transaction

Licensee with trust account filing bankruptcy petition
- GREC must immediately be notified in writing
  - by licensee if licensee owning a trust account files bankruptcy petition
  - by qualifying broker if qualifying broker or firm files bankruptcy petition

Trust accounts for property management or association management
- Brokers who manage real property or community associations may maintain designated rental or assessment trust or escrow accounts separate from other trust or escrow accounts

Monthly reconciliation
- Brokers required to maintain trust account must make a monthly written reconciliation statement

Account summary required for renewal

- When renewing broker's license, broker must submit
  - summary of broker's trust account data on GREC form, or
  - report on trust account from CPA with form similar to GREC form

Abandoned funds in trust account

- Licensee may not disburse abandoned funds from trust account unless
  - licensee's written authorization requires a particular disbursal
  - licensee has complied with requirements of Disposition of Unclaimed Property Act and other applicable statues and court ordered requirements

Part IX. Advertising

Advertising Rules and Regulations

Advertising definitions
- **Advertising or advertisement**: any activity through the use of any media makes known to general public real estate for sale, rent, lease or exchange
- **Media:** print, photographs, broadcast, and Internet including newspapers, magazines, flyers, posters, business cards, billboards radio, videos, television, signs (including office, directional, "for sale," "for lease", "sold", or vehicle signs), newsletters, voicemail, email, facsimile transmissions, Internet websites, blogs, video blogs, property listing database services, email farming, news groups, discussion lists, bulletin boards, social networking/social media, instant text messages, multimedia advertising, banner ads, pop-ups, and similar media
- **Misleading advertising:** Advertising that is misleading or inaccurate in any material fact or in any way misrepresents real estate

Noncompliance by principal
- If license becomes aware that a principal is advertising in a manner that does not comply, licensee must immediately take steps to stop the advertising until it complies

Advertising under supervision and in name of firm
- All advertising must be under direct supervision of broker and in the name of the firm

Written permission required to advertise
- To advertise property, licensee must obtain prior written permission of owner or owner's authorized agent

Advertising another firm's listings
- Advertising real estate listed with another firm must clearly and conspicuously disclose that fact and name the listing firm unless listing firm has agreed in writing to waive disclosures

Non-discriminatory advertising
- Ad content must be confined to information related to the real estate.
- Any advertisement directed at persons of any particular race, color, religion, sex, handicap, familial status, or national origin is a violation.

Internet Advertising

Disclosure of advertiser
- Internet advertising must disclose name and phone number of licensee's firm on every viewable web page, except
  - when advertising in electronic messages of limited information or characters, licensee must provide direct link to a display that complies
  - on website not owned or controlled by licensee or firm, that website's terms of use limit the licensee's ability of comply, ad must have direct link to a display that complies
- Information on website maintained by licensee that is outdated must be updated or removed within 30 days of information becoming outdated
  - if licensee's website is maintained by authorized third party, licensee must provide third party timely written notice of outdated information or information to be removed. if third party fails to effect change, licensee is not in violation
  - licensee not responsible for information taken from licensee's website or other advertising, if placed on a website or in other ads outside licensee's ownership and/or direct control and without licensee's consent

112

Trade names and franchise names
- In all ads and office signs, firm or franchisee must:
  - clearly include firm's name as registered with GREC
  - place firm's name adjacent to any real estate firm so the public may identify firm listing the real estate
    - name of firm must appear in equal or greater size, prominence, and frequency than name of any affiliated licensees or groups of licensees
  - clearly include firm's name as registered with GREC on all contracts or other documents relating to real estate transaction

Firm name and telephone number
- Ads must include name of firm as registered, telephone number of firm
- Firm's name must be adjacent to any real estate the firm is advertising
  - name of firm must appear in equal or greater size, prominence, and frequency than name of any affiliated licensees or groups of licensees
- Firm's phone number must appear in equal or greater size, prominence and frequency than number of affiliated licensee and must be a number at which the public can reach a broker or manager of firm without going through affiliated licensees listed in ad
- Name of firm must be in equal or greater in size, prominence and frequency than name of any affiliated licensee or groups of licensees
- Block advertisement in any print media advertising listings and including name of listing agent next to each listing must be in compliance
  - in compliance if name of firm appears only once at top of advertisement in equal or greater prominence and print size than any listing agent names
  - firm name may be in other positions in advertisement if appearing clearly and larger and more prominently than name of licensees

Licensees advertising as principal
- Licensee may not advertise that offer is being made by private, unlicensed party
- Associate brokers, salespersons, and community association managers prohibited from advertising under own name -- must be under direct supervision of broker and in name of firm
- When advertising own property without a listing, licensee may, provided
  - broker holding license has been notified in writing of specific real estate to be advertised
  - broker gives written consent and approves ad
  - ad includes the disclosure " _____ (seller, buyer, landlord, tenant) holds a real estate license", or "Georgia Real Estate License # _____."
- Licensees must make every reasonable attempt to assure the public knows they are being contacted by a licensee

Part X. Handling Transactions

Presenting offers: requirements
- Licensees must promptly present all offers
- If offeror is not a client or customer of licensee, licensee receiving offer must provide copy to licensee working with or representing offeree
- Licensee must include GREC issued license number of each firm and each licensee participating in transaction on all offers
- Licensee must provide copy of any document used in transaction to any individual signing document
  - if offer to is accepted and signed by all parties, copies of document must be distributed to each person signing document and to each brokerage firm involved in transaction
- Transaction documents must be maintained for three years and must be made available to GREC upon reasonable request. Documentations include
  - any broker identified in sales contract, brokerage engagement, closing statement, lease, or other document related to transaction
  - any firm that participates in negotiations of transaction
  - any broker required to maintain a trust account
- Records may be in any record storage system that utilizes paper, film, electronic, or other media if
  - licensee can produce true copies of documents and records, and
  - copies can be made available to GREC authorized representative upon reasonable request and at reasonable cost to GREC

Falsification of documents and misleading representations
- Licensees prohibited from falsifying transaction documents related and from knowingly misrepresenting:
  - true sales, lease or exchange price or earnest money, security deposit, or other trust funds tendered
  - payment of trust funds in cash when some other method is made

Disclosure of commissions, fees, rebates or other valuable consideration
- Required disclosure regarding commissions and other fees may be made by licensee to principal in advance of payment or receipt based on pre-established terms in brokerage engagement or management agreement

- When licensee refers principal to another broker, and broker receiving referral knows of referring licensee's expectation to receive compensation, payment of commission must be disclosed in writing to principal by broker working with principal no later than closing of transaction

- "Licensee's principal" in a specific transaction for which disclosure is required means both client and customer of broker if customer is working primarily with broker and is not represented by another broker

- Licensee may rebate to principal any part of commission or other compensation received by licensee related to transaction if disclosed on closing statement, if not misleading

- No disclosure required for gifts, products, services or other things of value given as gifts given to principal by licensee if they are not contingent upon consummation of transaction

Licensee as Transaction Principal

Disclosure requirements

- Licensee's position as buyer to seller, or seller to buyer
- Licensee's position as tenant to landlord or landlord to tenant
- Disclosure must also be included in contract.

Prior notice to broker

- Licensees may not list, sell, buy, exchange, rent, lease or option in licensee's own name or name of firm without first advising licensee's broker in writing
- Agent employed to sell may not be the purchaser, and agent to buyer may not be the seller without consent of the principal after full knowledge of all facts

Part XI. Other Real Estate-Related Georgia Laws

Georgia laws affecting fair practices and anti-trust issues
- **Georgia Fair Business Practices Act**
  - prohibits unfair and deceptive acts involving sale, lease or rental of goods, services or property for personal, family or household purposes. Activities prohibited by Act include
    - making false or misleading statements about another business or its products or services.
    - advertising goods or services with the intent not to sell them as advertised; "bait-and-switch" tactics
- **Uniform Deceptive Trade Practices Act**
  - prohibits deceptive acts or omissions and permits injured party to take legal action

Georgia Condominium Act
- A condo is created when developer or owner of existing building records a Declaration of Condominium with floor plans and plats.
- Condos can be created with any type of property
- Sales contract must disclose
  - oral representation cannot be relied upon
  - for correct representation, buyer should refer to documents required in Disclosure Package
- Buyer has at least seven days after all items in Disclosure Package have been received by buyer.

Uniform Electronic Transactions Act
- Legal effect of contracts cannot be denied due to use of electronic communications; signature cannot be denied legally because of legal format

Georgia Property Owners Association Act
- Optional participation can be chosen by developer, or by owners through amendment to bylaws
- Creates automatic liens; allows interest to be charged on unpaid assessments

Georgia Land Sales Act
- Regulates land subdivided into more than 150 lots when lots are less than five acres.
- **Rescission right**: if required documents are not provided to consumer at least 48 hours prior to signing contract, consumer has until midnight of **seventh day** to rescind

Georgia Land Conservation Program (GLCP)
- Funds Georgia Conservation Tax Credit Program which offers tax incentives for eligible donations for conservation
- Provides financing for local governments, state agencies and non-government organizations for permanent land conservation projects, striving to protect
  - water quality, flood protection, natural habitat for native plants and animals
  - wetlands
  - erosion reduction
  - prime agricultural and forestry lands
  - cultural sites, archaeological and historic resources
  - recreation provisions

Georgia Department of Natural Resources and Georgia Land Conservation Program
- Responsibility for protection of environment
- Purchasers of property listed on the hazardous site inventory can buy the property without liability from damages arising hazardous waste

No tenancy by the entirety or community property in Georgia
- Ownership as tenants by entirety not available in Georgia
- Georgia is not a community property state

Georgia Residential Mortgage Fraud Act
- Violations of the Act
  - making deliberate misrepresentations, or omissions during mortgage lending process
  - receiving any funds in connection with residential mortgage closing caused by such misrepresentations
  - filing with registrar of deeds any document knowing it contains a deliberate misstatement, misrepresentation, or omission
- Punishment: imprisonment or fines or both

Georgia Lead Paint Protection Act of 1994
- Established requirements for Lead Abatement Program and Lead Renovation Program
- Provides regulations for residential dwellings and child-occupied facilities built prior to 1978

Georgia Illegal Immigration Reform and Enforcement Act 2011
- Requires real estate license applicants and appraisal applicants to provide proof of lawful presence in the U.S.

No compensation-related lawsuits against licensees:
- No person may bring action in state courts unless licensed at the time cause of action arose
  - for collection of compensation or performance of licensing act
  - for collection of compensation without proving that any person acting in broker's behalf was licensed in Georgia at time cause of action arose
  - against another broker for collection of compensation

Timeshares

Georgia Code on Timeshare Projects and Programs
Timeshares are regulated by Georgia Code on Timeshare Projects and Programs

Georgia timeshare definitions
- **Agent**: person authorized by developer in offering or managing time-share intervals including employees or independent contractors of developer, managing agents, sales agents, and escrow agents
- **Exchange company**: person owning or operating an exchange program
- **Exchange program**: arrangement whereby owners may exchange occupancy rights with persons owning other time-share intervals or units
- **Public offering statement**: required written statement given to prospective purchasers by developer disclosing information about the time-share project as required by law
- **Time-share estate**: ownership or leasehold interest divided into measurable chronological periods
- **Time-share use**: contractual right of exclusive occupancy which does not fall within definition of a time-share estate including vacation license, prepaid hotel reservation, club membership, limited partnership, or vacation bond

Timeshare sales is a licensed activity
- Timeshares included in GREC's definition of licensing activity
- Georgia Timeshare Act governs developers
- Act is enforced through civil action or criminal prosecution
- Selling in Georgia timeshares to principals located in other states requires a Georgia real estate license
- Purchaser has seven days after signing contract in which to rescind

Taxes, Liens and Foreclosures

Real estate taxes
- Real estate taxes and special assessments taxes have priority over all other liens
- Real estate tax year is calendar year
  - due dates vary from county to county; December 20 is a common due date
  - real estate taxes must be paid prior to recording deed
  - Georgia property is assessed at 40% of fair market value

Real estate transfer tax
- Based on property sale price at the rate of $1 for first $1,000 or fractional part of $1,000, and 10 cents for each additional $100 or fraction part of $100
- Seller is liable for transfer tax; buyer may pay if stipulated in sales contract

Intangible recording tax
- Tax on long-term notes secured by real estate
- Lenders must record security instrument in county where real estate is located within 90 days from date instrument is signed
- Lender is responsible for payment, but may pass amount on to borrower
- Rate is $1.50 per $500 or fractional part for face amount of loan

Mechanic's liens
- Take priority over other liens except:
  - tax liens
  - general and specific liens for laborers
  - general landlord liens for rent
  - liens for purchase money for persons who have given bonds for titles,
  - general liens when actual notice was given prior to furnishing materials or labor provided
- Priority determined by date work commenced or materials delivered
  - must be filed within 90 days of completion of work
  - within two days of filing, must send owner notice by registered or certified mail or overnight delivery
- Priority of other liens are ranked based on the date of the lien (oldest lien has priority)

Leases

Basic requirements of leasehold
- Must contain legal address when entire property is leased
- Must be in writing if longer than one year to be enforceable in court
- Landlord and tenant may not waive certain duties and rights in the lease
- Landlord has duty to keep property repaired; tenant must pay rent

Security deposit regulations
- Tenants must be notified in writing of bank and account number of account holding security deposit
  - must be deposited in escrow account for that purpose
- Security deposit must be returned within one month or tenant provided with written statement for retention
- Prior to landlord accepting security deposit, tenant must be given list of any existing damage
  - tenant has the right to inspect and verify accuracy of list
  - both parties sign list
- **Premises surrender**: landlord must inspect premises 3 days before lease termination and list any damages that are basis for keeping any portion of security deposit

- tenant may inspect within five business days after termination to verify accuracy
- landlord and tenant sign damages list
- If tenant terminates occupancy without notifying landlord, landlord may make final inspection within reasonable amount of time
- Tenant may bring court action when disputing final damages list to recover deposit held for dissented items.
  - if tenant refused to sign list, he/she is not entitled to recover security

Tenancy at will termination notice
- Sixty days' notice from landlord or 30 days' notice from tenant

Eviction
- Landlord gives notice and reasonable time to respond
- If tenant does not give up possession, a dispossessory affidavit is filed in court, sheriff requires tenant to respond within seven days
- If no response, court provides landlord writ of possession, and tenant can be removed by sheriff

Flooding disclosure
- Prior to entering a written lease, owner must notify tenant in writing if flooding has damaged any portion of living space three or more times during the five-year period immediately preceding date of lease

Disclosure of owner's name
- No later than beginning of tenancy, landlord must provide in writing name and address of owner or person authorized to act for owner
  - any change during tenancy requires tenant to be notified within 30 days

GA-specific Variations of National Real Estate Laws & Practices

Rights of owner in property foreclosure
- Georgia has equitable right of redemption, or owner's right to redeem delinquent obligation prior to foreclosure sale
- Owner does not have statutory right of redemption after sale

Net listings
- Illegal in Georgia

Illegal or unauthorized practice of law
- Only licensed attorneys are permitted to close real estate transactions
- Illegal practice examples include
  - licensees closing a transaction
  - preparing legal documents
  - charging a fee for completing real estate forms
  - providing legal opinion

Statute of limitations
- Six years for written contracts not under seal. If under seal, 20 years

Wills
- Wills can be superseded by Georgia law requiring surviving spouse to receive a year's support
  - purpose: to ensure that surviving spouse and minor children are provided a year of support
  - if not included in will, spouse may demand from estate of deceased
- Wills for transfer of real estate cannot be oral or hand-written and must have two witnesses

Adverse possession
- Must be accompanied by claim of right and must be without fraud
- Adverse claim and actual notice must be given to other party
- Required prescriptive time with good title 20 years
  - with color of title seven years

Estate on condition
- Ownership limited by some condition requiring performance before owner will have complete right of ownership
- Conditions may be precedent (require performance prior to estate ownership) or subsequent (may result in forfeiture of ownership)

Georgia mortgage instruments
- Called security deed, deed to secure debt loan deed, or warranty deed to secure debt -- is most common financing instrument for Georgia real estate loans
- Security deed transfers legal title to lender with equitable title held by borrower
- Constitutes less risk for lender
- Permits non-judicial foreclosure through "power of sale" clause; expedites recovery of lender losses

Georgia legal descriptions
- Use county, district, land lot, and then metes and bounds, or lot and block (plat map) description
- Portions of Georgia use special areas referred to as sections, headrights, and Georgia Militia Districts
- To see how each county is legally described, go to: https://www.grec.state.ga.us/infobase/table%20of%20contents%20pdf/Chapter%2027.pdf

General warranty deeds guarantees
- Covenant of title (similar to covenant of seisin). Seller guarantees he owns legal title and right to sell property
- Covenant of quiet enjoyment
- Covenant against encumbrances

Title search
- Normal title history search period is 50 years

Appraiser categories
- State Trainee Appraiser: may perform appraisal activities only under direct control and supervision of Certified Residential or Certified General appraiser
- State Registered Appraiser: may perform appraisals on any type of property **except** when the purpose of the appraisal is for use in federally related financial transaction
- State Licensed Appraiser: may perform any appraisal not to be used in federally related financial transaction and may perform appraisals for use in federally related financial transactions for:
  - non-complex one to four unit residential properties where the value of the financial transaction does not exceed $1,000,000.00, and
  - any type of property where the transaction value is less than $250,000.00
- In federally related transactions licensed appraisers may not appraise real estate where a development analysis/appraisal is necessary and utilized
- State Certified Residential Appraiser: may perform any appraisal not to be used in a federally related financial transaction and may perform appraisals for use in federally related financial transactions for
  - one to four residential units without regard to t value or complexity, and
  - any type of property where value is less than $250,000.00
- State Certified General Appraiser: may appraise any type of property for any purpose

Section IV: National Practice Tests

Test 1: Rights; Interests and Estates; Ownership

1.1   Which of the following would be defined as real estate as opposed to real property?

   a. Wells, driveways, and signs on a parcel of land.
   b. Mobile homes temporarily parked on a parcel of land.
   c. Timber that has been cut and is lying on a parcel of land.
   d. Business equipment an owner or tenant has placed on a parcel of land.

1.2   Which of the following would be considered a property improvement?

   a. An alteration to land to make it more useful.
   b. An increase in the value of a property.
   c. A chicken coop permanently attached to land.
   d. A parcel of land that has passed a percolation test.

1.3   Which of the following best describes the physical boundaries of land?

   a. The surface of the earth and infinite space above the surface.
   b. The center of the earth and infinite space above the earth.
   c. The surface of the earth and all water and minerals on or below the surface to the center of the earth.
   d. The surface of the earth and the air rights above the surface to the point defined by local zoning.

1.4   The "bundle of rights" refers to a set of rights

   a. enjoyed by the owner of a property.
   b. that is synonymous with the Bill of Rights.
   c. guaranteed to citizens by the Statute of Rights.
   d. specified in a deed or land contract.

1.5   Which of the following best describes the legal concept of personal property?

   a. Any item which is acquired in a fee simple sale transaction.
   b. Any item of property that is not definable as real property.
   c. Any movable property owned by an individual, partnership, or corporation.
   d. Any item that is not a natural item affixed to the earth.

1.6   The right to encumber a property means that the owner can

   a. sell the property to an encumbered party.
   b. pledge the property as collateral for debt.
   c. lease the property.
   d. assign the bundle of rights to another.

1.7   A property owner leases 60 acres of agricultural land for a renewable period of 5 years. In the context of real estate rights, this lease represents a(n)

   a. transfer of a portion of the bundle of rights.
   b. encroachment on the bundle of rights.
   c. conveyance of the complete bundle of rights.
   d. encumbrance of the tenant's rights.

1.8   A homeowner is very upset over a drone that a neighbor flies over his house. He takes his case to court to end this possible violation of rights. Does he have a case, and on what basis?

a. No. The neighbor is not physically on his property.
b. No. The drone is in the air, so he cannot exercise any surface rights.
c. Yes. The owner has the right to stop encroachments.
d. Yes. The drones infringe on his air rights.

1.9   Littoral rights apply to which of the following?

a. Boatable ponds entirely contained within the boundaries of an owner's property.
b. Streams and rivers.
c. Navigable lakes, seas, and oceans.
d. Navigable streams and rivers.

1.10   A retired couple has just bought a retirement home with a pier on a large lake. In this case the retirees' water rights extend to

a. the high water mark of the body of water at the shoreline.
b. the low water mark of the body of water at the shoreline.
c. the center of the lake.
d. the end of the pier.

1.11   A waterfront homeowner has just died. What will become of the water rights the owner enjoyed while living in the home?

a. They revert to the state when the property is sold.
b. They are extinguished.
c. They are a personal right belonging to an individual owner, not attaching to the real property.
d. They transfer with the property when the property is sold.

1.12   Riparian rights concern which of the following bodies of water?

a. Lakes.
b. Seas and oceans.
c. Streams and rivers.
d. Navigable lakes.

1.13   Which of the following best describes a "fixture?"

a. Any item of personal property positioned within the boundaries of a parcel of real estate.
b. An item of personal property that has been converted to real property.
c. An item of real property temporarily placed on land for the purpose of conducting a business.
d. An item of personal property that has been left in one location for a period of six months.

1.14   An item may be considered personal property as opposed to real property provided that

a. the owner intended to remove it after a period of time.
b. it can be removed without altering the appearance of the structure.
c. it is unnecessary to the physical integrity of the structure.
d. the owner installed it at some time after acquiring the real property.

1.15   Two people own a house, each having an undivided equal interest. Which of the following best describes what each party owns?

a. Fifty percent of the physical house and the land it rests on.
b   One hundred percent of the home and the land.
c. Fifty percent of the estate consisting of the indivisible whole of the real property.
d. Each owns one hundred percent of the estate represented by the real property and fifty percent of the physical house and the land it rests on.

1.16   A real property interest that includes the right to possess is considered

    a. an estate in land.
    b. a leasehold estate.
    c. a fee simple estate.
    d. the bundle of rights.

1.17   The right to control land usage by zoning and eminent domain is an example of

    a. a public interest.
    b. a police interest.
    c. an encumbrance.
    d. an estate in law.

1.18   If the duration of an owner's rights in an estate is not determinable, the owner has

    a. a tenancy at sufferance.
    b. a leased fee simple estate.
    c. a freehold estate.
    d. a leasehold estate.

1.19   The distinguishing feature of a leasehold estate is

    a. ownership of an interest by a tenant.
    b. temporary ownership of the full bundle of rights in a property.
    c. unlimited ownership of one right in the bundle of rights in a property.
    d. that the estate is limited by a lease term.

1.20   A landowner conveys a parcel of property with the provision that the land cannot be developed for retail purposes. The new owner immediately begins to develop a retail shopping outlet, the grantor finds out and takes the property back. What kind of estate did this landowner convey?

    a. Fee simple absolute.
    b. Life estate with reversion.
    c. Life estate with condition subsequent.
    d. Fee simple defeasible.

1.21   Ned grants his sister Alice an estate for as long as she lives. Her descendants, however, cannot inherit the estate. What kind of estate is it?

    a. An estate pur autre vie.
    b. An estate for years.
    c. An ordinary life estate.
    d. A legal life estate.

1.22   Homestead estates are examples of

    a. a conventional life estate.
    b. a legal life estate.
    c. an estate created by an owner's agreement.
    d. a fee simple absolute.

1.23 Louis owned a boat and a house before marrying Barbara. While she was single, Barbara owned a new car. The two got married and bought a second home. As a wedding present, Barbara's father bought Louis a motorcycle. Under the law of community property, what property can Louis sell without his wife's consent or signature?

a. The boat and house.
b. The boat, house, and motorcycle.
c. The second home and the motorcycle.
d. The boat and motorcycle.

1.24 Katelyn rents an apartment for one year. What rights has she acquired under the leasehold?

a. The right to exclude everyone from the premises.
b. The right to encumber the fee interest.
c. The right to sell the premises.
d. The right to possess and use the premises.

1.25 An estate from period-to-period will continue as long as

a. the tenant makes, and landlord accepts, regular rent payments.
b. the term specified in the lease.
c. the period is less than a year.
d. the landlord has not sold the property.

1.26 An estate at will

a. cannot be terminated.
b. is terminated only if so stated in the lessee's last will and testament.
c. terminates on the death of lessor or lessee.
d. terminates on the date specified in the lease agreement.

1.27 A tenant continues to occupy an apartment after lease expiration without the consent of the landlord. This type of estate is called

a. an estate at sufferance.
b. a holdover estate.
c. a canceled leasehold.
d. a hostile leasehold.

1.28 A tenant without a lease has been sending the landlord monthly rent checks, and the landlord continues to accept the payments. What kind of leasehold estate exists?

a. Estate for years.
b. Estate from period to period.
c. Estate at will.
d. Estate at sufferance.

1.29 A fee or life estate is held by an individual. This form of estate is referred to as a(an)

a. tenancy in severalty.
b. tenancy by the entireties.
c. absolute fee simple.
d. legal fee simple.

1.30   Six people have identical rights in a property and enjoy an indivisible interest. However any of the owners may sell or transfer his/her interest without consent of the others. This form of ownership is a

a. joint tenancy.
b. homestead ownership.
c. tenancy in common.
d. estate in severalty.

1.31   The "four unities" required to create a joint tenancy include which of the following conditions?

a. Parties must acquire respective interests at the same time.
b. Parties must be residents of the same state at the time of acquiring the interest.
c. Parties must be family members.
d. Parties must have joint financial responsibility.

1.32   Unlike tenants in common, joint tenants

a. own distinct portions of the physical property.
b. cannot will their interest to a party outside the tenancy.
c. may own unequal shares of the property.
d. cannot encumber their interest to outside parties.

1.33   Which of the following life estates is created by operation of law rather than by the owner?

a. Conventional life estate.
b. Ordinary life estate.
c. Legal life estate.
d. Community property life estate.

1.34   Which of the following is true of a homestead?

a. A homestead interest cannot be conveyed by one spouse.
b. A homestead interest cannot be passed to the children of the head of household.
c. A homestead interest is a form of conventional life estate.
d. A homestead is a primary or secondary residence occupied by a family.

1.35   A tenant in common can

a. sell or transfer his interest without the consent of the other tenants in common.
b. use his or her interest in the estate to encumber the entire estate.
c. sell, encumber or transfer his or her interest only to the other tenants in common.
d. sell, encumber or transfer his or her interest only with the consent of all the other tenants in common.

1.36   Which of the following would be considered community property?

a. Property acquired before marriage
b. A motorcycle bought after the marriage with separate property funds
c. Income derived from community property
d. A mother's heirloom wedding ring gifted to the wife after her wedding

1.37   When real property is held in a land trust, who controls the property?

a. The trustor
b. The trustee
c. The beneficiary
d. The mortgagee

1.38   In a community property state, John marries Patricia. Prior to the marriage John owned an SUV. During the marriage, John bought a Buick, John and Patricia bought a second property with money earned from Patricia's job, and each individual received a motorcycle from Patricia's uncle as a gift. What property is community property in this marriage?

a. The SUV, the Buick, and the second property.
b. The SUV, the Buick, the second property, and the motorcycles.
c. The Buick and the second property.
d. The Buick, the second property, and the motorcycles.

1.39   Which of the following is true of a cooperative?

a. A cooperative may hold an owner liable for the unpaid operating expenses of other tenants.
b. The owners have a fee simple interest in the airspace of their respective apartments.
c. Owners may sublease their apartments even if they sell their stock in the cooperative.
d. The proprietary lease is guaranteed to have a fixed rate of rent over the life of the lease term.

1.40   Which of the following is true of a tenancy in common?

a. The co-owners must be related.
b. The owners enjoy an indivisible interest.
c. The tenants must acquire their interests at the same time.
d. The tenants must pay equal amounts for their interest in the estate.

1.41   Carissa and Robert acquire a condominium as tenants in common. In this circumstance, Carissa can

a. sell her interest to a third party without the consent of Robert.
b. use her interest in the estate to mortgage the entire estate.
c. sell her interest only to Robert.
d. sell encumber or transfer her interest only with the consent of Robert.

1.42   When a tenant in common dies, what happens to the tenant's interest in the estate?

a. It is divided equally among the surviving tenants in common.
b. The surviving tenants must buy the interest from the deceased tenant's heirs or sell their interests to the heirs.
c. It becomes a joint tenancy.
d. It passes by probate to the deceased tenant's heirs.

1.43   Which of the following is true of a joint tenancy?

a. The tenants can determine the size of the share owned by each tenant.
b. The size of the tenant's shares is determined by the amount of equity each has invested in the property.
c. The tenants have an equal and indivisible ownership interest.
d. There can be no more than two co-owners, and each has a fifty percent interest.

1.44   In contrast to a tenancy in common, in a joint tenancy

a. there is a single title to the property.
b. there are as many titles to the property as there are co-owners.
c. title is held by a trustee.
d. co-owners who are married hold separate titles.

1.45 If a joint tenant sells his or her interest to an outside party,

    a. the new owner becomes a tenant in common with the other owners, who continue to hold a joint tenancy with each other and a tenancy in common with the new owner.
    b. the joint tenancy continues with the new owner as the third joint tenant.
    c. the joint tenancy terminates and all owners become tenants in common.
    d. the joint tenancy terminates and the owners must create a new joint tenancy to include the new owner.

1.46 When a joint tenant dies, what happens to the tenant's interest in the estate?

    a. It passes to the decedent's heirs, who become joint tenants.
    b. It passes as a tenancy in common to the decedent's heirs.
    c. The joint tenancy terminates and becomes a tenancy in common with the decedent's heirs and the surviving tenants as co-owners.
    d. It passes to the surviving joint tenants.

1.47 Under what conditions can two individuals own a property as tenants by the entireties?

    a. If they so elect at the time of acquiring title.
    b. If they are blood relatives.
    c. If they are married.
    d. If they incorporate.

1.48 When an estate is held in a trust, which party holds legal title?

    a. The beneficiary.
    b. The trustor.
    c. The trustee.
    d. The grantor.

1.49 Tanya buys a 4-bedroom condominium. As the new owner, she has the right to

    a. sell or mortgage the unit without impediment from individual owners of neighboring units.
    b. sell the interest in the physical unit separately from the interest in the common elements.
    c. prevent non-owners from using the unit owner's portion of the common elements.
    d. exclusively possess and use those portions of the common areas structurally or functionally necessary for the operation of the unit.

1.50 A condominium owner's share of maintenance and operations expenses are based on

    a. the unit's pro rata share of floor space.
    b. the unit's pro rata share of the property value as defined in the declaration.
    c. the number of shares the owner purchased in the condominium association.
    d. the assessed value of the condominium unit.

1.51 By contrast to a condominium, the owner of a cooperative owns

    a. shares in a corporation or association and a proprietary lease in a physical unit.
    b. a fee simple interest in a physical unit plus a tenancy in common in common elements.
    c. a tenancy in common in a physical unit and the common areas.
    d. a ground lease in the physical unit's pro rata share of land and a proprietary lease in the unit.

1.52 In a cooperative, real property is owned only by

    a. the individual unit owners.
    b. the individual unit owners and the cooperative association.
    c. the cooperative developer.
    d. the corporate entity of the cooperative association.

1.53 In a time-share freehold, owners acquire

    a. undivided interests in the property as tenants in common.
    b. a renewable periodic tenancy from for a portion of a year.
    c. a pro rata share of a leased fee.
    d. a tenancy in severalty for a portion of a year.

1.54 A party has just purchased a manufactured housing unit. When is this property considered real property?

    a. As soon as it is purchased
    b. As soon as it is constructed
    c. As soon as it is affixed to the ground.
    d. This form of property is considered personal property at all times.

Test 2: Encumbrances; Liens; Title Transfer and Recording; Leases

2.1   Which of the following describes an encumbrance?

   a. A third party's right to encroach upon a property without the permission of the property owner.
   b. A third party's right to claim the sale proceeds of a property that has been mortgaged as collateral for a loan.
   c. A third party's interest in a real property that limits the interests of the freehold property owner.
   d. Another's right to acquire a freehold interest in a property against the property owner's wishes.

2.2   Which of the following is true of easements in general?

   a. They involve the property that contains the easement and a non-owning party.
   b. They apply to a whole property, not to any specific portion of the property.
   c. They only involve the legal owner of the property.
   d. They may require a specific use, but cannot prohibit one.

2.3   Mr. King wants to offer 100 acres of his property for sale. Since the property is landlocked, he will have to put in a driveway to the road that will run across his remaining property. What kind of easement will he have to grant?

   a. An easement in gross.
   b. A commercial easement.
   c. A personal easement.
   d. An easement appurtenant.

2.4   If property Alpha has a court-ordered easement across property Beta in order for Alpha to have access to a public road, the easement is a(n)

   a. easement by prescription.
   b. personal easement.
   c. easement by necessity.
   d. easement in gross.

2.5   An encroachment is

   a. an easement that has not been recorded on the title of the burdened property.
   b. an unauthorized physical intrusion of one property into another.
   c. a right granted by a property owner to the owner of an adjoining property to build a structure that protrudes across the property boundary.
   d. a structure that does not comply with a zoning ordinance.

2.6   A court might grant an easement by prescription if

   a. a town needs to dig a trench across an owner's property to install a sewer line to a neighboring property, and the owner refuses permission.
   b. a property owner sells the front half of a lot and wants to continue using the driveway to access the rear of the lot.
   c. a trespasser has been using an owner's property for a certain period with the owner's knowledge but without permission.
   d. a property owner wants to prevent the owner of an adjoining property from building a an improvement that blocks her view.

2.7   The purpose of a deed restriction is to enable an owner to specify

a. the form of ownership in which a property may be held.
b. how long a property must be owned before it can be legally transferred.
c. what groups of people are legally excluded from future ownership of a property.
d. how a property may be used and what improvements may be built on it.

2.8   Melinda purchases a house and finances it. The lender in turn places a lien on Melinda's title. The lien in this mortgage transaction is

a. evidence of debt incurred by a property owner.
b. a promissory note granted by a property owner as security for a debt.
c. the creditor's claim against the property as collateral security for the loan.
d. the document required to clear clouded title.

2.9   In a lien-theory state, what kind of interest does a mortgage lender have in the liened property?

a. A possessory interest.
b. A tenancy-by-mortgagee interest.
c. A legal interest in a pro rata share of the property.
d. An equitable interest.

2.10   How is a lien terminated?

a. Payment of the debt that is the subject of the lien and recording of the satisfaction.
b. Transfer of the property that has the lien.
c. Recording of another lien that is superior.
d. Death of the lienor or lienee.

2.11   A judge rules in favor of the creditor in a court proceeding and places a judgment lien against all the debtor's assets, including his real property. This is an example of a(n)

a. voluntary junior lien.
b. involuntary superior lien.
c. involuntary specific lien.
d. involuntary general lien.

2.12   A real estate tax lien, a federal income tax lien, a judgment lien, and a mortgage lien are recorded against a property. Which lien will be paid first when the property is sold?

a. Real estate tax lien.
b. Federal income tax lien.
c. Judgment lien.
d. Mortgage lien.

2.13   A lien holder can change the lien priority of a junior lien by agreeing to

a. change the date of recording.
b. lower the amount of the claim.
c. cancel the lien.
d. subordinate the lien.

2.14   Which of the following accurately describes the act of foreclosure?

a. A court-ordered acceleration of loan payments.
b. The final step in a bankruptcy filing.
c. A proceeding to enforce a lien by forcing the sale or transfer of a secured property.
d. A proceeding to take equitable title to a property that was liened as security for a mortgage loan.

2.15 A property is secured by a mortgage that does not contain a "power of sale" clause. To foreclose, the lien holder will have to

a. file a deficiency suit.
b. file a foreclosure suit.
c. file a suit to quiet title.
d. obtain a quit claim deed.

2.16 A homeowner defaults on his mortgage loan. In the subsequent foreclosure action, the lender takes title to the liened property directly instead of initiating a court-ordered public sale. This is an example of

a. strict foreclosure.
b. judicial foreclosure.
c. non-judicial foreclosure.
d. deed in lieu of foreclosure.

2.17 A property owner gives Deanna permission to cross his property as a shortcut to her kindergarten school bus. One day the property owner dies. What right was Deanna granted originally, and will it survive the owner's death?

a. A personal easement in gross, which continues after the owner's death.
b. An easement by prescription, which continues after the owner's death.
c. A license, which continues after the owner's death.
d. A license, which terminates upon the owner's death.

2.18 On two adjacent properties, there is an easement that allows property A to use the driveway that belongs to property B. Here, property A is said to be which of the following in relation to property B?

a. Subservient estate.
b. Servient tenement.
c. Senior tenant.
d. Dominant tenement.

2.19 A property owner who is selling her land wants to control how it is used in the future. She might accomplish her aim by means of

a. an injunction.
b. a deed restriction.
c. an easement.
d. a land trust.

2.20 What distinguishes a lien from other types of encumbrance?

a. It involves a monetary claim against the value of a property.
b. It lowers the value of a property.
c. It is created voluntarily by the property owner.
d. It attaches to the property rather than to the owner of the property.

2.21 Which of the following defines actual notice?

a. It is notice published in a newspaper.
b. It is knowledge one could have or should have obtained.
c. It is notice explicitly stated in a legal document.
d. It is knowledge received or imparted through direct experience.

131

2.22 Which of the following defines constructive notice?

    a. It is notice published in a newspaper.
    b. It is knowledge one could have or should have obtained.
    c. It is notice explicitly stated in a legal document.
    d. It is knowledge received or imparted through direct experience.

2.23 Ownership of real estate can be transferred voluntarily or involuntarily. The three ways title can be transferred voluntarily are by

    a. grant, deed, and will.
    b. escheat, deed, and covenant.
    c. title certificate, will, and deed.
    d. sale contract, deed, and warrant of seizin.

2.24 What is the function of recording a deed?

    a. It makes the deed valid.
    b. It causes title to pass.
    c. It gives constructive notice of ownership.
    d. It removes all prior recorded encumbrances.

2.25 The only clause that is actually required in a deed is the

    a. habendum clause.
    b. granting clause.
    c. reserving clause.
    d. tenendum clause.

2.26 The type of deed that offers the grantee the fullest protection against claims to the title is the

    a. general warranty deed.
    b. special warranty deed.
    c. quitclaim deed.
    d. bargain and defend deed.

2.27 What is one of the purposes of a lawsuit to "quiet title"?

    a. To force the grantor to defend the title against a third party claim.
    b. To terminate a co-ownership estate when one co-owner is unwilling.
    c. To keep the owner's name out of the title records.
    d. To have an encumbrance removed if the lienholder cannot prove its validity.

2.28 Which of the following best describes the documentary stamp tax?

    a. A transfer tax based on the price of the property being conveyed.
    b. A tax a title company must pay in order to examine title records in the recorder's office.
    c. A tax collected by attorneys and paid to the state when transfer documents are prepared.
    d. A tax on stamps used to certify the authenticity of a conveyance.

2.29 The court proceeding that generally settles a decedent's estate is called

    a. testate.
    b. probate.
    c. escheat.
    d. distribution.

2.30 If an owner of real property dies intestate and has no legal heirs, what will happen to the property?

a. It will escheat to the state or county.
b. It will transfer to the decedent's executor.
c. It will be divided equally among adjoining property owners.
d. It will become a public easement.

2.31 A municipality wants to build a sewage treatment facility which will require the acquisition of several parcels of privately owned land. What legal power enables the municipality to buy the necessary properties, even against the owners' wishes?

a. Estoppel.
b. Escheat.
c. Alienation.
d. Eminent domain.

2.32 An adverse possessor must be able to successfully demonstrate that he or she has been

a. openly possessing and claiming the property without the owner's consent.
b. occupying the property without an occupancy permit.
c. using the property intermittently and without permission over a period of years.
d. building a permanent structure on the property.

2.33 A buyer has signed a contract to purchase a property, but is uncertain of the condition of the title. Which of the following parties is legally responsible for knowing the condition of the title?

a. The County Recorder.
b. The seller's agent.
c. The buyer.
d. The mortgage lender.

2.34 A break in the chain of title to a property results in

a. a clouded title.
b. a title plant.
c. a lien of indeterminate ownership.
d. a duplicate title.

2.35 Wayne and Leota obtain an insurance policy that protects them from liabilities and losses resulting from title defects. The kind of policy they bought is a

a. homeowner's insurance policy.
b. standard owner's title insurance policy.
c. lender's title insurance policy.
d. private mortgage insurance policy.

2.36 An owner transfers title to a property to a buyer in exchange for a motorcycle. This is an example of

a. voluntary alienation.
b. involuntary liquidation.
c. hypothecation.
d. 1031 exchange.

2.37 A person wishes to convey any and all interests in a property to another without assurance of the property's marketability. This party would most likely use which of the following types of deed?

a. A sheriff's deed.
b. A special warranty deed.
c. A partition deed.
d. A quitclaim deed.

2.38 Jennifer owns a one-half interest in a condominium as a tenant in common with her business partner. If Jennifer has several heirs and dies without a will, the property will

a. pass to the heirs by the laws of descent and distribution.
b. escheat to the state.
c. pass to the surviving spouse based on homestead law.
d. pass to the surviving heirs according to the provisions of the will.

2.39 A drifter secretly lives in an abandoned shack on a large ranch property. After twenty years, the person makes a claim of ownership to the shack and the land immediately surrounding it that he had cleared. This claim will likely be

a. upheld through adverse possession.
b. upheld because of the length of possession.
c. declined through the doctrine of prior appropriation.
d. declined because possession was secretive.

2.40 To be marketable, title must be

a. insured.
b. free of undisclosed defects and encumbrances.
c. abstracted by an attorney.
d. guaranteed by a title certificate.

2.41 Which of the following types of leasehold estate lacks a specific term?

a. Estate for years.
b. Estate from period-to-period.
c. Estate at will.
d. Estate by the entireties.

2.42 A landlord generally has the right to enter the leased premises

a. at any time without notice.
b. for specified reasonable purposes.
c. provided the tenant gives prior permission.
d. only thirty days prior to lease expiration.

2.43 When a tenant rents an apartment, he or she is usually responsible for

a. compliance with the rules and regulations of the building.
b. payment for any alterations to the leased space.
c. recording the lease in title records.
d. occupying the premises throughout the lease term.

2.44 Under landlord-tenant laws, landlords must treat tenants fairly and honestly. In a residential leasehold, this requirement would include

a. insuring the tenant against loss of personal property.
b. providing required building support and services.
c. guaranteeing that a fair rent is being charged.
d. insuring the property for the value of the leasehold.

2.45 While a one-year lease is in effect, the tenant dies of a sudden illness. In this situation,

a. the lease automatically terminates.
b. the tenant's estate has the option of canceling the contract.
c. the landlord can record a lien against the leased fee interest.
d. the tenant's estate is still obligated under the lease.

2.46 Three students rent a house together, and all three sign a one-year lease. Six months later, two students move out. Which of the following is true of the remaining rent obligation?

a. The remaining tenant is responsible for the full rent obligation.
b. The remaining tenant is responsible for one third of the rent obligation.
c. The lease is cancelled due to abandonment. Therefore, the rent obligation is extinguished.
d. The departing tenants have no further rent obligation.

2.47 A tenant transfers a portion of the leasehold interest to another party. The instrument that accomplishes this transfer is a(n)

a. deed.
b. novation.
c. sublease.
d. reconveyance

2.48 Vijay enters into a lease for his new store. The provisions of the lease require Vijay to pay the operating expenses of the premises such as janitorial and repair expenses. This is an example of a

a. gross lease.
b. percentage lease.
c. land lease.
d. net lease.

2.49 A tenant obtains a full-service lease where the landlord agrees to pay all operating expenses in exchange for an additional $5.00 rent per square foot. Another term for this lease is a(n)

a. gross lease.
b. proprietary lease.
c. exchange lease.
d. full service net lease.

2.50 Which of the following circumstances is the most likely scenario for a ground lease?

a. A developer wants to acquire a necessary parcel that separates two parcels she already owns.
b. An owner-developer wants to retain ownership of the land portion of the improved real property.
c. A fast food company wants to place a restaurant in an existing building without buying either land or improvement.
d. A farmer wants to sell his property to a mining company.

2.51 A tenancy at will can usually be terminated by

a. either party giving proper notice.
b. either party without notice.
c. a sublease, with the lessor's approval.
d. an assignment by the lessor.

2.52 Under the Uniform Residential Landlord and Tenant Act, if a lease does not state a clear expiration date, the lease is regarded as

a. invalid.
b. a tenancy from period-to-period.
c. a tenancy at will.
d. a tenancy for years.

2.53 The Uniform Residential Landlord and Tenant Act generally does not apply to

a. a hotel.
b. a single-family residence.
c. a unit in an apartment building that has fewer than ten units.
d. a duplex in which the owner occupies one of the units.

2.54 In executing a condominium lease, a tenant has acquired

a. a temporary transfer of legal title.
b. a limited freehold interest in the air space of her unit.
c. a temporary possessory interest.
d. a title conveyance in exchange for rent.

2.55 When a tenant acquires a leasehold estate through a lease, what does the property owner acquire?

a. A freehold estate for years.
b. A reduced leasehold estate.
c. A defeasible estate.
d. A leased fee estate.

2.56 When an owner leases her property, she temporarily relinquishes the right to

a. transfer the property.
b. encumber the property.
c. occupy the property.
d. maintain the property.

2.57 Which of the following happens when a leased property is sold?

a. The buyer acquires title subject to the lease, which remains in effect.
b. The lease is cancelled.
c. The lease expires within thirty days unless renewed.
d. A new lease is automatically executed.

2.58 If a lease does not state a specific ending date, when does it terminate?

a. Immediately, since it is an invalid lease.
b. After one year.
c. When either party gives proper notice.
d. Whenever the property is sold.

2.59 In accordance with the statute of frauds,

a. leases in excess of one year must be recorded to be enforceable.
b. oral leases are not enforceable.
c. a five-year lease must be in writing to be enforceable.
d. an unwritten lease is fraudulent.

2.60 Which of the following is true of a sublease?

a. The subtenant takes over sole responsibility for performance of the original lease contract.
b. The original tenant retains primary responsibility for performance of the original lease contract.
c. It does not convey any of the leasehold interest.
d. It conveys the entire leasehold interest.

2.61 A homeowner goes bankrupt and the lender forecloses on her residence. In the foreclosure sale, the proceeds are insufficient to pay off the loan, and the court orders other property sold to cover the shortfall. This action is called a(n)

   a. strict foreclosure.
   b. suit for specific performance.
   c. equity foreclosure judgment.
   d. deficiency judgment.

2.62 To make a successful claim of adverse possession, the adverse possessor must satisfy which of the following criteria?

   a. The possession must have been concealed, without permission, and for a statutory period of time.
   b. The possession must have been unconcealed, for the necessary length of time, and without permission.
   c. The possession must be with intent, secretive, notorious and hostile.
   d. The possession must be open, without permission, for the statutory period of time, and within the number of permitted intervals.

2.63 One of the primary benefits of recording conveyances is to give evidence to the public that the new owner actually owns the property. What is another benefit of recording to the homeowner?

   a. Recording instruments establishes the title's marketability.
   b. Recording the deed prevents any future clouds on title.
   c. Recording prevents lienholders from illegal credit practices.
   d. Recording the deed of conveyance nullifies any and all claims of adverse possession.

Test 3: Land Use; Legal Descriptions; Contract Law

3.1 Which of the following is true regarding master planning and zoning?

    a. The aggregate of zoning ordinances is the master plan.
    b. A master plan eliminates the need for zoning ordinances.
    c. Master planning is a county-level function; zoning is limited to the city level.
    d. Zoning ordinances are a primary means of keeping land use in harmony with the master plan.

3.2 The basic intent of zoning ordinances is to

    a. establish the basis for public ownership of land for the common good.
    b. establish subdivision rules and regulations.
    c. specify usage for every parcel within the zoning authority's jurisdiction.
    d. restrict development in unincorporated areas.

3.3 Why do zoning authorities create different types of zones?

    a. To ensure that a variety of building structures are available in the community.
    b. To separate land uses so that they do not interfere with each other.
    c. To preserve high density land uses.
    d. To discourage industrial and commercial users from relocating.

3.4 The key consideration in granting a zoning exception known as a special exception is which of the following?

    a. Hardship
    b. Change of zones
    c. The public interest
    d. The use was legal prior to the new zone creation

3.5 The intensity of land usage generally refers to what?

    a. The number of residential building lots per acre.
    b. The number of people per square mile.
    c. The number of building permits issued per year within a zoning jurisdiction.
    d. The area of a commercial or industrial facility in relation to the size of the site.

3.6 How does Planned Unit Development zoning vary from ordinary zoning?

    a. It applies only to office parks.
    b. It incorporates a number of different zones within a single property boundary.
    c. It requires that multiple tracts of land be developed according to a single design.
    d. It requires developers to obtain a separate building permit for every structure.

3.7 Which of the following situations is most likely to represent an illegal nonconforming use?

    a. A homeowner in a residential zone converts her residence to a private school.
    b. A homeowner builds a toolshed in a neighborhood where there are no toolsheds.
    c. A storeowner remodels a storefront in accordance with regulations, and then the zoning is changed to residential.
    d. A new zoning ordinance outlaws two-story additions after a homeowner completes an addition.

3.8 What is the difference between a variance and a nonconforming use?

    a. A variance, once granted, is unconditional and permanent.
    b. A variance is granted by the zoning board if the owner has a justifiable reason.
    c. A nonconforming use is allowed if the owner requests it in advance of building.
    d. A nonconforming use violates current zoning, but a variance does not.

3.9 A document certifying that a structure complies with building codes and is ready for use is referred to as a(n)

    a. inspection report.
    b. satisfaction bond.
    c. certificate of occupancy.
    d. user permit.

3.10 Which of the following is true of an eminent domain proceeding?

    a. It cancels the property owner's mortgage loan balance.
    b. It leaves the property owner with equitable title in place of legal title.
    c. It conveys legal title to the acquiring entity.
    d. It clouds the chain of title by canceling the original grant.

3.11 Among other provisions, the Superfund Act (CERCLA) and Superfund Amendment and Reauthorization Act of 1986 provided that

    a. large development projects undergo an environmental impact survey immediately after completion of construction.
    b. industrial users of real estate comply with air quality standards.
    c. the EPA would give financial help to homeowners to remedy any hazardous situation resulting from radon, asbestos, or lead-based paint.
    d. parties responsible for improper disposal of hazardous waste could be charged for the cleanup costs.

3.12 Public land use planning strives to balance which of the following potentially conflicting interests?

    a. Individual property rights and the public's interest.
    b. Public policy makers and community business leaders.
    c. Tenant occupancy specifications and construction contractors.
    d. Individual property owners and municipal planning agencies.

3.13 Zoning, building codes, and environmental restrictions are forms of local land use control known as

    a. master planning.
    b. preemption.
    c. police power.
    d. concurrency.

3.14 If a municipality exerts its power of eminent domain against a certain property owner, what happens?

    a. The owner must pay higher property taxes or give up the property.
    b. The owner must cede an easement without receiving any compensation.
    c. The municipality annexes the property.
    d. The owner must sell the property in exchange for market-value compensation.

3.15 To be valid, a local zoning ordinance must

    a. reasonably promote community health, safety and welfare.
    b. comply with federal zoning laws.
    c. apply only to unique properties.
    d. published periodically in the local newspaper.

3.16 Why do communities require building permits?

    a. To promote development.
    b. To establish the basis for an inspection.
    c. To promote certificates of occupancy.
    d. To ensure that improvements comply with codes.

3.17 What is the purpose of residential zoning?

    a. To increase home values in a neighborhood.
    b. To regulate the density of dwellings in the residential zone.
    c. To prevent families from residing in commercial and industrial sites.
    d. To maximize intensity of usage.

3.18 A non-profit organization wants to erect an urgent care facility in a residential zone. Given other favorable circumstances, the local authorities may grant permission by allowing

    a. a special exception.
    b. an illegal nonconforming use.
    c. an easement.
    d. a license.

3.19 A property that conformed with zoning ordinances when it was developed but does not conform to new ordinances is said to be

    a. an illegal special exception.
    b. a variance.
    c. a legal nonconforming use.
    d. unmarketable.

3.20 The approval process for development of multiple properties in an area includes submission of

    a. a covenant of restriction.
    b. a plat of subdivision.
    c. a court order.
    d. a developer's pro forma.

3.21 A legal description of a property is one which

    a. accurately identifies the boundaries of the property as distinct from all other properties.
    b. accurately describes the location and dimensions the lot and improvements on the property.
    c. is accepted by a licensed surveyor as suitable for inclusion in a survey of the property.
    d. is written by an attorney licensed to practice real estate law in the state in which the property is located.

3.22 The essential elements of the metes and bounds system are

    a. parallels, base lines, and meridians.
    b. boundaries, distances, and a base line.
    c. reference points, angles, and distances.
    d. lot numbers, sections, and ranges.

3.23   In the Rectangular Survey System, a range is the area in between

   a. any row of sections in a township.
   b. two consecutive meridians.
   c. a principal meridian and a base line.
   d. a parallel and a meridian.

3.24   In the Rectangular Survey System, a tier is defined by

   a. six consecutive sections of a township.
   b. two consecutive meridians.
   c. two consecutive parallels.
   d. a parallel and a meridian.

3.25   In the Rectangular Survey System, what are the dimensions of a township?

   a. One mile square.
   b. Six miles by six miles, or 6 miles square.
   c. Thirty-six miles square.
   d. The north and south boundaries are one mile apart; the east and west boundaries are
       indeterminate.

3.26   What portion of a section is ten acres?

   a. 1/8.
   b. 1/16.
   c. 1/32.
   d. 1/64.

3.27   The lot and block system of legally describing property is used for

   a. farm properties.
   b. any property in an unincorporated area.
   c. properties where metes and bounds is not acceptable.
   d. properties in a subdivision.

3.28   A certain legal description contains the phrase, "...northwesterly along Erie Road to the POB...".
       What kind of description is this?

   a. Plat survey.
   b. Government grid.
   c. Metes and bounds.
   d. Rectangular survey.

3.29   How many sections are there in a township?

   a. One.
   b. Six.
   c. Twelve.
   d. Thirty-six.

3.30   In the Rectangular Survey System, a section contains how many acres?

   a. 640.
   b. 320.
   c. 160.
   d. 40.

3.31 The valuable consideration necessary to make a contract valid must be

  a. money.
  b. something tangible.
  c. something of value traded in exchange for something of value.
  d. something of equal value with whatever is received in exchange.

3.32 A real estate sales contract, to be enforceable, must

  a. contain a legal description of the property.
  b. be written on a form approved by the state bar association.
  c. be acknowledged by three witnesses.
  d. be recorded within three days to be enforceable.

3.33 How much time does a seller have to accept a buyer's offer?

  a. Forty-eight hours from the time of the offeror's signing of the offer.
  b. Twenty-four hours from the time of the offer's delivery to the seller.
  c. Within 24 hours following the stated expiration.
  d. A reasonable time, or until the expiration date on the offer.

3.34 A buyer submits an offer to a seller and then dies in a car accident. Before learning of the buyer's death, the seller accepts the offer. Which of the following is true?

  a. The seller can force the buyer's estate to go through with the purchase.
  b. The buyer's death terminated the offer.
  c. The seller must make a new offer with the same terms to the buyer's heirs.
  d. The buyer's heirs have the option of enforcing the contract.

3.35 Which of the following contracts can be assigned to another party?

  a. An exclusive listing agreement.
  b. A personal services agreement.
  c. A contract for the sale of undeveloped land.
  d. An employment contract between a broker and a salesperson.

3.36 An implied agency relationship may be deemed to exist if

  a. the parties do not disavow an express contract that has expired.
  b. the parties act is if there is a contract.
  c. an offering party does not receive written notice that the offer has been rejected.
  d. the parties promise to perform their part of the agreement if the other party performs.

3.37 Which of the following is an executory contract?

  a. An expired lease.
  b. A sale contract before closing.
  c. A recorded sale contract.
  d. An option to buy after it is exercised.

3.38 A bilateral contract is one in which

  a. both parties promise to do something in exchange for the other party's performance.
  b. both parties receive equal consideration.
  c. two parties agree to perform a service together.
  d. both parties promise to do something if the other party performs first.

3.39 A homeseller signs a listing agreement with a broker then subsequently revokes the listing. Which of the following is true?

a. The seller continues to have contractual obligations to the broker.
b. The contract remains in full force until the expiration date.
c. The broker may have a claim for marketing expenses expended during the listing term.
d. The seller cannot sign a listing agreement with another broker.

3.40 A breach of contract is

a. a termination of the contract by the mutual consent of the parties.
b. financial damage suffered by a party because another party has nullified a contract provision.
c. a lawsuit to force a party to discharge the contract.
d. the failure of a party to perform according to the terms of the contract.

3.41 What is rescission?

a. The act of withdrawing an offer before it has been accepted.
b. The act of declaring that a contract is no longer in effect for a given party.
c. The act of declaring a contract unenforceable.
d. The act of modifying the terms of an offer.

3.42 To be valid, a valid contract must

a. reflect a mutual understanding or agreement.
b. use precise wording in a document.
c. not be executable.
d. be created only by an attorney.

3.43 Two parties enter into a contract. The agreement fulfills all the requirements for a valid contract, with no disqualifying circumstances. Given this situation, it is still possible that the contract may be

a. void.
b. illegal.
c. unenforceable.
d. voidable.

3.44 The guardian for a mentally incompetent party enters into an oral contract with another party to buy a trade fixture on behalf of the incompetent party. This contract

a. does not meet validity requirements.
b. is possibly valid and enforceable.
c. must be in writing to be valid.
d. is valid but unenforceable.

3.45 A prospective homebuyer submits a signed offer with the condition that the seller pay for the inspection at closing. The seller disagrees, crosses out the provision, then signs and returns the document to the buyer. At this point, assuming all other contract validity items are in order, the original offer is now

a. an accepted offer, therefore a valid contract.
b. an executable option.
c. a counteroffer.
d. an invalid offer.

3.46 A construction contractor executes a contract with a buyer. In the agreement, the contractor promises to complete construction by November 20. This promise can be construed as

a. an option.
b. mutual consent.
c. a meeting of the minds.
d. valuable consideration.

3.47 A seller contracts to sell a property that she does not own. The sale contract for this transaction

a. is executable.
b. must be in writing.
c. is void.
d. is illegal yet potentially enforceable.

3.48 The statute of limitations requires that parties to a contract who have been damaged or who question the contract's provisions

a. must act within a statutory period.
b. must select a specific, limited course of action for recouping their losses.
c. must arbitrate prior to taking court action.
d. must wait a statutory period before they may take legal action.

3.49 The purpose of the statute of frauds is to

a. invalidate certain oral contracts.
b. require certain conveyance-related contracts to be in writing.
c. nullify oral leases and listing agreements.
d. eliminate fraud in real estate contracts.

3.50 A seller immediately accepts a buyer's offer but waits ten days before returning the accepted document to the buyer. Meanwhile, the offer has expired. Which of the following is true?

a. The buyer is bound to the contract since it was accepted immediately.
b. The buyer has no obligations to the seller whatsoever.
c. The buyer may not rescind the expired offer.
d. The seller may sue for specific performance.

Test 4: Agency; Listing Agreements

4.1   The agency relationship is defined by

    a. the Realtor Code of Ethics.
    b. the laws of agency, or in some states, by statute.
    c. the law of real estate contracts.
    d. the agreement between a principal and an agent.

4.2   Which of the following is true of the connection between compensation and the agency relationship?

    a. An agreement to give and receive compensation creates an agency relationship.
    b. If an agency relationship exists, the principal must provide valuable consideration to the agent.
    c. The relationship is independent of any compensation arrangement.
    d. If an agency relationship exists, the agent is entitled to compensation.

4.3   One of the parties to an agency relationship defaults, and the agreement terminates. Which of the following is true?

    a. All obligations are extinguished.
    b. Both parties must continue to perform all other obligations of the agreement.
    c. The defaulting party may have a financial consequence.
    d. The damaged party has no claim against the defaulting party.

4.4   Among the fiduciary duties imposed on a real estate agent is the requirement to

    a. refuse offers the agent knows will be unacceptable to the principal.
    b. present all offers to the principal regardless of their amount.
    c. advise the principal against accepting an offer that is below full price.
    d. advise a prospect that the principal will not accept the prospect's offer in order to elicit a better offer.

4.5   One of the agent's fiduciary duties that continues even after a listing agreement expires is

    a. obedience.
    b. diligence.
    c. confidentiality.
    d. disclosure.

4.6   The standard of care and competence that a principal can expect from an agent is generally that which is

    a. specified in the agency agreement.
    b. necessary to earn the promised compensation.
    c. necessary to procure a customer.
    d. comparable to that of other practitioners in the area.

4.7   Agent Michael is showing his new listing to a buyer who informs him that he has just inherited five million dollars. Michael is now bound by fiduciary duty to

    a. keep the information in confidence.
    b. disclose the information to the buyer's agent.
    c. disclose the information to the seller.
    d. verify the buyer's statements before disclosing them to the client.

4.8   Agent Gerry has executed an exclusive buyer broker agreement with the Andersons. The agent subsequently places an offer with Melinda, the exclusive selling agent for the Lincolns, to buy their lakefront property. The offer contains provisions for the Lincolns to pay the brokerage commission, which the Lincolns agree to. Given this set of circumstances, Gerry owes the full set of fiduciary duties to

a. the Andersons.
b. the Lincolns.
c. Gerry's broker.
d. Melinda's broker.

4.9   A subagent is the agent of

a. the seller.
b. the buyer.
c. a broker who has an agency relationship with a client.
d. the client's and the customer's agents.

4.10   Which of the following is a dual agency situation?

a. Two agents share the exclusive right to represent the same client on all transactions.
b. One agent represents both sides in a transaction.
c. A selling agent from one brokerage works with a listing agent from another brokerage to complete a transaction.
d. One agent represents two sellers at the same time.

4.11   The duties of a transaction broker or facilitator include

a. preserving the confidentiality of information received from either party.
b. helping the two parties achieve their respective objectives.
c. disclosing material facts that affect the value of the property to both parties.
d. choosing to obey the instructions of one party and informing the other party of the decision.

4.12   In which of the following contact situations would a seller's agent be expected to disclose his agency relationships?

a. The agent is showing the client's property to a prospective buyer.
b. The agent tells an acquaintance at a party about the client's property.
c. The agent answers questions about the client's property for a telephone caller responding to a newspaper ad.
d. The agent is showing a potential buyer houses in a certain price range in the multiple listing book.

4.13   The essential foundation of the agency relationship consists of

a. mutual respect, compensation, and confidentiality.
b. diligence, results, and compensation.
c. service, marketing, and respect.
d. good faith, trust and confidence.

4.14   Audrey wants to take a vacation. To do so, she authorizes an agent to conduct the operations of one of her business enterprises. The kind of agency she has established is

a. limited.
b. general.
c. universal.
d. special.

4.15   A property seller empowers an agent to market and sell a property on his behalf. The kind of agency represented is

a. general.
b. special.
c. universal.
d. no agency.

4.16   Implied agency arises when

a. an agent accepts an oral listing.
b. a principal accepts an oral listing.
c. a party creates an agency relationship outside of an express agreement.
d. a principal agrees to all terms of a written listing agreement, whether express or implied.

4.17   An agency relationship may be involuntarily terminated for which of the following reasons?

a. Condemnation of the property.
b. Mutual consent.
c. Full performance.
d. Renewal of the agent's license.

4.18   A principal discloses that she would sell a property for $500,000. During the listing period, the house is listed and marketed for $530,000. No offers come in, and the listing expires. Three weeks later, the agent confides to a customer that the seller would have sold for less than the listed price. Which of the following is true?

a. The agent has violated the duty of confidentiality.
b. The agent has fulfilled all fiduciary duties, since the listing has expired.
c. The agent is violating the duties owed this customer.
d. The agent has created a dual agency situation with the customer.

4.19   A principal instructs an agent to market a property only to families on the west side of the university campus. The agent refuses to comply. In this case,

a. the agent has violated fiduciary duty.
b. the agent has not violated fiduciary duty.
c. the agent is liable for breaching the listing terms.
d. the agent should obey the instruction to salvage the listing.

4.20   An owner's agent is showing a buyer a residential property for sale. The buyer notices water stains on the foundation walls and floor, and informs the agent. The appropriate course of action for the agent is to

a. immediately contract to paint the ceiling.
b. immediately contract to repair the roof.
c. suggest the buyer make a lower-price offer.
d. inform the seller.

4.21   The meaning and salient characteristics of the agency relationship should be disclosed to the client

a. prior to completing a listing agreement.
b. prior to or upon completion of an offer.
c. upon the initial contact with the person.
d. prior to showing properties.

147

4.22 When must a listing agent disclose his or her agency relationship to prospective tenants or buyers?

    a. Immediately prior to the initial contact.
    b. Upon initial contact.
    c. Whenever substantive communication is made beyond casual conversation.
    d. Immediately following any offer executed by the customer.

4.23 A buyer agent or tenant representative should disclose his or her agency relationship to the owner's agent

    a. immediately prior to the initial contact.
    b. upon initial contact.
    c. immediately prior to substantive contact.
    d. immediately following any offer executed by the landlord.

4.24 An agent is operating as a disclosed dual agent on a transaction. In this case, the agent

    a. may not represent one party's interests to the detriment of the other.
    b. must operate without a listing agreement.
    c. must be obedient and loyal to both parties.
    d. must require that the principals refrain from disclosing any material facts to him.

4.25 An agent informs a buyer that a provision in a contract is very commonplace. After explaining the clause, the agent assures the buyer that the clause does not mean anything significant. If something goes wrong with the transaction, the agent could be liable for

    a. violating duties owed a customer.
    b. misinterpreting the clause.
    c. intentional misrepresentation.
    d. practicing law without a license.

4.26 When a broker enters into a listing agreement, the broker has agreed to accept which of the following?

    a. Fiduciary and contractual obligations with the client.
    b. Fiduciary relationships with client and customer.
    c. Contractual obligations with cooperating brokers.
    d. Fiduciary obligations with the customer.

4.27 The degree of authority granted by a residential brokerage listing agreement generally allows the agent to

    a. create contractual obligations for the client.
    b. negotiate the selling price between client and customer.
    c. hire inspectors, and other individuals to prepare the property for marketing.
    d. market, sell and show the property.

4.28 A salesperson, without an oral or written listing agreement, brings potential buyers to the seller. The seller says, "You can bring me buyers if you want, but I'm not paying you a commission." The salesperson then continues to direct buyers to the property. Which of the following is true about this situation?

    a. There is no agency relationship, and therefore the seller will owe no commission if one of the salesperson's buyers buys the property.
    b. An implied agency may have been created, with obligations to perform for both seller and agent.
    c. The seller and agent have an illegal, undisclosed agency relationship.
    d. The agent has an open exclusive agency listing with no commission agreement, and therefore owes no fiduciary duties to the seller.

4.29 An agent enters into a listing agreement with a homeseller, but then becomes too busy to professionally fulfill the terms of the agreement. To solve the dilemma, the agent assigns the agreement to another licensee in the office. Which of the following is true about this situation?

a. The agent cannot assign the listing agreement.
b. The new listing agent acquires the full set of fiduciary duties owed to the client.
c. The new broker has to split any commission that results with the assigning broker.
d. The original broker has to disclose the assignment to the seller.

4.30 From an agent's point of view, the most desirable form of listing agreement is a(n)

a. exclusive agency.
b. exclusive right to sell.
c. open listing.
d. net listing.

4.31 What is a multiple listing?

a. A listing shared by a listing agent and a selling agent.
b. A listing that a listing agent delegates to a subagent.
c. A listing that is entered in a multiple listing service to enable cooperation with member brokers.
d. A listing that authorizes a listing agent to market more than one property for a seller.

4.32 Which of the following conditions is necessary for a customer to qualify as "ready, willing, and able" in the context of a commissionable transaction?

a. The customer's offer must be accepted.
b. The customer must be legally competent to undertake the transaction.
c. The customer must have a commitment from a lender.
d. The customer must have no business relationship with the agent.

4.33 Although a listing broker may delegate listing tasks to an employed licensee, the broker may not delegate the authority to

a. obtain and distribute compensation.
b. provide cooperating brokers with information about the property.
c. advertise the property.
d. inspect the property for hazardous substances.

4.34 Agent Peter has an open listing with Frank. Paul is Peter's broker. Agent Perry's customer buys Frank's house. Patrick has a commission agreement with Frank. Who is most likely to be compensated in this scenario?

a. Peter, since he has a written listing agreement.
b. Paul, since he is Peter's broker
c. Perry, since he found the customer.
d. Patrick, since he has a commission agreement.

4.35 If an agent has an exclusive listing to sell a property, and the property is then taken by eminent domain, what is the status of the listing?

a. The seller's obligations under the listing are assigned to the agency that takes the property.
b. It becomes a voidable contract.
c. The commission clause of the agreement is canceled.
d. It may be terminated against the agent's will.

4.36 A broker obtains an exclusive listing to sell a house, but after two months, he abandons the listing because the seller is too demanding and hot-tempered. What can the seller do in this situation?

a. Have the licensee's license revoked for negligence.
b. Sue the broker for money damages.
c. Sign a listing agreement with another broker and force the first broker to pay the commission.
d. Force the broker to perform the contract without compensation.

4.37 An owner agrees to pay a broker for procuring a tenant unless it is the owner who finds the tenant. This is an example of a(n)

a. exclusive right-to sell agreement.
b. exclusive agency agreement.
c. open listing.
d. net listing.

4.38 A landlord promises to compensate a broker for procuring a tenant, provided the broker is the procuring cause. This is an example of a(n)

a. exclusive right-to rent agreement.
b. exclusive agency agreement.
c. open rental listing.
d. net lease listing.

4.39 A property owner agrees to pay a broker an open-ended commission as the difference between the sale price and a net amount, provided the owner receives a minimum amount of proceeds from the sale at closing. This is an example of a(n)

a. exclusive right-to sell agreement.
b. exclusive agency agreement.
c. open listing.
d. net listing.

4.40 In the context of agency law, the legal difference between an owner representation agreement and a buyer representation agreement is

a. the client.
b. the commission amount.
c. fiduciary duties.
d. regulatory approvals.

4.41 A multiple listing authorization gives a broker what authority?

a. To list the owner's property in a multiple listing service.
b. To sell several properties for the owner at once.
c. To represent both seller and buyer, if necessary, in selling the property.
d. To delegate the listing responsibilities to other agents.

Test 5: Brokerage Business; Sale Contracts

5.1 Which of the following business entities is generally prohibited from brokering real estate?

a. Sole proprietorship.
b. Partnership.
c. Corporation for profit.
d. Non-profit corporation.

5.2 A joint venture may generally broker real estate if the co-venturers

a. form a business trust.
b. form a co-operative association.
c. are properly licensed.
d. are limited partners.

5.3 A licensed salesperson may work only for

a. a client who has signed a listing agreement with a licensed broker.
b. a single employing broker who has an active broker's license.
c. a client who has signed an authorization agreement with a licensed salesperson.
d. an employer who has an active or inactive broker's license.

5.4 Which of the following activities is a licensed salesperson allowed to engage in?

a. Accept a listing that is in an associate's name.
b. Accept a commission directly from the MLS.
c. Offer a property for lease on behalf of the employing broker.
d. Sign a contract with a management company on behalf of a client.

5.5 If a salesperson has worked on a completed transaction that involved a listing agent, a selling agent, and several subagents for each of these, from whom will the salesperson receive any compensation that is due?

a. The listing agent.
b. The selling agent.
c. The seller.
d. The employing broker.

5.6 A property has sold for $380,000. The listing agreement calls for a commission of 6.5%. The listing broker and selling broker agree to share the commission equally. What will the listing agent receive if the agent is scheduled to get a 40% share?

a. $4,445.
b. $3,556.
c. $2,667.
d. $4,940.

5.7 A real estate salesperson finds a buyer to a For Sale By Owner property. The home sells for $245,000, and the seller agrees to pay a commission of 3%. The salesperson is on a 65% commission schedule with her broker, who pays her 65% minus office expenses of $500. How much will the salesperson receive from this transaction?

a. $4,778.
b. $4,452.
c. $4,278.
d. $3,175.

5.8 A salesperson makes a listing presentation to a homeseller and obtains a signed listing agreement. The first thing the salesperson must now do is

a. make a final pricing determination for the property.
b. negotiate the commission with the client.
c. complete the signing of the listing.
d. explain the agency relationship to the client.

5.9 Juan shows a customer a property that is listed by another brokerage firm. He obtains an offer that is $5,000 less than the listing price. How should Juan deal with this offer?

a. Advise the buyer that the offer will be rejected.
b. Present the offer to the seller at the earliest possible moment.
c. Ask the listing broker to lower the listing price.
d. Counter the offer.

5.10 A broker receives an earnest money deposit from a buyer and signs the check over to the listing agent as a partial commission advance. What is wrong with this procedure?

a. Nothing, provided the deposit clears the bank and doesn't bounce.
b. The broker and the agent are guilty of price fixing.
c. The broker has illegally converted security funds for business use.
d. The agent may not be able to return the advance if the transaction falls through.

5.11 Under what circumstance may a property listed for sale with a brokerage be advertised without identifying the broker?

a. When the salesperson is an out-of-state licensee.
b. When the ad is restricted to the brokerage's website.
c. When the advertisement is a silent ad.
d. Never.

5.12 Competing brokers in a county seat agree on a standard commission rate for principals within the county. This is a possible violation of

a. fair trade and anti-trust laws.
b. the Statute of Frauds.
c. contract law.
d. the Uniform Commercial Code.

5.13 What is co-brokerage?

a. An owner agent and a buyer agent combine efforts to complete a sale.
b. Outside brokers assist a listing agent in procuring a buyer.
c. An owner or buyer lists with several brokers to complete a transaction.
d. Agents from a single agency cooperate to generate listings for the broker.

5.14 Which of the following may associate his or her name or title with the term "Realtor®"?

a. Any active or inactive broker in the country.
b. Any duly licensed, active agent or broker.
c. Any member in good standing in a properly chartered real estate trade organization.
d. Only members of the National Association of Realtors®.

5.15 Real estate sales agents are legally authorized to

a. represent their employing broker in procuring clients and customers.
b. act directly on a client's behalf to discharge the broker's listing responsibilities.
c. negotiate and execute contracts for sale on behalf of the client.
d. take on the listing responsibilities for other listings in MLS.

5.16 How does the position of an independent contractor licensee (IC) differ from that of an employee licensee?

a. The IC is responsible for his or her own taxes; the broker does not withhold.
b. The IC must obtain his or her own training; it is not provided by the broker.
c. The employee is not entitled to company benefits.
d. The IC must abide by all office meeting schedules.

5.17 A salesperson's commission rate and structure is established by

a. state regulation.
b. competitive conditions.
c. agreement with other brokers in the market.
d. negotiations with the client.

5.18 In obtaining offers from a buyer, an agent must be careful to

a. pursue only those offers which are at or near the listing price.
b. balance the owner's price expectations with the buyer's opinion of value.
c. avoid disclosing what price the owner will accept.
d. avoid completing offers that are beneath market value.

5.19 Commingling is the practice of

a. blending escrow funds on a number of properties in one escrow account.
b. mixing socially with prospects at open houses or other marketing functions.
c. allocating commission funds from a transaction for use in the agency's business.
d. mixing escrow funds with the broker's operating funds.

5.20 Three leading agencies charge identical commission rates for brokering office properties in Phoenix. Based on this information alone, which of the following is true?

a. There is insufficient evidence of anything other than a normal business practice.
b. The brokers have engaged in legal collusion.
c. The brokers have allocated the Phoenix market.
d. The brokers have illegally fixed prices.

5.21 A real estate sale contract is an executory contract until

a. the completed sale transaction is recorded.
b. the buyer and seller have agreed to all provisions and have signed the contract.
c. all the obligations and promises are performed and the transaction is closed.
d. the loan has been approved, the title insurance has been obtained, and the closing date is set.

5.22 In assisting a buyer or seller to complete an offer to purchase, what should an agent do to reduce the risk of committing an unauthorized practice of law?

a. Use a standard contract promulgated by a state agency or a real estate board.
b. Observe ethical standards promulgated by real estate trade organizations.
c. Offer legal advice only on points of the contract that the agent is absolutely certain about.
d. Write contract terms that are fair to both buyer and seller.

5.23 To be enforceable, a contract for the conveyance of real estate must

a. be acknowledged by witnesses.
b. be written.
c. be recorded.
d. have an expiration date.

5.24 A buyer makes an offer to purchase a house, and the seller accepts the offer. However, before the salesperson can inform the buyer of the seller's decision, the buyer delivers a written notice that she is opting out and cancelling the agreement. At this point, which of the following is true?

a. The contract has been legitimately cancelled and is null and void.
b. The seller must give the buyer an opportunity to make a new offer.
c. The buer must perform under the terms of the contract
d. The seller must notify the buyer in writing that the buyer is in default.

5.25 Which of the following is an essential element of a valid contract for the sale of real estate?

a. A valid blank form that the contract is written on.
b. A habitable property.
c. An offer and acceptance.
d. A marketable title.

5.26 What kind of interest does the buyer acquire once a real estate sale contract is signed by the principal parties?

a. Legal title.
b. Lienholder interest.
c. Reversionary interest.
d. Equitable title.

5.27 A contingency in a sale contract is

a. a promise by buyer or seller to perform a specific action.
b. a condition that, if unmet, renders the contract unenforceable.
c. one of several alternative actions that buyer or seller may take to satisfy contract requirements.
d. an optional, unilateral action that either party may take at the request of the other party.

5.28 A clause in a sale contract stipulates that the seller must provide evidence that the property is free of active termite infestation. On the day of closing, the buyer learns that inspection service did not provide the required written documentation. The buyer then proceeds to declare that the sale is off. Which of the following is true of this situation?

a. The seller can sue for specific performance.
b. The buyer will be in default, and liable for damages, if he does not complete the transaction.
c. The buyer may be able to have the contract canceled.
d. The contract is automatically void.

5.29 A buyer signs an earnest money agreement and gives it to the broker who showed her the property she is buying. After leaving the broker's office, she reconsiders and decides she prefers a different property. How long does she have to take back her offer?

a. Until the seller communicates acceptance of the offer.
b. Until the earnest money deposit check is cashed.
c. She can take it back at any time, but must forfeit the earnest money.
d. She cannot take it back until after the expiration date of the offer.

5.30 On Wednesday, Fred offers to sell his property to Jack for $275,000, with the offer to remain open until 5 p.m. the next day. On Thursday morning, Sally offers Fred $280,000 for the property and Fred accepts. At 1 p.m. on Thursday afternoon, Jack accepts. Which of the following is true of this situation?

a. The acceptance by Sally creates a contract and terminates Fred's offer to Jack.
b. Fred has entered into contracts with both Jack and Sally to sell the same property.
c. Fred's acceptance of Sally's offer is invalidated by Jack's acceptance, because Fred's offer to Jack was made prior to Sally's offer to Fred.
d. No contract has been created because it is impossible to have two valid sale contracts for the same property.

5.31 Among the items that normally must be disclosed in a sale contract or its addenda is/are the

a. buyer's financial capability.
b. buyer's source of funds for the down payment.
c. seller's acceptable price range.
d. agency relationships and property condition.

5.32 To create an enforceable option-to-buy contract, there must be an exchange of

a. a promise to sell and a promise to buy.
b. valuable consideration and a right to buy.
c. valuable consideration and a promise to buy.
d. a down payment and a post-dated contract for sale.

5.33 Mary Carboy buys a house from Jim Schmidt and at the same time obtains an option to purchase the adjoining vacant lot for $10,000 within one year. A few months later, Carboy informs Schmidt that she is ready to exercise her option, but finds that Schmidt has received an offer of $12,000 from another party. Schmidt states that he will accept the offer unless Carboy is willing to match the $12,000 offer. Which of the following is true of this situation?

a. Schmidt must sell to Carboy for $10,000.
b. Carboy must pay $12,000 or lose the property.
c. Schmidt may sell to Carboy or the other party, but the price cannot exceed $10,000.
d. If the other party delivers payment before Carboy does, the option is canceled.

5.34 Which of the following is true regarding the assignability of an option?

a. It is assignable only if the contract specifically allows assignment.
b. It is never assignable.
c. It is assignable only if the option is exercised.
d. It is always assignable unless the contract prohibits assignment.

5.35 Which of the following is true of a contract for deed transaction?

a. At the end of the contract period, the vendee receives equitable title, provided all required periodic payments have been made.
b. The vendee has no right to possess or occupy the property during the contract period.
c. At the end of the contract period, the vendor conveys legal title, provided the vendee has fulfilled all obligations.
d. The vendor may cancel the contract at any time before the final payment has been received.

5.36 Several buyers are competing for the last available home in a desirable new subdivision. One buyer calls the owner-developer directly on the phone and offers $20,000 over and above the listed price. The developer accepts the offer. At this point,

a. the parties have a valid, enforceable sale contract on the home.
b. the parties have completed a verbal, executory contract.
c. the parties may not cancel their contract.
d. the developer could not entertain other offers on the property.

5.37 An owner completes a sales contract on her property with a buyer. Before closing, the seller runs into financial trouble and assigns the contract to her principal creditor. The buyer cries foul, fearing the property will be lost. Which of the following is true?

a. The buyer can sue the assignee to disallow the illegal assignment.
b. The buyer can take legal action against the assignor.
c. The assignor has completed a legal action.
d. The sale contract is nullified.

5.38. A due-on-sale clause in a sale contract puts parties on notice that

a. the full price of the property is due the seller at closing.
b. any loans surviving closing become immediately payable.
c. all of the seller's debts must be retired before or upon closing.
d. any conveyance may trigger an acceleration of any loans secured by the property.

5.39 A tenant has an option-to-purchase agreement with the landlord that expires on June 30. On July 1, the tenant frantically calls the landlord to exercise the option, offering the apology that she was busy with a death in the family. Which of the following is true?

a. Since options contain grace periods, the landlord must sell.
b. The tenant loses the right to buy, but can claim the money paid for the option from the landlord.
c. The landlord does not have to sell, but must renew the option.
d. The option is expired, and the tenant has no rightful claim to money paid for the option.

5.40 Two parties enter into a contract for deed agreement. In this form of agreement,

a. title is conveyed to the buyer, but the seller retains possession for a stipulated time period.
b. the buyer contracts to pay all cash at closing in exchange for the deed.
c. the seller retains legal title while the buyer makes partial payments until the contract is fully executed.
d. the buyer immediately acquires legal title and takes possession.

5.41 The federal law that produced the Do-Not-Call list and related protections is referred to as the

a. Solicitation Regulation Act.
b. Telemarketing Prohibition Act.
c. CAN-SPAM Act.
d. Telephone Consumer Protection Act

5.42 New federal regulation in advertising requires email advertisers to give recipients an option to discontinue receiving emails from such advertiser. This legislation is called

a. the CAN-SPAM Act.
b. the Truth-in-Advertising Act
c. the Telephone Consumer Protection Act
d. the Email Advertising Prohibition Act, or EAPA.

Test 6: Economics; Appraisal

6.1 If the price of an item is increasing, one can usually assume that

    a. demand for the item is decreasing in relation to supply of the item.
    b. demand for the item is increasing in relation to supply of the item.
    c. supply of the item is increasing.
    d. demand for the item and supply of the item are increasing.

6.2 When the market for an item has achieved market equilibrium, which of the following statements is true?

    a. New suppliers will enter the market and drive the price down.
    b. Demand will slowly taper off, driving the price down.
    c. Unmet demand for the item is directed toward demand for some other item.
    d. Supply and demand are equal, and price and value are equal.

6.3 As an economic product, real estate is distinguished by

    a. its homogeneity.
    b. its variety.
    c. the uniqueness of every parcel.
    d. its ability to appreciate in value.

6.4 The city of Stevensville has declared a moratorium on new construction. If demand is increasing, what will be the likely effect on real estate prices in the area?

    a. Prices level off.
    b. Prices continue to follow the trend that preceded the moratorium.
    c. Prices fall.
    d. Prices rise.

6.5 If Okapi, Inc., a company that markets its sports clothing worldwide, moves into Stevensville and hires 100 employees, it is reasonable to expect that the town will experience

    a. an immediate rise in the demand for industrial real estate, but no other changes in the real estate market.
    b. an increase in demand for all types of real estate.
    c. a housing boom, but no other changes in the real estate market.
    d. an immediate increase in the prices for industrial and office real estate, but no impact on the residential market.

6.6 What is "absorption?"

    a. The amount of new space that is added to available space over a period of time.
    b. The number of houses that are built over a period of time.
    c. The amount of space that is occupied at any given time.
    d. The number of available units that become occupied over a period of time.

6.7 When vacancies are declining in a real estate market, it is common for the market to experience

    a. rising prices.
    b. falling prices.
    c. falling construction activity.
    d. falling absorption.

6.8 The price for any product is a function of four fundamental determinants of value. These are

    a. durability, feasibility, mobility, and location.
    b. desire, utility, scarcity, and purchasing power.
    c. popularity, recognizability, promotion, and rebate.
    d. fungibility, costs, convenience, and uniqueness.

6.9 A town is rapidly growing, but all the buildable vacant lots in the most desirable area have already been occupied. In this case, it is likely that the price of existing homes in that area

    a. will stabilize, since the population must stabilize.
    b. will increase.
    c. will decline, since no further building can take place.
    d. will not show any predictable movement.

6.10 If there is a significant undersupply of homes in a market, construction will tend to increase. This is an example of

    a. supply outstripping demand.
    b. demand outstripping value.
    c. consumer optimism.
    d. the market tending toward equilibrium.

6.11 If commercial real estate rental prices are falling in a market, it is likely that

    a. demand has outstripped supply of space.
    b. the market is in equilibrium.
    c. the market is over-supplied.
    d. employment is increasing.

6.12 A construction boom in a market is an indication that prices

    a. have been increasing.
    b. have been declining.
    c. have been in equilibrium.
    d. have exceeded supply.

6.13 Why is real estate traditionally considered a relatively illiquid economic product?

    a. Its physical form is fixed.
    b. Real estate is defined as land, not water.
    c. It is often difficult to convert to cash.
    d. It cannot be moved.

6.14 What does "base employment" refer to in the context of real estate demand?

    a. The lowest category of employment in terms of wages and desirability
    b. The number of persons employed in base industries in an area
    c. The number of persons employed on military bases in an area
    d. The labor pool available for employment in all industries in an area

6.15 What is "vacancy" in real estate market economics?

    a. A property that has no owner-occupant
    b. The total number of properties of a certain type that are on the market at a given time
    c. The absence of certain types of users in a given market area
    d. The total existing space of a certain type that is unoccupied at a given time

6.16 A moratorium on new construction is an example of

    a. local government influencing the real estate market, regardless of demand.
    b. the natural result of demand exceeding supply in a local market.
    c. government promotion of the free market concept in the local real estate market.
    d. a government policy that aims to restrain a trend of rising prices in the local real estate market.

6.17 Of the following potential influences on a local real estate market, which one would be considered local, rather than regional, national, or global?

    a. Changes in money supply
    b. Federal Reserve interest rates
    c. In- and out-migrations of major employers
    d. Trade imbalances with foreign trading partners

6.18 There is a lot of new construction going on in the town of Florence. Which of the following would most likely be the immediate effect on the real estate market?

    a. Demand increases and prices rise.
    b. Vacancy rises and prices fall.
    c. Absorption and vacancy decrease.
    d. Supply decreases relative to demand.

6.19 What kind of real estate users are most concerned with neighborhood quality, access to services, property amenities, and quality of life in their demand for real estate?

    a. Retail
    b. Office
    c. Industrial
    d. Residential

6.20 One distinguishing feature of real estate as an economic product is

    a. its easy convertibility to cash.
    b. its quick response to changes in supply-demand balance.
    c. its susceptibility to swings in the local economy.
    d. the easy substitutability of one item for another.

6.21 Bill Parsons paid $150,000 for a house to operate as a rental property, figuring that he could rent it out at a rate of $900 a month. In paying a price based on the property's ability to generate a desired future income, Parsons was motivated by the economic principle known as

    a. substitution.
    b. anticipation.
    c. supply and demand.
    d. utility.

6.22 Which of the following situations illustrates the principle of contribution?

    a. A homebuyer makes a down payment of 20% instead of the 10% the lender requires.
    b. A homeowner adds a third bathroom to a house and thereby increases the appraised value by $10,000.
    c. The appraised value of a house goes up by $20,000 over a two-year period because of the prices recently paid for other houses in the neighborhood.
    d. Because of a decline in mortgage interest rates, a homeowner in a certain market is able to list her house at a higher price.

6.23 When a property owner combines two adjacent properties to create a single property with a higher value than the sum of the values of the two separate properties, the applicable principle of value is called

a. assemblage.
b. accretion.
c. progression.
d. subdivision.

6.24 What is the difference between market value and market price, if any?

a. There is no difference.
b. Market value is a broker's estimate; market price is a precise number derived by a licensed appraiser.
c. Market value is an average price derived from comparable sales; market price is a price based on the cost of creating the property.
d. Market value is an estimate; market price is the price at which a property sold.

6.25 The first step in the appraisal process, regardless of the appraisal method, is to

a. identify the highest and best use of the property to be appraised.
b. collect and analyze property data.
c. estimate the value of the land as if it were vacant.
d. define the appraisal problem and the purpose of the appraisal.

6.26 In the final step of an appraisal, the appraiser reconciles the value estimates derived by the various appraisal approaches by

a. disregarding the high and low extreme results.
b. averaging the results of all three approaches.
c. weighing the applicability of the approaches and considering the quality of data supporting each approach.
d. choosing the result that is closest to the average for properties in the immediate neighborhood.

6.27 Which of the following statements properly describes the central concept of the sales comparison approach?

a. Find the median price of recently sold comparable properties and add or subtract dollar amounts in the subject property to account for competitive differences.
b. Make dollar adjustments to the sale prices of comparable properties to account for competitive differences with the subject.
c. Find at least three comparable properties that are currently for sale and make dollar adjustments to the listing prices to account for competitive differences with the subject.
d. Apply an appreciation factor to the price at which the subject property most recently sold and make dollar adjustments to account for competitive differences with comparable properties currently for sale.

6.28 One of the strengths of the sales comparison approach is that it

a. takes into account the subject property's investment value.
b. reveals the profit margin of the builder or developer of the subject property.
c. discovers the underlying value of the subject property apart from the influence of competing properties.
d. takes into account the competitive value of specific amenities of the subject property.

6.29 In making dollar adjustments in the sales comparison approach, the appraiser

   a. adds value to a comparable that is inferior to the subject property.
   b. adds value to the subject property if it is inferior to a comparable.
   c. subtracts value from a comparable that is inferior to the subject property.
   d. subtracts value from the subject property if it is inferior to a comparable.

6.30 The best comparable property for use in the sales comparison approach is the one that

   a. requires the most and largest adjustments.
   b. requires the fewest and smallest adjustments.
   c. sold most recently at the highest price.
   d. is located closest to the subject property.

6.31 A house is being appraised using the sales comparison approach. The house has three bedrooms, two bathrooms, and a patio. The appraiser selects a comparable house that has three bedrooms, 3 bathrooms, and no patio. The comparable house just sold for $200,000. A bath is valued at $7,000, and a patio at $2,000. Assuming all else is equal, what is the adjusted value of the comparable?

   a. $202,000.
   b. $207,000.
   c. $195,000.
   d. $205,000.

6.32 Which of the following statements properly describes the central methodology of the cost approach to appraisal?

   a. Apply a depreciation factor to the reported actual cost of acquiring and improving the subject property.
   b. Estimate the cost of building the improvements on the subject property.
   c. Estimate the land value and add to this the actual cost of the improvements adjusted for competitive differences with similar properties.
   d. Add the estimated land value and cost of improvements and subtract the accrued depreciation of the improvements.

6.33 One of the strengths of the cost approach is that it

   a. takes into account the amount of money required to develop a similar property.
   b. is very accurate for a property with new improvements that represent the highest and best use.
   c. results in an actual price in dollars instead of an estimated value.
   d. reveals the owner's return on money invested in the cost of development.

6.34 The principle underlying depreciation from physical deterioration is that

   a. eventually, a property loses all of its value.
   b. a property loses a portion of its value each year because of economic obsolescence.
   c. a property loses the same increment of value each year over the economic life of the property.
   d. the value lost to depreciation is incurable.

6.35 A property is being appraised by the cost approach. The appraiser estimates that the land is worth $30,000 and the replacement cost of the improvements is $95,000. Total depreciation from all causes is $10,000. What is the indicated value of the property?

   a. $135,000.
   b. $130,000.
   c. $125,000.
   d. $115,000.

6.36 Which of the following statements properly describes how to apply the income capitalization approach to appraisal?

   a. Apply a rate of return to the price paid for an income property.
   b. Divide the income a property generates by a rate of return.
   c. Estimate the amount of income a property must generate to return the capital amount invested in it.
   d. Estimate the rate of return a property owner receives from income generated by the property.

6.37 A strength of the income capitalization approach is that it

   a. uses a rate of return that is required for all potential purchasers in a market.
   b. yields an accurate projection of investment income.
   c. uses a method that is also used by investors to determine how much they should pay for an investment property.
   d. can be used with any type of property in any market.

6.38 A property is being appraised using the income capitalization approach. Annually, it has an estimated gross income of $60,000, vacancy and credit losses of $3,000, and operating expenses of $20,000. Using a capitalization rate of ten percent, what is the indicated value (to the nearest $1,000)?

   a. $370,000.
   b. $400,000.
   c. $570,000.
   d. $600,000.

6.39 An apartment building that sold for $450,000 had monthly gross rent receipts of $3,000. What is its monthly gross rent multiplier?

   a. 12.5
   b. .01.
   c. .08.
   d. 150.

6.40 A rental house has monthly gross income of $1,200. A suitable gross income multiplier derived from market data is 14.1. What estimated sale price (to the nearest $1,000) is indicated?

   a. $169,000.
   b. $102,000.
   c. $203,000.
   d. $173,000.

6.41 A certified appraiser is one who has received certification by

   a. a licensed real estate school.
   b. the Appraisal Institute.
   c. the state in which the appraiser operates.
   d. the Appraisal Review Board.

6.42 The act that required federally-related appraisals to be conducted by a certified appraiser is known as

   a. The Financial Institutions Reform, Recovery and Enforcement Act (FIRREA).
   b. The Uniform Standards of Professional Appraisal Practice Act (USPAPA).
   c. The Appraisal Foundation Authorization and Reform Act (AFAR).
   d. The Federal Institution for Regulation and Enforcement of Appraisal Act (FIREAA).

6.43   As a component of real estate value, the principle of substitution states that

a. if two similar properties are for sale, a buyer will purchase the cheaper of the two.
b. if one of two adjacent homes is more valuable, the price of the other home will tend to rise.
c. if too many properties are built in a market, the prices will tend to go down.
d. people will readily move to another home if it is of equal value.

6.44   Highest and best use of a property is that use which

a. is physically and financially feasible, legal, and the most productive.
b. is legal, feasible, and deemed the most appropriate by zoning authorities.
c. entails the largest building that zoning ordinances will allow developers to erect.
d. conforms to other properties in the area.

6.45   Lynne just bought a house. She paid $187,500, for it, even though it had been listed at $195,000. An adjoining property owner, Ken, had tried to buy the property for $185,000, but had been refused. He now offers Lynne $190,000 for the house. Lynne is interested, so she hires an appraiser. The appraiser returns an estimate of value of $200,000. Which of these numbers can be called the market value?

a. $187,500.
b. $190,000.
c. $195,000.
d. $200,000.

6.46   A notable weakness of the sales comparison approach to value is that

a. there may be no recent sale price data in the market.
b. the approach is not based on the principle of substitution.
c. the approach is only accurate with unique, special purpose properties.
d. sale prices cannot be compared, since all real estate is different.

6.47   In the market data approach, an appraiser

a. chooses nearby comparables, adjusts the subject for differences, and estimates the value.
b. gathers relevant price data, applies the data to the subject, and estimates the value.
c. selects comparable properties, adjusts the comparables, and estimates the value.
d. identifies the price previously paid, applies an appreciation rate, and estimates the value.

6.48   In the sales comparison approach, an adjustment is warranted if

a. the buyer obtains conventional financing for the property.
b. the seller offers below-market seller financing.
c. a comparable is located in another, albeit similar neighborhood.
d. one property has a hip roof and the other has a gabled roof.

6.49   To complete the sales comparison approach, the appraiser

a. averages the comparable values.
b. weights the comparables.
c. identifies the subject's value as that of the middle value of the comparables.
d. identifies the subject's value as that of the nearest comparable.

6.50   One weakness of the cost approach for appraising market value is that

a. builders may not pay market value for materials or labor.
b. market value is not always the same as what the property cost.
c. comparables used may not have similar quality of construction.
d. new properties have inestimable costs and rates of depreciation.

6.51 The cost of constructing a functional equivalent of a subject property is known as

a. reproduction cost.
b. replacement cost.
c. restitution cost.
d. reconstruction cost.

6.52 An office building lacks fiber optic cabling to accommodate the latest communications equipment. This is an example of

a. physical deterioration.
b. economic obsolescence.
c. incurable depreciation.
d. functional obsolescence.

6.53 A home is located in a neighborhood where homeowners on the block have failed to maintain their properties. This is an example of

a. curable external obsolescence.
b. incurable economic obsolescence.
c. functional obsolescence.
d. physical deterioration.

6.54 In appraisal, loss of value in a property from any cause is referred to as

a. deterioration.
b. obsolescence.
c. depreciation.
d. deflation.

6.55 In the cost approach, after estimating the value of the land and the cost of the improvements, the appraiser

a. estimates depreciation, subtracts depreciation from cost, and adds back the land value.
b. subtracts deterioration from cost, estimates land depreciation, and totals the two values.
c. estimates depreciation of land and improvements and subtracts the total from original cost.
d. estimates obsolescence and subtracts from the cost of land and improvements.

6.56 Which regulatory entity/code establishes standards for an appraiser's methods, reporting methods and disclosures?

a. Financial Institutions Reform, Recovery, and Enforcement Act (FIRREA)
b. Uniform Standards of Professional Appraisal Practice (USPAP)
c. National Association of Realtors®' Code of Ethics
d. Federal Appraisal Regulation and Licensing Board.

7.1   What is a lien-theory state?

    a. A state in which a mortgagee holds legal title to a secured property.
    b. A state in which a mortgagee has equitable title to a secured property.
    c. A state that allows a real estate owner's creditors to record liens against the owner's property.
    d. A state in which a lien is considered as a conveyance.

7.2   What is the function of a note in a mortgage or trust deed financing arrangement?

    a. It is the lender's security instrument in the collateral property.
    b. It is evidence of ownership of the mortgage or trust deed.
    c. It contains the borrower's promise to maintain the value of the property given as collateral for a loan.
    d. It is evidence of the borrower's debt to the lender.

7.3   When homebuyer Henry pledges his newly purchased home as collateral for a mortgage loan, the evidence of the pledge is the

    a. trust deed or mortgage.
    b. promissory note.
    c. loan commitment.
    d. loan receipt.

7.4   The borrower in a mortgage loan transaction is known as the

    a. mortgagee.
    b. mortgagor.
    c. lienor.
    d. trustee.

7.5   If a borrower obtains an interest-only loan of $200,000 at an annual interest rate of 6%, what is the monthly interest payment?

    a. $1,200.
    b. $600.
    c. $500.
    d. $1,000.

7.6   If a borrower's monthly interest payment on an interest-only loan at an annual interest rate of 6% is $500, how much was the loan amount?

    a. $72,000.
    b. $100,000.
    c. $120,000.
    d. $50,000.

7.7   A borrower of a $50,000 interest-only loan makes annual interest payments of $3750. What interest rate is the borrower paying?

    a. 7.5%.
    b. .75%.
    c. 3.75%.
    d. 8.5%.

7.8 Maria borrows $100,000 and pays two points for the loan. How much does she pay in points?

   a. $200.
   b. $2,000.
   c. $1,200.
   d. It depends on the interest rate.

7.9 Which of the following is true of an amortizing loan?

   a. The amount of annual interest paid is the same for every year of the loan term.
   b. Part of each periodic payment is applied to repayment of the loan balance in advance and part is applied to payment of interest in arrears.
   c. Except for any points that may be paid, the interest on the loan balance is usually paid in advance.
   d. The interest rate is reduced each year to maintain equal payments even though the outstanding loan balance is smaller.

7.10 For a loan that is not backed by the Federal Housing Administration or Veterans Administration, and for which the borrower is making a down payment of less than 20%, the lender is likely to require the borrower to obtain

   a. a subrogation agreement.
   b. private mortgage insurance.
   c. a letter of credit.
   d. a co-signer on the note.

7.11 What is a loan-to-value ratio?

   a. The percentage of a lender's portfolio that is composed of mortgage loans.
   b. The ratio of borrowed principal plus total interest to the appraised value of the collateral property.
   c. The ratio of a lender's return on a mortgage loan to the value of the collateral property.
   d. The fraction of the appraised value of the property offered as collateral which the lender is willing to lend.

7.12 The difference between what a borrower has to pay to purchase a property and the amount a lender will lend on the property is the

   a. mortgage insurance coverage amount.
   b. lender's profit margin.
   c. buyer's down payment.
   d. origination fee.

7.13 The Equal Credit Opportunity Act prohibits a lender from

   a. refusing a loan because the borrower does not match the lender's target market.
   b. including income from self-employment in the borrower's qualifying income.
   c. requiring both spouses to sign the loan application form.
   d. refusing a loan because a borrower has a defective credit report.

7.14 A loan applicant has an annual gross income of $72,000. How much will a lender allow the applicant to pay for monthly housing expense to qualify for a loan if the lender uses an income ratio of 28%?

   a. $2,160.
   b. $1,680.
   c. $1,068.
   d. $840.

7.15 AMC Bank discovers, in considering buyer Bob's application for a mortgage loan, that Bob has borrowed the down payment from an uncle and has to repay that loan. Bob should expect that AMC Bank will

a. refuse the application.
b. adjust the applicant's debt ratio calculation and lower the loan amount.
c. increase the loan amount to enable the borrower to pay off the loan to the relative.
d. require the borrower to make payments to an escrow account for repayment of the relative's loan.

7.16 The Federal Reserve's Regulation Z applies to which loans?

a. All loans.
b. All loans secured by real estate.
c. All loans secured by a residence.
d. All loans over $25,000.

7.17 If a particular loan falls under Regulation Z's right of rescission provision,

a. the lender has the right to change the terms of the loan within a certain period.
b. the lender has the right to accelerate repayment of the loan because of a change in the borrower's credit status.
c. the borrower has the right to pay off the loan ahead of schedule with no penalty.
d. the borrower has a limited right to cancel the transaction within a certain period.

7.18 Under the Equal Credit Opportunity Act, a lender, or a real estate agent who assists a seller in qualifying a potential buyer, may not

a. tell a rejected loan applicant the reasons for the rejection.
b. ask the buyer/borrower about his/her religion or national origin.
c. ask the buyer/borrower to explain unconventional sources of income.
d. use a credit report that has not been provided to the borrower.

7.19 A conventional mortgage loan is one that is

a. backed by the Federal National Mortgage Association.
b. insured under Section 203(b) of the Federal Housing Administration loan program.
c. guaranteed by the Government National Mortgage Association.
d. not FHA-insured or VA-guaranteed.

7.20 The assumability of an FHA-insured loan is

a. unrestricted.
b. limited by when the loan was originated.
c. limited to owner-occupied properties.
d. prohibited on all existing loans under current regulations.

7.21 A VA certificate of eligibility determines

a. how long an individual served in the military.
b. the maximum loan amount an approved lender can give to veterans.
c. how much of a loan the VA will guarantee.
d. whether a lender is approved to issue VA-guaranteed loans.

7.22 A borrower obtains a 30-year, fully amortizing mortgage loan of $50,000 at 8%. What is the principal balance at the end of the loan term?

a. $2,000.
b. $50,000.
c. $220.
d. Zero.

7.23 Which of the following describes a purchase money mortgage financing arrangement?

a. A bank gives a buyer a senior mortgage loan that fully covers the cost of purchasing the property.
b. The buyer gives the seller a mortgage and note as part of the purchase price of the property.
c. A land trust holds title to the property while the buyer makes periodic installment payments to the seller.
d. The seller uses the purchase money obtained from the buyer's mortgage loan to repay the seller's outstanding loan balance.

7.24 A homeowner borrows money from a lender and gives the lender a mortgage on the property as collateral for the loan. The homeowner retains title to the property. This is an example of

a. intermediation.
b. forfeiture.
c. hypothecation.
d. subordination.

7.25 Which of the following correctly describes the flow of money and documents in a mortgage loan transaction?

a. The borrower gives the lender a note and a mortgage in exchange for loan funds.
b. The lender gives the borrower a mortgage and receives a note in exchange for loan funds.
c. The borrower receives a note in exchange for a mortgage from the lender.
d. The lender gives the borrower a note, loan funds and a mortgage.

7.26 In a deed of trust transaction, which of the following occurs?

a. The beneficiary conveys title to a trustee in exchange for loan funds.
b. The trustee conveys title to a beneficiary in exchange for loan funds.
c. The trustor conveys title to a trustee in exchange for loan funds from the beneficiary.
d. The trustee conveys title to a trustor in exchange for loan funds from the beneficiary.

7.27 A lender lends money to a homeowner and takes legal title to the property as collateral during the payoff period. They are in a

a. title-theory state.
b. lien-theory state.
c. state allowing land trusts.
d. state where hypothecation is illegal.

7.28 A lender who charges a rate of interest in excess of legal limits is guilty of

a. redlining.
b. usury.
c. profit-taking.
d. nothing; there are no legal limits to interest rates.

7.29 A lender is charging 2 points on a $60,000 loan. The borrower must therefore pay the lender an advance amount of

a. $120.
b. $300.
c. $1,200.
d. $3,000.

7.30 The difference between a balloon loan and an amortized loan is

a. an amortized loan is paid off over the loan period.
b. a balloon loan always has a shorter loan term.
c. an amortized loan requires interest-payments.
d. a balloon loan must be retired in five years.

7.31 A distinctive feature of a promissory note is that

a. it is not assignable.
b. it must be accompanied by a mortgage.
c. it is a negotiable instrument.
d. it may not be prepaid.

7.32 When the terms of the mortgage loan are satisfied, the mortgagee

a. may retain any overage in the escrow account.
b. may inspect the property before returning legal title.
c. may be entitled to charge the borrower a small fee to close the loan.
d. may be required to execute a release of mortgage document.

7.33 In addition to income, credit, and employment data, a mortgage lender requires additional documentation, usually including

a. an appraisal report.
b. a criminal record report.
c. a subordination agreement.
d. a default recourse waiver.

7.34 The three overriding considerations of a lender's mortgage loan decision are

a. points, interest rate, and loan term.
b. the location of the mortgaged property, the borrower's cash, and the amount of the borrower's equity.
c. the ability to re-pay, the value of the collateral, and the profitability of the loan.
d. the amount of the loan, the borrower's income, and the down payment.

7.35 The reason lenders consider the loan-to-value ratio important in underwriting is that

a. they don't want to lend borrowers any more money than necessary.
b. they want to ensure there is more than enough collateral to cover the loan amount.
c. borrowers can only afford to borrow a portion of the entire purchase price.
d. the higher the loan-to-value ratio, the more profitable the loan.

7.36 The Equal Credit Opportunity Act (ECOA) requires lenders to

a. extend equal credit to all prospective borrowers.
b. consider the income of a spouse in evaluating a family's creditworthiness.
c. discount the income of a person involved in child-rearing or child-bearing.
d. specialize lending activity by geographical area for improved customer service.

7.37 Lenders use an income ratio in qualifying to

a. insure a borrower has the earning power to make the loan payments.
b. compare a borrower's earnings to the borrower's short-term debt.
c. identify the highest possible interest rate that the borrower can afford.
d. quantify the borrower's assets to the fullest extent.

7.38 The debt ratio formula used to qualify borrowers is

a. total debt divided by debt payments.
b. gross income divided by assets.
c. gross income divided by debts.
d. debt payments divided by gross income.

7.39 At the closing of a mortgage loan

a. the borrower pays off the note and receives clear title.
b. the lender issues a firm loan commitment.
c. the parties complete all loan origination documents and the loan is funded.
d. the borrower's loan application is complete and the file closed.

7.40 Which laws or regulations require mortgage lenders to disclose financing costs and annual percentage rate to a borrower before funding a loan?

a. The Equal Credit Opportunity Act.
b. Truth-in-Lending laws and Regulation Z.
c. The Real Estate Settlement and Procedures Act.
d. Federal Fair Housing Laws.

7.41 Which laws or regulations prevent mortgage lenders from discriminating in extending credit to potential borrowers?

a. The Equal Credit Opportunity Act.
b. Truth-in-Lending laws.
c. The Real Estate Settlement and Procedures Act.
d. Federal Fair Housing Laws.

7.42 Which laws or regulations require mortgage lenders to provide an estimate of closing costs to a borrower and forbid them to pay kickbacks for referrals?

a. The Equal Credit Opportunity Act.
b. Truth-in-Lending laws.
c. the Real Estate Settlement and Procedures Act.
d. Federal Fair Housing Laws.

7.43 Which of the following are methods used by the Federal Reserve System to regulate the money supply?

a. Selling securities, printing money, and controlling lending underwriting requirements.
b. Buying securities, changing the discount rate, and controlling banking reserves.
c. Printing money, changing interest rates, and selling T-bills.
d. Controlling the prime rate, trading securities, and purchasing loans.

7.44 How does the secondary mortgage market aid borrowers seeking a mortgage loan?

a. It cycles funds back to primary lenders so they can make more loans.
b. It issues second mortgages and sells them in the home equity market.
c. It lends funds to banks so they can make more loans.
d. It pays off defaulted loans made by primary mortgage lenders.

7.45 The major organizations operating in the secondary mortgage market are

a. Fannie Mae, Freddie Mac, and Ginnie Mae.
b. Fannie Mae, GMAC, and MGIC.
c. Freddie Mac, FHA, and VA.
d. Fannie Mae, Freddie Mac, and the Federal Reserve.

7.46   What is the role of Fannie Mae in the secondary mortgage market?

    a. It guarantees FHA-backed and VA-backed loans.
    b. It insures FHA-backed and VA-backed loans.
    c. It purchases FHA-backed and VA-backed loans.
    d. It originates FHA-backed and VA-backed loans.

7.47   What is the role of the Federal Housing Authority in the mortgage lending market?

    a. It guarantees loans made by approved lenders.
    b. It insures loans made by approved lenders.
    c. It purchases loans made by approved lenders.
    d. It originates loans made by approved lenders.

7.48   What is the role of the Veteran's Administration in the mortgage lending market?

    a. It guarantees loans made by approved lenders.
    b. It insures loans made by approved lenders.
    c. It purchases loans made by approved lenders.
    d. It originates loans made by approved lenders.

7.49   In a graduated payment mortgage loan,

    a. loan funds are disbursed to the borrower on a graduated basis.
    b. the interest rate periodically increases in graduated phases.
    c. the loan payments gradually increase.
    d. the loan payments gradually increase and the loan term gradually decreases.

7.50   In a buydown,

    a. the lender lowers the interest rate on a loan in exchange for a prepayment of principal.
    b. the borrower pays additional interest at the onset in order to obtain a lower interest rate.
    c. the lender requires the borrower to buy down the price of the property by increasing the down payment.
    d. the borrower pays the lender additional funds to buy down the term of the loan.

Test 8: Investments; Taxation; Professional Practices

8.1   When an investor has to pay a lender more to finance the investment than the investment property generates in income, the investor suffers from

a. negative amortization.
b. negative leverage.
c. a reverse mortgage.
d. a debt investment.

8.2   Cost recovery is allowed as a federal tax deduction on

a. principal residences that do not have a home office.
b. income properties.
c. land.
d. commercial properties owned by the federal government.

8.3   A homeowner paid $200,000 for a house three years ago. The house sells today for $239,000. How much has the property appreciated?

a. 8.4 %.
b. 6.5 %.
c. 19.5 %.
d. 16.3 %.

8.4   The primary tax benefit in owning a non-income property such as a residence is

a. depreciation of improvements.
b. appreciation of land.
c. a deduction for costs of operating the property.
d. a deduction for mortgage interest.

8.5   A house sold for $250,000. The seller paid a brokerage commission of six percent, legal fees of $600, and had other closing costs of $1,500. What are net proceeds from the sale?

a. $235,000.
b. $234,000.
c. $233,500.
d. $232,900.

8.6   A homeowner bought a house five years ago for $150,000. Since then, the homeowner has spent $3,000 to pave the driveway and has added a central heating/airconditioning system at a cost of $4,000. What is the homeowner's adjusted basis if the house is sold today?

a. $156,000.
b. $157,000.
c. $144,000.
d. $145,000.

8.7   A homeowner sold her house and realized a net proceeds amount of $210,000. Her adjusted basis in the home was $176,000. She immediately bought another house for $200,000. What was her capital gain?

a. $10,000.
b. $24,000.
c. $34,000.
d. None.

8.8   After five years of owner-occupancy, Simon Wilson sells his principal residence for a gain of $150,000, and the next month buys another principal residence that costs more than the adjusted sale price of the old home. Which of the following is true of the treatment of the tax on gain?

a. There is no taxable gain.
b. It must be paid in the year of the sale.
c. The homeowner may choose to pay it or defer it.
d. Tax is due on the difference between the cost of the new home and adjusted basis of the old one.

8.9   Ralph Roberts buys a small office building as an investment and participates actively in the management and operation of the building. This is an example of

a. syndication.
b. equity investment.
c. direct investment.
d. illiquidity.

8.10   Elmo Gilmore owns a small retail property that he inherited from his father. There are no mortgages or interest expenses connected with the property. Elmo takes an annual cost recovery expense of $5,000. The property has a monthly gross income of $1,500 and monthly operating expenses of $500. Elmo's taxable income from this property will be taxed at a rate of 30%. What is the tax liability for the year?

a. $2,100.
b. $3,600.
c. $3,900.
d. $7,000.

8.11   All investors desire their investments to increase in value. However,

a. the degree of return is inversely related to the degree of risk.
b. the more the investor stands to gain, the greater the risk that the investor may lose.
c. investments requiring intense management have lesser returns.
d. the more liquid an investment is, the greater the chances are that the investment will not appreciate.

8.12   Two of the financial rewards that investments offer are

a. income and tax benefits.
b. negative leverage and appreciation.
c. appreciation and taxation.
d. positive leverage and prestige.

8.13   Because a real estate investment can take a long time to sell, real estate investments are considered to be

a. management intensive.
b. insensitive to marketing.
c. vulnerable to seller's markets.
d. relatively illiquid.

8.14   Compared to a stock portfolio, a real estate investment would be considered

a. a riskier investment.
b. a more management-intensive investment.
c. a shorter-term investment.
d. a more leveraged investment.

8.15 Six investors purchase a shopping center. One investor manages the tenants and another handles the marketing and leasing. Two investors manage accounting and finance, and the remaining two run the management office. This is a possible example of

a. a general partnership.
b. a limited partnership.
c. a real estate investment trust.
d. an investment conduit.

8.16 The formula for determining taxable income produced by an income property is

a. gross income minus expenses plus land and building depreciation.
b. gross income minus expenses minus land and building depreciation.
c. gross income minus building depreciation plus land depreciation.
d. gross income minus expenses minus building depreciation.

8.17 In deriving taxable income on an investment property, it is generally legal to

a. deduct principal and interest payments from income.
b. deduct principal payments from income.
c. deduct interest payments from income.
d. deduct principal and interest payments from income and capital gain.

8.18 Jake does not use any part of his principal residence as a home office. Which of the following is true of the tax treatment of this property?

a. The owner may deduct the property's interest and principal from ordinary income.
b. The owner may depreciate the property and deduct depreciation expenses from ordinary income.
c. The owner can deduct any capital gain when the property is sold.
d. The owner may be able to avoid capital gain tax when the property is sold.

8.19 An investment property seller pays $14,000 in closing costs. These costs

a. may be deducted from personal income.
b. may be deducted from the property's income.
c. may be deducted from the sale price for gains tax purposes.
d. may be deducted from the adjusted basis for gains tax purposes.

8.20 The formula for calculating capital gain tax is the taxpayer's tax bracket multiplied by

a. the sum of the beginning basis plus gain.
b. the difference between amount realized and adjusted basis.
c. the sum of net sale proceeds and capital gain.
d. the difference between net sale proceeds and capital gain.

8.21 Which of the following entities can legally levy annual real property taxes?

a. The Internal Revenue Service.
b. A utility company.
c. A tax district.
d. A court of law.

8.22 Certain classes of property owner and types of property are exempted or immune from real property taxation in many areas. The protected categories usually include

a. recreational properties.
b. properties owned by a government agency.
c. properties that comply with the Americans with Disabilities Act.
d. properties occupied by single-parent families.

174

8.23 What is the purpose of an equalization factor in ad valorem taxation?

    a. It modifies a local tax rate to bring it into conformity with statutory tax rates.
    b. It changes the assessed value of an individual property to make it reflect the assessed values of other properties in the same neighborhood.
    c. It adjusts assessments in a locality to make them more consistent with an average level for the state or other higher level jurisdiction.
    d. It adjusts the amount of the homestead exemption in a certain area to make it proportionally equivalent to the average homestead exemption in other areas.

8.24 A school district's tax rate is 10 mills. The school district's required revenue from real estate taxes is $20,000,000. What is the tax base of the area?

    a. $20,000,000.
    b. $200,000,000.
    c. $2,000,000,000.
    d. $200,000,000,000.

8.25 A homeowner receives a tax bill that includes an amount for the library district, taxed at $1.00 per $1,000, and the fire protection district, taxed at $2.00 per $1,000. How much does the taxpayer have to pay for these two items if the property's taxable value is $147,000?

    a. $1,567.
    b. $157.
    c. $1,410.
    d. $441.

8.26 A town is replacing a sidewalk that serves five homes. The length of the sidewalk is 200 feet. Mary's property has 38 feet of front footage. If the cost of the project to be paid by a special assessment is $30,000, what will Mary's assessment be?

    a. $6,000.
    b. $5,700.
    c. $789.
    d. $1,579.

8.27 What is a tax deed?

    a. A conveyance instrument for a property that is sold to enforce a tax lien.
    b. A document recorded in title records showing that property taxes have been paid.
    c. A notice to a homeowner that a tax lien has been entered against the property.
    d. A document that gives a municipal authority the power to collect an individual tax bill.

8.28 If a property owner has the right to redeem his or her property after a tax sale, the owner has

    a. a legal right of rescission.
    b. an equitable right to acquire title.
    c. a right of homestead exclusion.
    d. a statutory right of redemption.

8.29 The formula for deriving a municipal jurisdiction's ad valorem tax base is

    a. the jurisdiction's annual budget times the tax rate.
    b. the total of all assessed values of properties minus exemptions.
    c. the total amount of ad valorem taxes required by the budget.
    d. the municipality's budget multiplied times the millage rate.

8.30 A homeowner's total tax bill is derived by

a. dividing the tax requirement by the tax base.
b. multiplying each district's tax rate times the market value of the property.
c. multiplying each district's tax rate times the taxable value of the property.
d. averaging the tax rate for each tax district, and multiplying the average tax rate times the assessed value.

8.31 The fair housing law that first protected people against discrimination in housing based on race was the

a. Civil Rights Act of 1866.
b. Civil Rights Act of 1968.
c. Executive Order 11063 of 1962.
d. Title VIII amendment to the Fair Housing Act.

8.32 The classes protected against discrimination by the Fair Housing Act of 1968 are

a. race only.
b. religion and gender only.
c. race, color, religion, and national origin.
d. age and gender only.

8.33 An agent is committing an act of discriminatory advertising by doing which of the following?

a. Telling prospective buyers about the positive and negative aspects of a certain neighborhood.
b. Telling a prospective seller that now would be a good time to put a property on the market.
c. Advertising a property as available to individuals of a particular race.
d. Telling a prospective buyer that the agent is too busy to show the buyer properties personally on a given day.

8.34 Which of the following is an example of blockbusting?

a. An agent shows a minority home buyer properties located in a neighborhood where there are no other minority home owners.
b. An agent persuades a minority home buyer to avoid looking in a neighborhood where there are no minority home owners.
c. An agent persuades a family to put their house on the market because ethnic minority families are beginning to move into the neighborhood.
d. An agent persuades a minority home buyer to buy a property located in an area where most of the home owners belong to minority groups.

8.35 The practice of redlining is specifically prohibited by

a. The Home Mortgage Disclosure Act.
b. The Real Estate Settlement Procedures Act.
c. The Civil Rights Act of 1866.
d. The Americans with Disabilities Act.

8.36 Title VIII of the Civil Rights Act of 1968 applies to the sale of

a. all single-family residences.
b. all privately owned single-family residences.
c. privately owned single-family residences listed with a broker.
d. privately owned single-family residences for sale by owner.

8.37 A broker signs a listing agreement to sell a home for $200,000. An immigrant couple are interested in the house and ask the agent the price. The agent states the price as $210,000. According to the fair housing laws, such an action is

a. illegal, because the agent changed the terms of the sale to discourage this particular couple.
b. illegal, because the agent violated the listing agreement.
c. legal, because the quoted price increase did not exceed 10% of the listing price.
d. legal, because the increased price does not necessarily exclude the couple.

8.38 Which of the following actions is allowed under federal fair housing laws?

a. A broker, following the instructions of the seller, advertises the property as for sale to Christian families only.
b. A home seller, acting without a broker, places a "for sale-- mature, single men only" sign in front of the house.
c. The owner of four rental houses advertises one of the properties for rent to married couples, no children, no pets.
d. The owner of a duplex who resides in one of the units refuses to rent the other unit to a non-Christian.

8.39 Cecily Longstreet believes a real estate agent has kept her from seeing a certain property for rent because she is a woman. What actions should she take if she wants legal satisfaction for her complaint?

a. File charges of illegal discrimination with the police department that has jurisdiction over the local area.
b. File a complaint with HUD and/or file suit against the offending parties in a state or federal court within the prescribed time period.
c. Wait two years and then file a civil suit in federal court.
d. Sue HUD for damages under the Civil rights Act of 1866.

8.40 George Scott hires Shannon Lang to sell his house, with the condition that he will not be the first one in the neighborhood to sell to members of a certain ethnic group. What should Shannon do about this condition?

a. Inform Scott that the condition is illegal and that she cannot comply with it.
b. Note the condition on the listing agreement and have Scott initial it.
c. Pretend that she did not hear the condition and proceed to market the property to all groups.
d. Tell Scott that she will try to discourage members of that group from looking at the property, but that she cannot control cooperating brokers.

8.41 Under federal fair housing laws, the owner of a ten-unit apartment building may legally

a. advertise that the property is not available to anyone requiring wheelchair access.
b. refuse to rent to aliens.
c. require families without children to pay the same security deposit that families with children must pay.
d. require tenants to move out when they become 62 years old.

8.42 Sam Gough wants to rent out his home, but wants to exclude families with children because of his belief that they cause damage. Under what conditions would federal fair housing laws allow Gough to rent on these terms?

a. The owner has a consistent no-children policy in all his rental properties.
b. The owner can prove that costs to repair damage caused by previous tenants with children exceeded the tenants' security deposit.
c. It is a single-family house that is part of a federally-designated planned unit development.
d. It is a single-family house, and the owner owns only one other rental home in addition to his own residence.

177

8.43 Which of the following laws or rulings extended discrimination to include gender, handicapped status, and family status?

a. Executive Order 11063.
b. the Civil Rights Act of 1968.
c. the Fair Housing Amendments Act of 1988.
d. Jones v Mayer.

8.44 The Wallaces, a minority family, would like to buy a home in a certain price range. Agent Ambrose shows the family all available properties in a neighborhood of families with similar backgrounds. Ambrose does not mention a number of homes in the family's price range in other neighborhoods. This agent could be liable for

a. blockbusting.
b. providing unequal services.
c. steering.
d. nothing; his services were legal and acceptable.

8.45 An agent does not like a particular minority buyer, and is very short with the person, refusing to engage in lengthy conversation or show him any properties. A second minority party visits the office the next day. The agent is very forthcoming, and shows the person five prospective properties. This agent could be liable for

a. providing unequal services.
b. steering.
c. misrepresentation.
d. nothing; both parties were minorities, and therefore no discrimination occurred.

8.46 Following the client's recommendation, an agent conceals the availability of a property from an employed but pregnant and unmarried minority woman. This agent could be liable for

a. discriminatory misrepresentation by omission.
b. steering.
c. violating fiduciary duty.
d. nothing: an agent may show or not show any property at his or her discretion.

8.47. When must a Property Condition Disclosure Statement be used?

a. With a newly-constructed single family home
b. Immediately following the closing of any residential property
c. Prior to the sale of an occupied 1-4 unit dwelling
d. Prior to the closing of any commercial or residential re-sale

8.48. If a single-family resident has listed her property with a licensee, the Seller's Property Condition Disclosure form

a. can be substituted by the licensee's material facts disclosure form.
b. does not have to be completed prior to closing.
c. can be completed by either the seller or the licensee.
d. must still be completed according to local requirements.

8.49. Which of the following would be a non-material fact that would not have to be included in the Seller's Property Condition Disclosure form?

a. A house has a leaking roof.
b. A basement floods.
c. A previous occupant died in the house.
d. A previous occupant contaminated the house by manufacturing methamphetamine in the basement.

178

Test 9: Closings; Risk Management; Property Management

9.1 The conditions of an escrow agreement cannot be met and the related transaction cannot be completed. In such a case, the escrow agent

    a. levies a fine against the defaulting party.
    b. assigns his or her fiduciary responsibilities to the seller's broker.
    c. returns funds to the buyer.
    d. cancels the sale contract and destroys the transaction documents.

9.2 To avoid violating the Real Estate Settlement Procedures Act, parties who are providing services to the buyer or seller in a transaction must

    a. be paid before the closing date for any service they provide.
    b. inform the closing agent of the cost of their services at least one week before the closing date.
    c. receive payment only from the funds held in escrow, not directly from buyer or seller.
    d. disclose in writing any business relationships they have with other parties involved in the transaction.

9.3 A certain item is to be prorated between a buyer and seller. If no outside party is concerned, which of the following statements is true?

    a. The item must be prorated and recorded as a debit to one party and a credit to the other party for the same amount.
    b. The item must be prorated and recorded as a debit to one party; the remainder is recorded as a credit to the other party.
    c. The party who is owed money receives a credit for the entire item and a debit for the prorated amount.
    d. The party who owes money receives a debit for the portion owed and a credit for the portion that is not owed.

9.4 An item is said to be paid in arrears if it is normally paid

    a. on a monthly or yearly basis.
    b. at some time after the expense is incurred.
    c. only after it is billed.
    d. whenever it is incurred.

9.5 A seller received a rental payment of $900 in advance. At closing, the seller has earned only $320 of this rent. What should appear on the closing statement?

    a. A debit to the seller and credit to the buyer for $320.
    b. A debit to the seller for $580 and a credit to the buyer for $320.
    c. A debit to the seller for $320 and a credit to the buyer for $900.
    d. A debit to the seller and credit to the buyer for $580.

9.6 A buyer will receive a water bill for an estimated $100 at the end of the month. At closing, the seller has used an estimated $43 in water. What should appear on the closing statement?

    a. A debit to the seller and credit to the buyer for $57.
    b. A debit to the seller and credit to the buyer for $43.
    c. A debit to the buyer and credit to the seller for $57.
    d. A debit to the buyer and credit to the seller for $43.

9.7 A sale transaction closes on April 1, the ninety-first day of the tax year. The day of closing belongs to the seller. Real estate taxes for the year, not yet billed, are expected to be $2,190. According to the 365-day method, what is the seller's share of the tax bill?

a. $1,644.00.
b. $546.00.
c. $959.30
d. $1,364.66.

9.8 A sale transaction closes on July 4. The day of closing belongs to the seller. On January 1, the seller paid a hazard insurance premium of $375 for the calendar year. According to the 12-month/30-day method, what is the seller's share of the insurance premium?

a. $183.33.
b. $187.50.
c. $189.05.
d. $191.67.

9.9 Waldo is buying Marianne's house. The closing date (day belongs to seller) of the sale transaction is September 1 (day 244 of the year). Current Year real estate taxes are $1,100 (will be billed to buyer next year). Use the 365-day method for prorating. What is Marianne's share of the real estate taxes?

a. $364.66.
b. $367.67.
c. $732.33.
d. $735.34.

9.10 Christie is buying John's house. The closing date (day belongs to seller) of the sale transaction is September 1 (day 244 of the year). Existing hazard insurance of $350 has been paid by John through December 31. Use the 365-day method for prorating. What is Christie's share of the existing hazard insurance already paid in full?

a. $116.03.
b. $117.99.
c. $232.01.
d. $233.97.

9.11 Julie is buying Florence's house. The closing date (day belongs to seller) of the sale transaction is September 1 (day 244 of the year). The buyer's loan amount is $78,750 (90%; 30 years @ 8%). The monthly payment on this loan is $577.84, with $525 going to interest in the first month. At closing, Julie must pre-pay interest for the period of Sept. 2-Sept. 30. Use the 365-day method for prorating. What is Julie's prepaid interest amount?

a. $507.50.
b. $525.00.
c. $543.10.
d. $558.58.

9.12 Melissa is buying Raymond's house. Melissa's loan amount is $88,750. She has agreed to pay 2 points at closing. How much will Melissa pay for points?

a. $157.50.
b. $177.50.
c. $1,775.00.
d. $887.50.

9.13 Tina is buying Terrell's house for $187,500. The broker's commission, to be paid by the seller, is 6%. How much will Terrell pay the broker?

a. $31,250.
b. $2,625.00.
c. $4,725.
d. $11,250.

9.14 A sale contract stipulates that a buyer is to pay the seller's transfer tax expenses. This practice is not customary in the area. In this case,

a. the buyer and seller must amend the contract before closing.
b. the contract is voidable, since the seller must pay the expense.
c. the buyer may pay or not pay the expense, at his or her option.
d. the buyer must pay the expense.

9.15 What a buyer has to pay at closing is equal to

a. the excess of the buyer's debits over the buyer's credits.
b. the excess of the buyer's credits over the buyer's debits.
c. the excess of the seller's debits over the seller's credits.
d. the excess of the seller's credits over the seller's debits.

9.16 The standard E & O policy covers damages resulting from

a. failure to disclose an environmental condition.
b. antitrust violations.
c. mishandling of earnest money deposits.
d. negligence, error or omission in carrying out professional services.

9.17 Which of the following is a common risk relating to the agency relationship?

a. Failing to inform and disclose properly.
b. Failing to take a personal interest in a transaction.
c. Acting as an exclusive agent without an oral agency agreement.
d. Forgetting to record the listing agreement.

9.18 Even after giving buyer and seller the required information about property condition disclosures, the licensee may still be subject to legal action for

a. failing to detect customer misrepresentations.
b. failing to disclose known adverse facts.
c. relying on publicly available market information.
d. advising the purchaser to exercise due diligence.

9.19 A licensee performing a comparative market analysis must be careful to

a. use the term "market value" whenever possible in the report.
b. show a low suggested selling price to avoid a complaint of misrepresenting the value.
c. include the results of a certified appraisal in the analysis.
d. avoid creating a false impression that the licensee is a certified appraiser.

9.20 One of the major risk areas in fulfilling a listing agreement is

a. finding a buyer who turns out to be unqualified.
b. exceeding the authority of the agreement.
c. showing the property without the presence of the owner.
d. cooperating with other licensees.

9.21　To reduce the risk of committing an error or omission in the contracting process, it is a good idea to

　　a. use a checklist of all items, contingencies, dates and responsibilities that must be met.
　　b. delegate some of your responsibilities to the licensee who represents the other party in the contract.
　　c. call the buyer and seller daily to check on progress.
　　d. cut the list of necessary tasks down to a few essentials and concentrate on tracking those.

9.22　Regarding contracts and forms,

　　a. once written and signed they cannot be changed except by a lawyer.
　　b. real estate licensees may alter forms but not contracts.
　　c. whoever originates them can make changes without the risk of unauthorized practice of law.
　　d. the principals may make changes as long as they sign or initial each change.

9.23　Fair housing laws are easily violated. An effective way for agents to minimize the risk of doing so is to

　　a. deal only with consumers who do not belong to a protected class.
　　b. obtain education in the content and intent of the laws.
　　c. make sure there is always a witness present at all meetings with consumers.
　　d. stay away from transactions involving public housing.

9.24　A licensee risks violating antitrust law by

　　a. being present at a conversation where the setting of commission rates is discussed.
　　b. being present at a discussion of antitrust laws.
　　c. charging a commission rate that happens to be the same as that charged by another firm.
　　d. cooperating with another firm to do market research.

9.25　How is an intentional misrepresentation penalized?

　　a. License discipline, fines, and possible incarceration.
　　b. License discipline and fines, but no incarceration.
　　c. License discipline only.
　　d. Fines only.

9.26　Of the following actions, the only one which avoids any risk of committing unintentional misrepresentation is

　　a. measuring and reporting property dimensions.
　　b. describing properties and amenities.
　　c. stating that a client should seek legal counsel.
　　d. making statements about the presence or absence of hazardous substances.

9.27　To reduce risks inherent in reporting transaction progress to a client, the licensee should

　　a. make reports orally only, never in writing.
　　b. leave progress reporting to the inspectors and other experts.
　　c. advise the client that it is company policy to make no progress reports until the contingency period is over.
　　d. avoid speculative statements in all reports

9.28　How does sharing the qualifying function with a lender protect a licensee?

　　a. It guarantees that a buyer will have a loan.
　　b. It reduces the chance of presenting an offer from an unqualified buyer.
　　c. It relieves the licensee of his or her due diligence responsibilities.
　　d. It allows the licensee to avoid asking embarrassing questions.

9.29 The area of agent activity where there is the greatest risk of failing to maintain client confidentiality is

    a. trust fund handling.
    b. office management.
    c. the agency relationship.
    d. the closing process.

9.30 The area of agent activity where there is the greatest risk of creating a false impression that the licensee is a certified appraiser is

    a. performing a comparative market analysis.
    b. writing property advertisements.
    c. presenting written offers.
    d. researching ownership documents

9.31 One of the major risk areas in advertising a listed property is that an advertisement will

    a. describe the property in excessively glowing terms.
    b. fail to appear at the same time in all available media.
    c. omit any mention of the owner's main selling points.
    d. make a substantial misrepresentation.

9.32 Property managers have a _____ relationship with the property owner.

    a. non-binding
    b. partnership
    c. fiduciary
    d. subagency

9.33 One of the property manager's fundamental responsibilities is

    a. obtaining construction loans for the principal.
    b. financial reporting to the principal.
    c. finding a buyer for the property.
    d. maintaining good standing in a managers' professional association.

9.34 Effective gross income is defined as

    a. the total of scheduled rents.
    b. the total of all rents and revenues generated by a property.
    c. potential gross income minus debt service and reserves.
    d. revenue from all sources minus losses from uncollected rents, vacancies, and evictions.

9.35 The efficiency of marketing activities can be measured in terms of

    a. cost per tenant prospect generated per lease.
    b. number of ads produced per marketing dollar.
    c. dollars expended per square foot of vacant space.
    d. percentage of reserves expended on marketing.

9.36 If a property's vacancy rate is significantly lower than market rates, it may be a sign that the manager needs to

    a. lower rental rates.
    b. raise rental rates.
    c. find better tenants.
    d. improve management quality.

9.37 What are the three kinds of maintenance a manager has to carry out for a managed property?

    a. Constructive, deconstructive, and reconstructive
    b. Routine, preventive, and corrective
    c. Scheduled, planned, and improvised
    d. Emergency, elective, and optional

9.38 The Americans with Disabilities Act requires property managers to

    a. ensure that disabled employees have the same level of access to facilities that all employees have.
    b. hire the disabled whenever possible.
    c. remove all existing barriers to the free movement of disabled persons within the property, regardless of the cost.
    d. remodel the ground floor of the property in accordance with ADA standards if it was built before 1978.

9.39 Commercial fire and hazard insurance policies usually require coverage to equal at least 80 percent of the property's

    a. replacement value.
    b. reproduction value.
    c. original cost.
    d. depreciated basis.

9.40 Trust funds to be handled by a property manager are likely to include all of the following except

    a. rents collected from tenants.
    b. cash for the management firm's operating expenses.
    c. security deposits.
    d. capital contributions from the property owner.

9.41 What kind of agency is commonly created by a management agreement?

    a. Universal
    b. Specific
    c. General
    d. Vicarious

9.42 Which of the following describes a gross lease?

    a. The tenant pays a base rent plus some or all of the operating expenses.
    b. The tenant pays a fixed rent, and the landlord pays all operating expenses.
    c. The tenant pays a base rent plus an amount based on income generated in the leased space.
    d. The tenant pays a rent that increases at specified times over the lease term.

9.43 If an apartment contains a refrigerator that is not included in the lease,

    a. the lessee is required to buy it from the landlord.
    b. the landlord is required to remove it.
    c. the lease is invalidated because of an incomplete property description.
    d. the property manager does not have to maintain it.

9.44 A basic responsibility of a landlord is to

    a. provide leased space at market rental rates.
    b. deliver a habitable property.
    c. keep the rental space freshly painted.
    d. refrain from entering the leased space at any time during the lease term.

9.45   How does a constructive eviction occur?

   a. A landlord obtains a court order to force the tenant to vacate the leased premises.
   b. A court officer forcibly removes the tenant from the premises.
   c. A tenant declares a landlord in default and vacates the leased premises.
   d. A landlord declares a tenant in default and takes possession of the leased premises.

9.46   Among the essential elements of a management plan is consideration of

   a. the competitive market for the property.
   b. the property manager's career goals.
   c. the property owner's net worth.
   d. the management firm's income goals.

10.1　A licensee sells 5/6 of an acre for $28,000, and receives a 6% commission. If she splits with her broker 50-50, what did she receive per square foot?

　　　a. $.023 / SF
　　　b. $.046 / SF
　　　c. $.037/ SF
　　　d. $.002 / SF

10.2　Lots in the South Hyde subdivision are selling for approximately $.50 / SF. The Grandersons want to build a 2,500 SF home on a 1.5 acre corner lot. The custom builder can build the home for $135 / SF. What will the completed property cost the Grandersons?

　　　a. $359,170
　　　b. $370,170
　　　c. $32,670
　　　d. $374,070

10.3　Ivan owned a 1/4 acre lot. He wanted to construct a 120' x 80' tennis court on the lot. What approximate percentage of the lot will be left over, if any, when he has completed the construction?

　　　a. 12%
　　　b. 88%
　　　c. 3%
　　　d. 15%

10.4　A developer wants to develop a 16-acre subdivision. He figures that the streets and common area will take up about 30% of this overall area. If the minimum lot size is to be 12,000 SF, how many lots can the developer have on this property?

　　　a. 42
　　　b. 487
　　　c. 40
　　　d. 57

10.5　A homeowner wants to insulate the new recreation room in her basement. She has been told that 3" of insulation would do the job. The walls are all 9' high and respectively measure 13', 13', 18', and 18' in length. How many rolls will she need if each roll measures 3" x 2' x 50'?

　　　a. 6
　　　b. 56
　　　c. 5
　　　d. 9

10.6　Maria plans to mulch the flower area around her house. The house measures 40' x 30', and she figures she'll mulch an area 8' in width to form a big rectangle all around the perimeter. What is the square footage of the resulting mulched area?

　　　a. 64 SF
　　　b. 2,576 SF
　　　c. 1,824 SF
　　　d. 1,376 SF

10.7. Calculate how many acres are in the Southeastern ¼ of the Western ½ of the Eastern ½ of Section 9.

    a. 20 acres
    b. 40 acres
    c. 60 acres
    d. 5 acres

10.8. Homeowner Savannah owns the Southeastern ¼ of the Southwestern ¼ of the Northwestern ¼ of Section 4. How many acres is that property?

    a. 4 acres
    b. 40 acres
    c. 10 acres
    d. 8 acres

10.9 Yard of Pizza has a percentage lease on its 1,800 SF space in Lincoln Shops. The terms are $1.40 / SF / month rent plus 1.75% of the store's gross income. If monthly sales averaged $41,500 last year, how much annual rent did Yard of Pizza pay last year?

    a. $38,955
    b. $43,420
    c. $30,240
    d. $21,525

10.10 A home appreciated 2 2/3% one year, then 5 1/5% the next year, then 7 1/4% the third year. What was the average appreciation over the 3-year period expressed as a decimal?

    a. 5.04%
    b. 15.24%
    c. 7.56%
    d. 4.8%

10.11 A homeowner paid $185,000 for a house three years ago. The house sells today for $239,000. How much has the property appreciated?

    a. 23 %
    b. 77 %
    c. 29 %
    d. 123 %

10.12 Seller Frank receives an offer of $290,000 on a property he listed at $308,000. How much is the offer as a percent of the listing price?

    a. 87%
    b. 91%
    c. 94%
    d. 106%

10.13 A property is being appraised using the income capitalization approach. Annually, it has potential gross income of $30,000, vacancy and credit losses of $1,500, and operating expenses of $10,000. Using a capitalization rate of 9%, what is the indicated value (to the nearest $1,000)?

    a. $206,000
    b. $167,000
    c. $222,000
    d. $180,000

10.14 If gross income on a property is $75,000, net income is $30,000 and the cap rate is 8%, the value of the property using the income capitalization method is

a. $625,000
b. $375,000
c. $3,750,000
d. $937,500

10.15 The roof of a property cost $16,000. The economic life of the roof is 20 years. Assuming the straight-line method of depreciation, what is the depreciated value of the roof after 3 years?

a. $16,000
b. $13,600
c. $18,400
d. $12,000

10.16 Lee had to report his home office depreciation for the tax year. He has a 2,500 SF home and a 500 SF office area. Lee paid $280,000 for his home, and he figures the land portion carries about 25% of that value. If Lee depreciates on a 39-year basis, how much can he write off for his home office depreciation per year?

a. $1,077
b. $1,436
c. $5,384
d. $2,108

10.17 A property is being appraised by the cost approach. The appraiser estimates that the land is worth $40,000 and the replacement cost of the improvements is $175,000. Total depreciation from all causes is $27,000. What is the indicated value of the property?

a. $148,000
b. $228,000
c. $162,000
d. $188,000

10.18 An apartment owner paid $500,000 for her complex 5 years ago. An appraiser at that time valued the land @ $100,000, but land has appreciated 25% over this period. The investor has used a 40-year straight-line depreciation method to depreciate the property. What is its current value using the cost approach?

a. $437,500
b. $462,500
c. $475,000
d. $546,875

10.19 An apartment building that recently sold for $400,000 had monthly gross rent receipts of $3,200. What is its monthly gross rent multiplier?

a. 80
b. .01
c. 110
d. 125

10.20 A rental home has monthly gross income of $1,100. A suitable gross income multiplier derived from market data is 14.7. What estimated sale price (to the nearest $1,000) is indicated?

a. $99,000
b. $162,000
c. $194,000
d. $173,000

10.21 Amy obtains a 75% LTV loan on her new $200,000 home with an annual interest rate of 6%. What is the first month's interest payment?

a. $900
b. $250
c. $1,000
d. $750

10.22 Emily has an interest-only home equity loan at an annual interest rate of 5.3%. If her monthly payment is $790, how much is the loan's principal balance (to the nearest $1,000)?

a. $222,000
b. $179,000
c. $95,000
d. $146,000

10.23 The loan officer at Sixth Fourth Bank tells Amanda she can afford a monthly payment of $1,000 on her new home loan. Assuming this is an interest-only loan, and the principal balance is $249,000, what interest rate is Amanda getting?

a. 4.82%
b. 5.03%
c. 6.25%
d. 3.69%

10.24 The Keegans obtain a fixed-rate amortized 30-year loan for $280,000 @ 6.25% interest. If the monthly payments are $1,724, how much interest do the Keegans pay in the second month of the loan?

a. $1,748.33
b. $1,456.95
c. $1,458.33
d. $1724.00

10.25 A lender offers the Greys two alternative loan packages for their $60,000 home equity application. One option is an interest-only loan for 5 years @ 6.5% interest with no points, and the second, a 6.25% interest-only loan for 5 years with 1 point to be paid at closing. Which loan will cost the Greys less total interest, and by how much?

a. The first option, by $150.
b. The second option, by 150.
c. The second option, by $750.
d. Both options charge the same amount of interest.

10.26 Jose recently obtained a 90% loan on his $410,000 home, and he had to pay $6,150 for points. How many points did he pay?

a. 1.4 points
b. 1.67 points
c. 2.48 points
d. 1.5 points

10.27 Mack is buying Roy's house for $500,000. Mack's loan amount is $325,000. He has agreed to pay 1.5 points at closing. How much will Mack pay for points?

a. $450
b. $4,500
c. $4,875
d. $7,500

189

10.28 A lender determines that a homebuyer can afford to borrow $130,000 on a mortgage loan. The lender requires an 80% loan-to-value ratio. How much can the borrower pay for a property and still qualify for this loan amount?

    a. $138,000
    b. $104,000
    c. $162,500
    d. $170,000

10.29 Home buyer Janet pays $1,600 / month for the interest-only loan on her new house. The loan's interest rate is 6.75%. If she obtained a 75% loan, what was the purchase price?

    a. $313,333
    b. $31,604
    c. $379,259
    d. $256,000

10.30 Loan applicant Taylor has an annual gross income of $76,000. How much will a lender allow Taylor to pay for monthly housing expense to qualify for a loan if the lender uses an income ratio of 30%?

    a. $2,160
    b. $1,900
    c. $1,215
    d. $4,433

10.31 An investor paid $80,000 for a lot and $600,000 to have an apartment building constructed on it. He has depreciated the property for the past 10 years on a 39-year straight-line schedule. If he sells the property this year and realizes $780,000, what is his capital gain?

    a. $253,846
    b. $274,000
    c. $100,000
    d. $179,000

10.32. A homeowner bought a house five years ago for $250,000. Since then, the homeowner has spent $2,000 to build a screened porch and has added a central air-conditioning system at a cost of $5,000. What is the homeowner's adjusted basis if the house is sold today?

    a. $256,000
    b. $257,000
    c. $244,000
    d. $245,000

10.33 A homeowner sold her house and had net proceeds of $265,000. Her adjusted basis in the home was $231,000. She immediately bought another house for $301,000. What was her capital gain?

    a. $265,000
    b. $36,000
    c. $34,000
    d. None

10.34 Debra bought a home for $120,000, paying $24,000 down and taking a mortgage loan of $96,000. The following year she had a new roof put on, at a cost of $5,000. What is Debra's adjusted basis in the house if she now sells the house for $150,000?

a. $29,000
b. $96,000
c. $101,000
d. $125,000

10.35 A certain investor wants an 11% return on investment from any real estate investment. A property priced at $360,000 has gross income of $60,000 and expenses of $22,000. Approximately how much too high or too low is the price of this property for the investor to obtain her desired return exactly?

a. $1,000 overpriced.
b. $8,000 underpriced.
c. $15,000 overpriced.
d. $16,000 underpriced.

10.36 An office building investor sees a listing of an office building which is priced at $2 million. He loves the property, but he knows he needs to make a return of at least 8% to satisfy his partners. If the building is 25,000 SF, rents for $10/SF per year, has 5% vacancy, and annual expenses of $70,000, should he buy it? What is his return?

a. No, since he will yield 2.00%.
b. Yes, since he will yield 8.375%.
c. Yes, since he will yield 8%.
d. Yes, since he will yield 9.125%.

10.37 Chad owns a small retail property that he inherited from his father. There are no mortgages or interest expenses connected with the property. Chad takes an annual cost recovery expense of $7,000. The property has a monthly gross income of $1,650 and monthly operating expenses of $600. Chad's taxable income from this property will be taxed at a rate of 30%. What is the tax liability for the year?

a. $1,680
b. $5,940
c. $2,100
d. $7,000

10.38 A property has a net income of $150,000, interest payments of $105,000, principal payments of $30,000, and annual cost recovery of $7,000. The property's tax rate is 28%. What is the property's annual tax on income?

a. $14,550
b. $40,040
c. $10,640
d. $2,240

10.39 An investor bought 4 oversized lots in order to subdivide. He paid $70,000 for the lots. After subdividing, the investor was able to sell each lot for $23,000. Excluding commissions and closing costs, what per cent profit did the investor realize?

a. 0%
b. 45%
c. 23.9%
d. 31.4%

10.40 A school district's tax rate is 10 mills. The school district's required revenue from taxes is $10,000,000. What is the tax base of the area?

a. $10,000,000
b. $100,000,000
c. $1,000,000,000
d. $100,000,000,000

10.41 A homeowner's residence has an assessed valuation of $140,000, and a market value of $170,000. The homestead exemption is $25,000. Tax rates for the property are 7 mills for schools; 3 mills for the city; 2 mills for the county; and 1 mill for the local community college. What is the homeowner's tax bill?

a. $1,495
b. $1,820
c. $1,150
d. $2,210

10.42 The village of Goodsprings has an annual budget requirement of $8,000,000 to be funded by property taxes. Assessed valuations are $400,000,000, and exemptions total $25,000,000. What must the tax rate be to finance the budget?

a. 2.00%
b. 2.13%
c. 1.32%
d. 21.33%

10.43 A property has sold for $127,000. The listing agreement calls for a commission of 7%. The listing broker and selling broker agree to share the commission equally. What will the listing agent receive if the agent is scheduled to get a 40% share from his broker?

a. $4,445
b. $3,556
c. $2,667
d. $1,778

10.44 Kevin, who works for selling broker Paul, sells a house listed by listing broker Adams. The house sells for $325,000. The co-brokerage split between Paul and Adams is 50-50. Kevin is on a 65% commission schedule with Paul. If the total commission rate is 6.5%, what is Kevin's commission?

a. $6,866
b. $5,282
c. $10,563
d. $13,731

10.45. A sale transaction closes on April 1, the ninety-first day of the tax year. The day of closing belongs to the seller. Real estate taxes for the year, not yet billed, are expected to be $3,150. According to the 365-day method, what should appear on the closing statement?

a. A debit to the buyer and credit to the seller for $2,364.62
b. A debit to the buyer and credit to the seller for $785.34
c. A credit to the buyer and debit to the seller for $785.34
d. A credit to the buyer and debit to the seller for $2,364.62

192

10.46 Alexis is buying Jack's house. The closing date (day belongs to seller) of the sale transaction is September 1 (day 244 of the year). Her loan has a monthly payment of $577.84, with $525 going to interest in the first month. At closing, Alexis must pre-pay interest for the period of Sept. 2-Sept. 30. Use the 365-day method for prorating. What is her prepaid interest amount?

    a. $507.50
    b. $525.00
    c. $543.10
    d. $558.58

10.47 A sale transaction on rental property closes on December 16. The landlord received the December rent of $1,380 on December 1. Assuming the closing day is the buyer's, and that the 365-day method is used for prorating, which of the following entries would appear on the settlement statement?

    a. Debit seller $667.74.
    b. Credit seller $1,380.00.
    c. Debit buyer $712.26.
    d. Credit buyer $712.26.

10.48 A home sells for $322,600 in Primm County. Here, transfer taxes are set at $1.00 per $500 of the sale price. Title insurance runs $450, and the attorney costs $550. The agent's commission is 7%, and the mortgage balance is $210,000. Annual real estate taxes are estimated to be $4,000, half of which will have to be charged to the seller. If the seller pays all of these expenses, what will she net at closing?

    a. $86,873
    b. $88,371
    c. $81,372
    d. $86,372

10.49 A farmer wants to net at least $5,000/acre on the sale of his 300-acre property. If he allows for 10% commissions and closing costs, and to allow for negotiating room, he wants to get 95% of the listing price as the selling price, what should his listing price be per acre?

    a. $5,750
    b. $5,882
    c. $4,250
    d. $5,848

10.50. The Wildes have purchased a $740,000 home. The land is worth 25%, and they insure the improvements @ 75% of their replacement value. If the Wildes suffer damage estimated at $500,000, and they have an 80% co-insurance clause, what will their recovery be from the policy?

    a. Zero
    b. $531,915
    c. $500,000
    d. $468,750

10.51 The Uptons carry a $140,000 property insurance policy which covers 75% of the replacement cost of their insurable property, valued at $190,000. They have an 80% co-insurance requirement in the policy. If the family incurs a $150,000 loss, what if any amount will the Uptons recover?

    a. $159,999
    b. $140,625
    c. $140,000
    d. $187,500

Section V: Georgia-Specific Practice Tests

Test 11: Definitions; RE Commission; Licensing Regulation; Disciplinary Actions; Violations & Sanctions

11.1. The Georgia Real Estate Commission consists of

   a. seven members appointed by the Governor.
   b. six members appointed by the Commissioner.
   c. nine members, seven appointed by the Governor.
   d. six members appointed by the Governor.

11.2 Georgia Real Estate Commission members serve terms of

   a. three years and may serve two terms.
   b. two years and may serve three terms.
   c. five years and serve until a replacement is named.
   d. four years.

11.3 The Commission is empowered to do which of the following?

   a. Pass rules and regulations relating to the real estate profession
   b. Specify maximum compensation of brokers
   c. Specify items included in the agreement between the broker and affiliated licensees
   d. Specify how affiliated licensees are compensated

11.4 Which of the following is true regarding the salesperson 25-hour post-license course?

   a. If not completed within one year, the license expires and the individual must retake the pre-license course and licensing exam in order to be licensed.
   b. If not completed within six months, the licensee will become inactive until the course is completed.
   c. If not completed within one year and licensee enrolled and paid for the course within one year, license is lapsed and licensee has an additional six months to comply.
   d. If not completed within license renewal period, license expires.

11.5 When a licensee fails to complete the required continuing education within the renewal period,

   a. the license is cancelled.
   b. the license will lapse.
   c. the licensee will be on inactive status.
   d. the license status is suspended.

11.6 Which of the following is the most accurate definition of real estate broker?

   a. A person who manages a real estate office
   b. One who buys, sells and manages real estate for clients
   c. A person who buys, sells, manages, or exchanges real estate on behalf of others for compensation
   d. A person who manages real estate on behalf of customers

11.7   If a general partnership applies for a real estate license,

  a. all participants in the partnership must practice real estate.
  b. the qualifying broker must be a general partner of the partnership.
  c. the limited partners may not practice real estate under any circumstances.
  d. all general partners must be licensed as active brokers.

11.8   Christine obtained her real estate license on June 3 of this year. When will her license expire?

  a. On December 31 of the fourth year
  b. On December 31 of the third year
  c. On last day of her birth month, in the fourth year
  d. On last day of her birth month, in the third year

11.9   Broker Walter had his licensed revoked six months ago. He would like to continue to practice real estate. What must Walter do?

  a. Wait ten years before reapplying for licensure
  b. Follow the procedure for a licensee whose license has been expired for more than 6 months
  c. Wait two years before reapplying for licensure
  d. Walter cannot be licensed after having his license revoked.

11.10 Any licensee who violates the provisions of the real estate license law

  a. is subject to license suspension, revocation, censure or reprimand by the Commission.
  b. will automatically have his or her license suspended.
  c. must face an investigation followed by due process in court.
  d. is, in most cases, guilty of a felony.

11.11 Licensees who are on inactive status may

  a. not engage in any real estate activity requiring a license.
  b. engage in activities limited to referrals
  c. engage in any real estate activity for others, provided no compensation is involved.
  d. act as brokers-in-charge.

11.12 In addition to continuing education requirements required for other licenses to renew, the broker must also

  a. complete an additional 12-hour broker continuing education course.
  b. complete a renewal form regarding status of any trust accounts of broker or affiliated licensees.
  c. pay an additional $50.
  d. complete an additional six-hour broker continuing education course.

11.13 After making application for a salesperson or community association manager license, the applicant may commence brokerage activity

  a. immediately.
  b. 30 days following the initial issuance of the license.
  c. immediately upon signing the agreement with the broker.
  d. when the wall certificate of licensure is received by the broker.

11.14 In addition to suspending and revoking licenses, the Commission is also empowered to

  a. issue a cease and desist order prohibiting a non-licensee from practicing without a license.
  b. pursue criminal charges against individuals for fraud.
  c. sue licensees for license law infractions.
  d. for certain serious infractions, take disciplinary action without affording the licensee a hearing.

11.15 The continuing education requirement for license renewal, other than the first renewal, consists of

    a. six hours per year.
    b. nine hours per year.
    c. 25 hours per renewal period.
    d. 12 hours per year.

11.16 The license renewal fee for real estate licensees is

    a. $150 for all licensees.
    b. $125 for all licensees.
    c. $75 for all licensees.
    d. $50 for salespersons and community association managers and $75 for brokers and associate brokers.

11.17 An associate broker is best defined as

    a. any broker associated with a real estate firm.
    b. a licensee with a broker-type license who acts on behalf of the broker.
    c. an office manager who is not the main broker.
    d. a broker-in-training.

11.18 A real estate license is required for which of the following individuals?

    a. Power of attorney transferring property for an owner
    b. Government agency employee conducting official business
    c. Auctioneer selling real estate
    d. Person employed full-time by community association to provide community association management services

11.19 Which of the following may be performed without a real estate license?

    a. Performing property management
    b. Prospecting for listings
    c. Performing community association management services if employed full-time by the association
    d. Providing real estate consulting services

11.20 Can a salesperson be legally affiliated with more than one broker?

    a. Yes, if the brokers are not in the same geographical area
    b. Yes, if one of the brokers is in another state
    c. No, License Law prohibits affiliation with more than one broker.
    d. Yes, if obtaining the brokers' permission and if one of the brokers is in another state that permits affiliation in both states

11.21 How are continuing education requirements affected by a new licensee completing the required 25-hour post-licensing course?

    a. The licensee must complete an additional 11 hours of continuing education prior to renewal.
    b. The licensee's continuing education requirement is unaffected by the post-licensing course.
    c. The licensee must complete an additional 27 hours of continuing education prior to renewal.
    d. The 25-hour course is in lieu of the continuing education requirement for first renewal.

11.22 A salesperson applicant has recently passed the licensing exam. How long does the applicant have in which to apply for a license without incurring a penalty?

    a. Three months
    b. Twelve months
    c. Six months
    d. Two years

11.23 Which of the following is required to have a real estate license?

   a. An employee of a non-profit organization acting for that organization
   b. A company assisting individuals in exchanging property
   c. Officer of government agency conducting official duties
   d. Private utility employee performing acts on property owned by utility company

11.24 Which of the following is NOT required for a salesperson to obtain a broker license?

   a. Be at least 21years old
   b. Having maintained an active license for past five years
   c. Completing a 60-hour broker course
   d. Passing the licensing exam

11.25 Which of the following actions would be a violation performed by a licensee?

   a. Guaranteeing future profits on a property
   b. Listing a property the licensee owns through the brokerage company
   c. Writing a sales contract for someone who is not a client
   d. Using the brokerage name in a newspaper ad

11.26 Which of the following actions by a broker would NOT be a license law violation?

   a. Failing to pay commission to a cooperating broker
   b. Failing to promptly deposit earnest money checks
   c. Failing to provide to the principal written notice of paying a fee to another broker for referral of the principal
   d. Placing misleading or inaccurate advertising

11.27 Which of the following is a license law violation?

   a. A broker paying a commission to a licensee affiliated with the company
   b. A broker paying a commission to a broker in another state not licensed in Georgia for performing licensing activity in Georgia
   c. The broker paying a referral fee to a referring broker
   d. A broker paying a referral fee to a broker in another country

11.28 All of the following are violations of law EXCEPT

   a. including a specific expiration date in a listing agreement.
   b. indicating that a price opinion given by the licensee is an appraisal.
   c. inducing someone to break an existing contract or brokerage engagement.
   d. failing to disclose that the principal in a transaction is a licensee.

11.29 Which of the following would be a license law violation?

   a. A broker sharing commission with an affiliated licensee
   b. A broker paying a commission to a licensee who was affiliated with the broker at the time the commission was earned
   c. A salesperson sharing a commission with another licensee affiliated with the same broker for assisting with a transaction
   d. A broker sharing commission with another Georgia broker as a referral

11.30 Jenna is the office manager for a large real estate firm. She supervises the secretarial staff, places ads, inputs listings in the multiple listing service, and ensures that required signs and contract forms are available for the licensees. Jenna in this case

    a. is required to have a salesperson or community association manager license.
    b. is required to have a broker license.
    c. may not input listings without obtaining a license.
    d. is exempt from licensure.

11.31 The Commission can revoke a license if the licensee

    a. takes a listing which reflects an interest rate higher than permitted by the Commission.
    b. represents a tenant but is paid by the owner.
    c. deposits earnest money into her personal account.
    d. enters into an open listing.

11.32 The purpose of the Real Estate Education and Recovery Fund is to

    a. provide funds for researching trends in the real estate industry.
    b. provide scholarships in the field of real estate.
    c. compensate individuals who have suffered financial loss due to licensees' violations of license law.
    d. provide resources for Commission expenses.

11.33 Which of the following statements is true regarding unlicensed support personnel?

    a. They may complete information on contract forms as directed by a licensee.
    b. They may be paid a portion of the commission after assisting in the transaction.
    c. They may advise brokerage clients regarding contract terms.
    d. They may assist brokerage clients with negotiations.

11.34 Which statement is true regarding net listings?

    a. Although rarely used, they are a type of legal listings in Georgia.
    b. They are illegal in Georgia.
    c. They are permitted if requested by the seller.
    d. They are permitted only with prior permission by the Commission.

11.35 The qualifying broker appoints one affiliated licensee to represent the buyer and another licensee to represent the seller in the transaction. In this case, the affiliated licensees are acting as

    a. dual agents.
    b. designated agents.
    c. appointed agents.
    d. implied agents.

11.36 Which of the following statements is true regarding complaints filed with the Commission?

    a. The Commission is not obligated to respond to a complaint if it feels the complaint is frivolous.
    b. The Commission may not investigate a licensee unless it receives a written, sworn request to investigate a licensee.
    c. The Commission may on its own motion investigate a licensee.
    d. The Commission may choose to pass the complaint to the courts rather than act on the complaint.

11.37 In which of the following circumstances is a person or business required to have a real estate license?

    a. A property manager who leases and sells his own apartment buildings
    b. An attorney who handles a purchase for a client
    c. A professional negotiator who assists clients in obtaining the best price for their properties
    d. A guardian acting under court order

11.38 Which of the following actions by a broker would NOT be a license law violation?

    a. Disclosing in a timely manner to all parties in a real estate transaction any agency relationship that the licensee may have with any of the parties
    b. Failing to promptly deposit earnest money checks
    c. Failing to provide written notice of paying a fee to another broker for referral of the principal
    d. Inducing anyone to change another licensee's commission without that licensee's written consent

11.39 An applicant for a community association manager's license must meet all the following qualifications EXCEPT
    a. being at least 21 years old.
    b. having a high school diploma or equivalent.
    c. providing a criminal history report to the Commission.
    d. completing a minimum of 25 hours in a community association manager's course.

11.40 Which of the following statements is true regarding license application and renewal?

    a. Salesperson and community association manager applicants must apply within six months of passing the licensing exam.
    b. A licensee will be charged an extra fee for renewing online.
    c. All licenses expire at the same time.
    d. If salesperson or community association manager applicant does not apply within three months of passing licensing exam, the fee doubles.

11.41 All of the following statements are true regarding the Real Estate Education, Research and Recovery Fund EXCEPT

    a. $75,000 is the maximum liability of the fund for the acts of any licensee.
    b. when the fund pays on behalf of a licensee, the licensee has six months in which to repay the amount or the license will be revoked.
    c. $25,000 is the maximum amount any one person may receive from the fund.
    d. $25,000 is the total paid out for any one act, regardless of the number of aggrieved persons.

11.42 Other than investigations of applicants for licensure, investigations of fraud, mishandling funds, or possible violations that have been litigated or arise from litigation, the Commission may not investigate unless the act which may constitute a violation occurred with _____ years of the initiation of the investigation.

    a. 2 years
    b. 3 years
    c. 5 years
    d. 7 years

Test 12: Management Responsibilities; Trust Accounts; Advertising; Handling Transactions

12.1. A qualifying broker may refuse to release the license of an individual transferring to another broker if

    a. the transferring licensee fails to return property belonging to the firm.
    b. the transferring licensee wants to hand-deliver the license to the new broker.
    c. the broker is aware that the transferring licensee has not fulfilled the terms of the licensee's agreement with the broker.
    d. under no circumstances.

12.2. Licensees may be disciplined by the Real Estate Commission for failing to deliver copies of signed transaction documents to

    a. buyers only.
    b. both parties in the transaction only.
    c. all parties in the transaction and any broker involved in the transaction.
    d. any party, if requested.

12.3. Which of the following is a required provision that must be included in a listing agreement?

    a. A property condition disclosure
    b. The standard commission rate
    c. License number of each firm and licensee participating in the transaction
    d. A liquidated damages clause

12.4. Within 30 days of termination of a community association management agreement, or as agreed in the contract, the community association must receive

    a. a list of all duties performed by the manager on behalf of the association.
    b. 12 months' report of trust account funds..
    c. 24 months' report of trust account funds, or if shorter than 24 months, report for entire period of the agreement.
    d. a complete record of transactions and funds handled during contract not previously accounted for.

12.5. A buyer's agent refers the principal to another licensee in order to avoid dual agency. The licensee working with the referred client must

    a. keep the referring agent informed of the transaction status.
    b. pay a referral fee immediately.
    c. inform the principal of the referral commission no later than closing of the transaction.
    d. share the referral commission with the buyer.

12.6. The broker must deposit earnest money, security deposits, rents and other trust funds into the escrow/trust account

    a. immediately.
    b. within three business days.
    c. within three calendar days.
    d. within 48 hours..

12.7. Is it legally permissible for a licensee to advertise a property listed by another broker?

a. No. Licensees are prohibited from advertising listings of other brokers.
b. Yes, if the property is listed through a multiple listing service
c. Yes, if the seller agrees
d. Yes, if permission is granted by the listing broker and the ad discloses the property is listed with another company and the name of listing licensee

12.8. Buyers made an offer on a property through ABC Realty, and the sellers accepted. During the contingency period, the buyers were unable to obtain a loan, and the deal fell through. In this case, ABC Realty

a. must retain records of this transaction for three years.
b. is not required to maintain records of the failed transaction, since it did not close.
c. must retain all records of the failed transaction for at least one year.
d. must retain records of the transaction for five years.

12.9 The broker must notify the Commission of the bank, account name and number within _____ of opening the account?

a. 30 days
b. 24 hours
c. three business days
d. seven calendar days

12.10 Agent Patrick has a buyer who is concerned about the wording of a contract and asks Patrick how it could be reworded. Patrick rewrites the paragraph in a way that he feels will accomplish what the buyer wants to achieve. In this case,

a. Patrick should also write an optional revision and let the buyer choose to avoid liability.
b. Patrick has correctly solved the client's concern.
c. Patrick should have consulted with his broker prior to rewriting the contract.
d. Patrick is guilty of illegally practicing law.

12.11 A broker may maintain an interest-bearing trust account, provided that

a. the principals approve of the account and agree in writing on who will receive the interest.
b. the principals understand that the broker will receive the interest.
c. the party depositing the funds receives the interest.
d. the account is named as a trust account and is not the broker's business account.

12.12 The deadline for the broker to deliver a closing statement to the seller is

a. one day after closing.
b. at the time of closing.
c. five days after closing.
d. 24 hours prior to closing.

12.13 Commission regulations require that brokers have trust accounts

a. if they are engaged in active brokerage practice.
b. regardless of whether their licenses are active or inactive.
c. for each brokerage office.
d. if they handle the funds of others.

12.14 Salesperson Jim wants to have a trust account in his name. Is this permissible?

    a. Yes, but the account must be a joint account with Jim's broker.
    b. Yes, if the Commission receives an annual summary statement on the account
    c. Yes, if Jim's broker approves and provides the Commission with Jim's name and the bank account information
    d. No, salespersons are prohibited from having trust accounts.

12.15 Licensees are prohibited from

    a. obtaining a brokerage agreement knowing or having reason to believe that another broker has exclusive brokerage agreement, unless licensee has written permission from that broker.
    b. listing a property the licensee owns through the brokerage.
    c. writing a sales contract for someone who is not a client.
    d. using the brokerage name in a newspaper ad.

12.16 Salespersons may accept commissions from

    a. a client wanting to provide the licensee with a bonus.
    b. their employing/sponsoring broker.
    c. any broker.
    d. any client represented by the licensee or their sponsoring broker.

12.17 Which of the following is prohibited for a broker?

    a. Paying a commission to a licensee affiliated with the company
    b. Failing to notify the Commission within 30 days of an address change of broker's place of business
    c. A broker sharing a referral fee to a referring broker
    d. A broker acting as a dual agent

12.18 Salesperson Jim ran into his friend, Bob, at the country club. Bob had just learned he was being transferred. He wanted Jim to list his property and start marketing it immediately. Jim had no listing forms with him. Can Jim begin marketing the property for sale?

    a. Yes, since the seller gave the verbal direction, and Jim must obey all legal directives of clients
    b. Yes, however Jim has 24-hours in which to get the agreement in writing.
    c. Yes, with his broker's approval
    d. No, licensees must have written approval to advertise property.

12.19 Which of the following statements is false regarding licensees advertising real estate?

    a. The ad must identify the brokerage firm.
    b. Ads must be under the supervision of the broker.
    c. The broker's license number must be included in all ads.
    d. Outdated information on websites must be removed within 30 days.

12.20 License law violations and practicing without a license are

    a. class 4 felonies.
    b. misdemeanors.
    c. either a misdemeanor or felony, depending on the severity.
    d. none of the above.

12.21 In order to more easily accommodate a busy executive, the broker provides an exclusive listing agreement that automatically renews unless the seller specifically cancels it. Is this listing legally acceptable?

a. No, the agreement must terminate at a specific time without prior notice by the seller.
b. No, the listing agreement is a binding contract and may expire only upon the broker's written consent.
c. Yes, the agreement is perfectly acceptable.
d. Yes, it is acceptable provided the agreement is in writing.

12.22 Based on Georgia license law, who is permitted to write sales contracts and other legal documents?

a. Any real estate licensee involved in the transaction
b. The listing broker only
c. An attorney
d. Either broker involved in the transaction

12.23 Which of the following is a true statement regarding escrow (trust) accounts?

a. The Commission must give the broker 48 hours' notice prior to examining the broker's trust account.
b. Nonresident brokers are not permitted to maintain a trust account in their state of residence.
c. The account is not required to be federally insured.
d. The Commission will examine brokers trust account during each renewal period, or accept a report of compliance or summary of data on the Commission's form.

12.24 A broker has a brokerage engagement to locate a suitable property for the buyer to purchase. The broker owes all the following duties to the buyer client EXCEPT

a. Actively seeking a property at price and terms in the engagement, or as acceptable to the buyer
b. Presenting all offers, even if the client currently has an accepted offer
c. Disclosing to the client any adverse material facts known to the broker
d. Disclosing to the client that the seller has AIDS

12.25 Is it permissible for a transferring licensee to continue to conduct real estate business for the former broker on transactions begun prior to being transferred?

a. No, licensees can work for only one broker at a time.
b. Yes, if both brokers agree in writing to details as specified in the law
c. Yes, nothing is required because the licensee was affiliated with the former broker at the time the transactions were begun.
d. Yes, if the former broker receives permission from the Commission

12.26 In which of the following situations could a broker disburse earnest money in compliance with Commission requirements?

a. The buyer signs a written release authorizing the broker to disburse funds.
b. When the transaction has closed
c. The buyer cancels the offer a week after acceptance.
d. The seller signs a written release authorizing the broker to disburse funds.

12.27 Support personnel may perform which of the following activities without a real estate license?

a. Explain contracts to clients of the brokerage firm
b. Host open houses
c. Prospect for clients for the firm
d. Assemble documents for closings

12.28 Regarding the business relationship of the broker and salesperson, the salesperson

    a. must be an independent contractor.
    b. must be an employee.
    c. may be either an independent contractor or employee.
    d. must be an independent employee.

12.29 Which of the following brokers who provide community management services is exempt from carrying fidelity insurance?

    a. Brokers who maintain separate accounts for each association
    b. There are no exemptions.
    c. Brokers who do not collect, maintain, control, or disburse more than $100,000 at any time
    d. Brokers who do not collect, maintain, control, or disburse more than $60,000 at any time

12.30 A broker could be disciplined by the Commission if the broker

    a. permitted the affiliated licensees to reduce commission rates charged to clients.
    b. required affiliated licensees to be employees rather than independent contractors.
    c. failed to have the affiliated licensees enter into an employment agreement with the firm.
    d. instituted a company policy that all listing commissions would be 10% with no negotiation as to the rate.

12.31 Dual agency agreements must contain all the following EXCEPT

    a. a description of transactions or types of transactions in which broker will serve as dual agent.
    b. a statement that, in serving as a dual agent, broker represents two clients whose interests are, or at times could be, different or adverse.
    c. a statement that the agent will disclose known, adverse material facts relevant to the transaction to all parties, excepting confidential information.
    d. a statement that the client must consent to dual agency.

12.32 Which statement is true regarding escrow accounts?

    a. Brokers may not use an electronic bookkeeping system.
    b. Brokers are prohibited from having more than one escrow account.
    c. Salespersons are prohibited from having escrow accounts.
    d. Affiliated licensees who have trust accounts must provide their broker with a reconciliation statement at least quarterly.

12.33 The written contract in which a client promises to pay the broker is a

    a. escrow agreement.
    b. designated agency agreement.
    c. brokerage engagement.
    d. purchase agreement.

12.34 If an affiliated licensee wants to be placed on inactive status, the broker would advise the licensee that the

    a. licensee must request inactive status prior to ceasing work.
    b. licensee may remain inactive for no longer than six months.
    c. licensee must request to be placed on inactive status by the Commission within 30 days of ceasing real estate activity.
    d. renewal fees are not required for inactive licensees.

12.35 When an affiliated licensee is leaving the firm, the broker must do all the following EXCEPT

    a.   hold the license until the broker receives a transfer request from the new broker.
    b.   sign a release form.
    c.   forward the wall certificate to the Commission or new broker.
    d.   if a licensee is leaving because of broker's request, send letter to the licensee indicating he/she must affiliate with another broker or be placed on inactive status within one month.

12.36 In response to the death of the qualifying broker,

    a.   the brokerage must surrender its license to the Commission within 15 days if a new qualifying broker is not secured during that time.
    b.   the brokerage must secure a new qualifying broker within 60 days to continue active licensure.
    c.   the brokerage must secure a new qualifying broker within 120 days to continue active licensure.
    d.   the brokerage may continue operating as usual indefinitely if an associate broker is in charge of the office.

12.37 A source, compiler, or supplier of information regarding real estate for sale or lease includes

    a.   multiple listing services.
    b.   community association managers.
    c.   real estate commissions.
    d.   support personnel.

12.38 Trust funds must be deposited in the broker's trust account

    a.   immediately.
    b.   within three business days of acceptance of the offer.
    c.   within three calendar days of acceptance of the offer.
    d.   within two business days of acceptance of the offer.

Test 13: Brokerage Relationships; Other Georgia-specific Laws

13.1 When and to whom is a licensee required to disclose agency relationship?

   a. To the client only, prior to closing
   b. To the client only, at the time of writing or presenting an offer
   c. To all parties, prior to closing
   d. To all parties, in a timely manner, but no later than when any party first makes an offer

13.2 Which of the following is NOT a duty owed to a client, based on BRRETA?

   a. Timely presentation of all offers, even if the property is subject to a contract
   b. Disclosing material facts concerning the transaction known to the licensee
   c. Discovering adverse material facts unknown to the licensee
   d. Advising the client to obtain expert advice regarding material matters beyond the licensee's expertise

13.3 Which of the following is NOT a legally recognized form of agency in Georgia?

   a. Designated agency
   b. Single agency
   c. Buyer agency
   d. Undisclosed dual agency

13.4 Which of the following is a protected class per Georgia fair housing law?

   a. Age
   b. Ancestry
   c. Marital status
   d. Family status

13.5 Which of the following duties is owed by a licensee to all parties to the transaction?

   a. confidentiality
   b. disclosure of material facts
   c. loyalty
   d. obedience

13.6 A home sold for $563,850, and the buyers obtained a loan of $507,000. What was the amount of the transfer tax?

   a. $563.90
   b. $562.85
   c. $507.00
   d. $506.00

13.7 Which of the following is true regarding disclosure of material facts?

   a. A licensee will be held liable for unknowingly providing false information if the licensee was unaware the information was false and disclosed to the client the source of information.
   b. A transaction broker must disclose to buyers and tenants adverse material facts known to the broker pertaining to the property and neighborhood within one mile of the property.
   c. A listing agent who has no agency relationship with a buyer is not required to disclose adverse material facts regarding the property to the buyer.
   d. A prospective buyer is not responsible to inspect the property for any adverse conditions if the buyer is represented by a licensee.

13.8   A broker engaged by the seller must present all offers to and from the seller

   a.   within 24 hours.
   b.   immediately upon receipt.
   c.   in a timely manner.
   d.   within 48 hours.

13.9   Which of the following statements is true regarding wills in Georgia?

   a.   Wills regarding real estate can be hand-written.
   b.   Wills regarding real estate can be oral.
   c.   A spouse's right to a year's support can supersede a will.
   d.   A will must have three witnesses to be valid.

13.10 Which of the following property rights is recognized in Georgia?

   a.   Equitable right of redemption
   b.   Statutory right of redemption
   c.   Tenancy by the entirety
   d.   Community property

13.11 In Georgia, the period of time required to establish adverse possession is

   a.   20 years with good title.
   b.   seven years with good title.
   c.   ten years with color of title.
   d.   four years with color of title.

13.12 The Georgia law governing agency relationships with clients and customers is known as

   a.   BRRETA
   b.   RESPA
   c.   CERCLA
   d.   GREC

13.13 Which of the following would be considered a ministerial act?

   a.   Assisting a buyer in negotiating a contract
   b.   Recommending to the seller a price the seller should accept
   c.   Coaching the buyer on an offer price
   d.   Providing a buyer with information on properties for sale in the area

13.14 Which of the following is true regarding a designated agent?

   a.   A designated agent may share confidential information of the client with other licensees affiliated
        with the brokerage firm.
   b.   A designated agent may share confidential information with his/her broker.
   c.   A designated agent must share all information with all parties to the transaction.
   d.   A designated agent may not share confidential information with anyone.

13.15 In Georgia, when may a broker represent both parties in a real estate transaction?

   a.   When the broker has obtained prior written consent of both parties
   b.   Only when the broker is acting as a designated agent in a firm
   c.   Only when the principal broker has agreed to the transaction
   d.   Never

13.16 In Georgia, a designated agent is

    a. an agent appointed to represent either the buyer or seller in a transaction to the exclusion of other company licensees.
    b. a subagent to the seller as assigned by a cooperative broker.
    c. a transaction broker.
    d. a general agent.

13.17 What right of rescission does a consumer have when entering into a contract to purchase a timeshare?

    a. 48 hours following the execution of a contract
    b. Seven days following the execution of a contract
    c. Three days following the execution of a contract
    d. 72 hours following the execution of a contract

13.18 What is the statute of limitations for contracts in Georgia?

    a. For written contracts not under seal, six years; if under seal, 20 years
    b. For written contracts not under seal, five years; if under seal, 25 years
    c. For written contracts not under seal, three years; if under seal, 10 years
    d. For all written contracts, 10 years

13.19 Which of the following DOES NOT terminate an agency relationship?

    a. Completion of performance of the engagement
    b. Any authorized termination of the relationship
    c. Written notice of the broker
    d. If no expiration is provided and no termination occurred, one year after initiation of engagement

13.20 Which of the following is a true statement regarding advertising?

    a. A broker can never advertise another firm's listings.
    b. All advertising must be under the direct supervision of the broker and in the name of the firm.
    c. The Commission does not require franchise names to be included in advertising.
    d. There are no requirements addressing the size of the brokerage name in comparison to the size of the name of licensees.

13.21 Which of the following statements is true regarding a licensee engaged by the seller?

    a. The licensee has a duty to discover potential adverse facts affecting the property.
    b. The licensee is liable for providing false information given to the licensee by the seller.
    c. The licensee must present all offers to and from the seller, even when the property is subject to a contract.
    d. The licensee owes confidentiality and loyalty to the buyer.

13.22 Which of the following statements is correct regarding agency relationships in Georgia?

    a. A broker must represent the party who is paying the broker's commission.
    b. Licensees have an obligation to advise clients on the legal aspects of real estate contracts.
    c. Ministerial acts are services performed to assist the licensee's client.
    d. Disclosure of information between the broker and an affiliated licensee representing the client is not a breach of confidentiality.

13.23 BRRETA requires that dual agency disclosure contain all the following statements EXCEPT
    a. description of transactions or types of transactions in which the broker will serve as a dual agent.
    b. that, as a dual agent, the broker represents two clients whose interests at time could be adverse.
    c. that the dual agent is prohibited from disclosing adverse material facts to either party in a dual agency relationship.
    d. that the client is not required to consent to dual agency.

13.24 Regarding a broker's legal relationship with customers and clients, BRRETA states that

    a. brokers who perform brokerage services for clients owe fiduciary duties to clients.
    b. brokers who perform brokerage services for customers owe fiduciary duties to customers.
    c. the broker is not considered to have fiduciary relationship or owe fiduciary obligations to the client but is responsible for exercising reasonable care in the discharge of duties.
    d. the broker has a duty to discover any potential adverse facts affecting the property.

13.25 BRRETA requires brokers to disclose brokerage relationships with a customer or client

    a. within 24 hours of beginning the agency relationship.
    b. immediately upon beginning the agency relationship.
    c. in a timely manner, but no later than when any party first makes an offer.
    d. prior to writing an offer.

13.26 Which of the following statements is accurate regarding property management transactions?

    a. Only the landlord has a duty to disclose adverse material defects.
    b. Only the broker has a duty to disclose adverse material defects.
    c. The broker and landlord are solely responsible for discovering and disclosing adverse material facts.
    d. Prospective tenants have an obligation to inspect and familiarize themselves with potentially adverse physical conditions of the property and neighborhood.

13.27 Responsibilities to clients engaged by broker include all the following EXCEPT

    a. seeking a sale or leasehold at the price and terms stated in the brokerage engagement, or as acceptable to seller or landlord client.
    b. seeking property at price and terms in the buyer or tenant brokerage agreement, or at price and terms acceptable to buyer or tenant client.
    c. advising the client on legal issues and matters beyond the expertise of the broker.
    d. disclosing to the client all material facts concerning the transaction of which the broker has actual knowledge.

13.28 A licensee providing preprinted forms and acting as a scribe in the preparation of real estate contracts

    a. can be performed only by an agent of the buyer.
    b. are ministerial acts performed for a customer.
    c. creates an agency agreement between the licensee and the potential buyer.
    d. is prohibited by a designated agent.

13.29 Closings of real estate transactions in Georgia must be conducted by

    a. the listing broker.
    b. either the listing broker or selling broker.
    c. both the listing broker and selling broker.
    d. an attorney.

13.30 A property sold for $250,500, and the buyers obtained a mortgage for $200,250. What is the amount of the intangible recording tax for this transaction?

    a. $600.00
    b. $601.50
    c. $750.00
    d. $751.50

13.31 The Georgia Condominium Act requires that potential buyers are given what period of time in which to rescind the purchase contract?

    a. Seven days
    b. 48 hours
    c. Three days
    d. There is no right of rescission when purchasing a condominium.

13.32 A transaction broker is best defined as

    a. a broker who represents both parties in the transactions.
    b. a broker whose affiliated licensees serve as designated agents.
    c. a broker who provides assistance to consumers by performing ministerial acts.
    d. a broker who represents only one of the parties to the transaction.

13.33 Which of the following is NOT a duty required of the transaction broker?

    a. Timely presentation of all offers to and from parties involving sale, lease, and exchange of property
    b. Timely accounting of all money and property received by broker on behalf of parties in transaction
    c. Timely disclosure to all buyers and tenants with whom broker is working, adverse material facts pertaining to property's physical condition
    d. Obeying all lawful directions of the customer

13.34 Required notices to terminate a tenancy at will are

    a. 60 days from the landlord or 30 days from the tenant.
    b. 30 days from the landlord or 60 days from the tenant.
    c. 30 days from either the landlord or the tenant.
    d. 60 days from either the landlord or the tenant.

13.35 Which of the following is an INCORRECT statement regarding security deposits?

    a. Security deposits must be returned within one month, or the tenant must be provided with written statement of the reason for retention.
    b. Prior to accepting a security deposit, the tenant must be given a list of any existing damages.
    c. Within three business days of occupancy termination, landlord or landlord's agent must inspect premises, list damages and estimate values for keeping any portion of deposit.
    d. If the tenant refuses to sign the damages list, he/she should not list in writing the items to which the tenant dissents.

13.36 The most common mortgage instrument for real estate loans in Georgia is a

    a. mortgage.
    b. promissory note.
    c. security deed.
    d. contract for deed.

13.37 Which of the following is a duty of a buyer's agent?

    a. Ensuring that the seller and seller's agent are aware of the buyer's financial situation to encourage acceptance of an offer
    b. Timely presentation of any offer, even if the subject property is under contract
    c. Investigating and discovering any material defects in the property or neighborhood
    d. Advising the buyer that a home inspection is not necessary because the seller must disclose any defects

13.38 Which of the following statements is NOT true regarding the brokerage in response to designated agency?

a. The broker may delegate assignment responsibility of designated agency to other management personnel.
b. Company policy must contain a provision to ensure each client is represented as required by law.
c. If the broker appoints designated agents, broker and brokerage will be deemed to be dual agents.
d. There is no imputation of information between broker, designated agents and clients.

13.39 Real estate in Georgia is assessed at _____% of market value.

a. 40
b. 33 1/3
c. 25
d. 35

13.40 Which of the following best defines agency?

a. A real estate licensee's relationship with a customer
b. Any relationship between a licensee and a consumer
c. A relationship in which the broker acts on behalf of a client with that client's authority
d. A real estate brokerage

13.41 Which of the following is NOT an example of a brokerage engagement?

a. Listing agreement
b. Buyer agency agreement
c. Escrow agreement
d. Property management agreement

13.42 Salespersons may accept commissions from

a. a client wanting to provide the licensee with a bonus
b. their employing/sponsoring broker
c. any broker involved in the transaction
d. any client represented by the licensee

13.43 To renew an inactive license to active status, the licensee must do all the following EXCEPT

a. obtain the signature of his/her broker.
b. meet continuing education requirements unless the licensee maintained an active license in another state with continuing education requirements while inactive.
c. pay a renewal fee.
d. retake the licensing exam but not the prelicense course.

13.44 Which of the following is NOT a penalty that can be levied by the Commission for license law violations?

a. Suspension
b. Revocation of license
c. Imprisonment
d. Fines

13.45 How many hours of coursework are required to obtain a community association manager license?

a. 60
b. 25
c. 35
d. 75

13.46 Practicing real estate without a license could result in

    a.   issuance of a cease and desist order and a fine of up to $1,000/day.
    b.   a fine of up to $5,000.
    c.   issuance of a cease and desist order but no fine.
    d.   imprisonment of up to one year.

13.47 Complaints may be filed against Georgia licensees by

    a.   clients only.
    b.   customers only.
    c.   consumers who are not licensees.
    d.   anyone.

Section VI: Georgia License Examination Sample Test

Sample Test: Georgia Practice Exam

S 1.   A farmer temporarily installs produce coolers in a leased farm stand in order to prevent spoilage. The coolers would be considered which of the following?

    a.   Trade fixtures that are real property.
    b.   Trade fixtures that are personal property.
    c.   Temporary real property.
    d.   Emblements.

S 2.   Property can be converted from real to personal property and from personal property to real property by means of which processes, respectively?

    a.   Assemblage and plottage.
    b.   Application and dissolution.
    c.   Severance and affixing.
    d.   Planting and harvesting.

S 3.   The highest form of ownership interest one can acquire in real estate is the

    a.   legal life estate.
    b.   conventional life estate.
    c.   defeasible fee simple estate.
    d.   absolute fee simple estate.

S 4.   The distinguishing feature of a defeasible fee simple estate is that

    a.   it can be passed on to heirs.
    b.   it has no restrictions on use.
    c.   the estate may revert to a grantor or heirs if the prescribed use changes.
    d.   it is of unlimited duration.

S 5.   Maria acquires a property from her uncle Alfonso. When Maria dies, the estate will pass to Alfonso's other niece, Serena. The type of estate that Maria has in the property is a

    a.   conventional life estate.
    b.   legal life estate.
    c.   fee simple defeasible estate.
    d.   tenancy by the entireties.

S 6.   One difference between a cooperative estate and a condominium estate is that

    a.   a condominium owner owns a unit of air space whereas the co-op owner owns a proprietary lease.
    b.   a condominium sale adversely affects other unit owners.
    c.   the coop owner owns stock and a freehold real estate interest whereas the condominium owner simply a proprietary lease.
    d.   the condominium owner owns the common elements and the airspace whereas the coop owner only owns the apartment.

213

S 7. Who are the essential parties involved in an estate in trust?

    a. Owner, trustor and lawyer.
    b. Owner, trustor and trustee.
    c. Trustee, title company, and beneficiary.
    d. Trustor, trustee and beneficiary.

S 8. A condominium owner enjoys a

    a. share in an association that owns one's apartment.
    b. tenancy in common interest in airspace and common areas of the property.
    c. fee simple ownership of the airspace in a unit and an undivided share of the entire property's common areas.
    d. fee simple ownership of a pro rata share of the entire property.

S 9. With various types of junior liens, the order of payment priority is generally established according to

    a. the date of recordation.
    b. what form of tax is in question.
    c. the order of disbursement.
    d. whether the lien was subordinated.

S 10. What is a lien-theory state in contrast to a title-theory state?

    a. A state in which liens are given priority over other encumbrances.
    b. A state in which a mortgagor retains title to the property when a mortgage lien is created.
    c. A state in which the holder of a mortgage lien receives title to the mortgaged property until the debt is satisfied.
    d. A state in which liens must be recorded to be enforceable.

S 11. A property owner has an easement appurtenant on her property. One day the property is sold to another party who is opposed to the easement. Following the closing, this particular form of easement

    a. terminates.
    b. transfers with the property.
    c. transfers with the owner to a new property.
    d. becomes a license on the property.

S 12. What fundamental legal purpose is fulfilled by title records?

    a. Keeping the county apprised of tax payments.
    b. Preventing identity theft.
    c. Giving constructive notice of one's rights and interests in the property.
    d. Assembling all relevant documents in a single place.

S 13. What is "chain of title?"

    a. The list of all parties who have ever owned real estate.
    b. The bundle of rights linked to the recorded title to a parcel.
    c. A chronology of successive owners of record of a parcel of real estate.
    d. Involuntary conveyance of title by statutory rules of descent.

S 14. Which of the following provides the strongest evidence of marketable title?

    a. A general warranty deed.
    b. A title certificate.
    c. Title insurance.
    d. An attorney's opinion.

S 15. A store owner enters into a lease that charges rent per square foot, a common area fee, and a portion of the store owner's gross income from the property. This kind of lease is a

    a. triple charge, or triple net lease.
    b. proprietor's lease.
    c. percentage lease.
    d. retailer's gross lease.

S 16. An owner leases a property to a business in exchange for rent. The tenant is required to pay all operating expenses as well. This is an example of a

    a. proprietary lease.
    b. percentage lease.
    c. gross lease.
    d. net lease.

S 17. A lease automatically terminates under which of the following circumstances?

    a. The tenant fails to pay rent.
    b. The leased property is foreclosed.
    c. The tenant goes out of business.
    d. The landlord cancels the lease.

S 18. A county or municipal authority usually grants a certificate of occupancy for new construction only after

    a. all contractors' work has been inspected.
    b. all work has been completed for at least sixty days.
    c. the construction conforms to building codes.
    d. the tax assessor has valued the improvement.

S 19. A property owner is precluded by deed restriction from developing a thirty foot boat dock. The limitation prompts the owner to sell to another party. The new owner

    a. is free to build the dock since the next door neighbor built a similar dock two weeks later.
    b. takes title subject to the same restriction.
    c. can build the dock with special permission from the zoning board.
    d. may build, since the restriction is extinguished by the sale.

S 20. Emily sells Rycole a property containing a deed condition. The condition stipulates that the forested portion of the property must never be razed for development. Three months later, Rycole proceeds to harvest the trees and turn the area into an executive golf course. What recourse, if any, does Emily have under the deed condition?

    a. She has the right to re-possess the property because the grantee has violated the condition.
    b. The condition has ceased to apply because she allowed the violation to continue for a certain period of time.
    c. She can claim the proceeds from the harvested trees.
    d. She can force Rycole to sell the property to a new owner who agrees to comply with the condition.

S 21. What is the essential purpose of legal descriptions of real property?

    a. To create a consistent, unchanging standard for uniquely locating a property.
    b. To enable courts and attorneys to calculate property size accurately.
    c. To comply with common law for real property.
    d. To eliminate cumbersome metes and bounds descriptions.

S 22. Which of the following characterizes metes and bounds descriptions?

    a. They use meridians and base lines.
    b. They identify an enclosed area, beginning and ending at the same point.
    c. They use lot and block numbers.
    d. They incorporate elevation into the descriptions.

S 23. A buyer agrees to all terms of a seller's offer except the length of time for a contingency to procure financing. The buyer extends the financing period in the offer by one week, signs the form, and mails it back to the seller. At this point, the seller's offer

    a. is void.
    b. becomes an executory contract.
    c. becomes a counteroffer.
    d. has been accepted, since the modification was a contingency.

S 24. Real estate contracts that are not personal service contracts

    a. may be assigned.
    b. are not assignable.
    c. must be in writing.
    d. are exempt from the statute of frauds.

S 25. Which of the following contracts must be in writing to be enforceable?

    a. A parol contract.
    b. A six-month lease.
    c. A two-year lease.
    d. An executory contract.

S 26. Agent Bob, who works for Broker Bill, obtains an owner listing to lease a building. Bill's other agent, Sue, locates a tenant for Bob's listing. Broker Bill in this instance is

    a. an implied agent.
    b. a dual agent.
    c. a single agent.
    d. a subagent.

S 27. A transaction broker should disclose his or her agency relationship to prospective buyers and sellers

    a. upon first substantive communication.
    b. upon completion of the listing agreement.
    c. immediately following completion of any offer.
    d. immediately prior to closing.

S 28. A transaction facilitator in a residential transaction represents

    a. the seller.
    b. the buyer.
    c. both seller and buyer.
    d. neither seller nor buyer.

S 29. A principal instructs an agent to inform minority buyers that the property for lease was just leased an hour ago and is no longer available. The agent refuses to comply. In this case,

    a. the agent should exercise caution until the listing expires, then decline to renew it.
    b. the principal has proposed an illegal act, which should not be obeyed.
    c. the agent is liable for breaching the listing terms.
    d. the agent may sue the principal for discrimination and misrepresentation.

S 30. The amount of a real estate broker's commission is established by

  a. agreement among competing brokers.
  b. negotiation with clients.
  c. the local Board of Realtors®.
  d. state real estate license law.

S 31. A client revokes an exclusive right-to-sell listing two months prior to expiration. The reason stated: the client is too busy to meet with the agent. In this case,

  a. the client is criminally liable for negligence.
  b. the client may be liable for a commission and marketing expenses.
  c. the agent can sue the client for specific performance, even if no customer had been located.
  d. the agent must accept the revocation without the possibility of damage recovery.

S 32. A protection period clause in an exclusive listing provides that

  a. the owner is protected from all liabilities arising from the agent's actions performed within the agent's scope of duties.
  b. the agent has a claim to a commission if the owner sells or leases to a party within a certain time following the listing's expiration.
  c. agents are entitled to extend a listing agreement's term if a transaction is imminent.
  d. an owner is not liable for a commission if a prospective customer delays in completing an acceptable offer.

S 33. Real estate advertising must conform to regulatory standards and requirements. One requirement is

  a. a broker may only place blind ads in social media outlets.
  b. a broker must have all advertising approved by the local real estate board.
  c. the advertising must not be deceptive.
  d. sales agents may only advertise in their own name.

S 34. The three principal brokerage firms in a market agree to pay sales agents 15% more than any other competitor currently in practice. This is an example of

  a. collusion.
  b. price fixing.
  c. allocation of markets.
  d. steering.

S 35. Two leading agencies jointly agree to raise commissions charged to residential sellers to 7.5% of the sales price. Which of the following is true?

  a. This is a perfectly legitimate business practice.
  b. The brokers have illegally fixed prices.
  c. The brokers have allocated markets.
  d. The brokers have engaged in legal collusion.

S 36. A sale contract contains an open-ended financing contingency: if the buyer cannot obtain financing within a reasonable time, the deal is off. Six months later, the buyer still cannot secure financing. Which of the following is true?

  a. The seller may cancel the contract, since it can be ruled invalid.
  b. The buyer can continue indefinitely to seek financing, and the seller's property must remain off the market, since "reasonable" is not defined.
  c. The escrow agent is entitled to the buyer's deposit.
  d. The seller can force a lender to commit to a loan under fair financing laws.

217

S 37. In the event of a buyer's default, a provision for liquidated damages in a sale contract enables a seller to

a. sue the buyer for specific performance.
b. force the buyer to quitclaim equitable title.
c. sue the buyer for the broker's marketing expenses.
d. claim the deposit as compensated damages for the buyer's failure to perform.

S 38. Which of the following is true of an option-to-buy agreement?

a. The potential buyer, the optionee, is obligated to buy the property once the option agreement is completed.
b. The optionor must perform if the optionee takes the option, but the optionee is under no obligation to do so.
c. The contract can be executed at no cost to the optionee.
d. It is a bilateral agreement.

S 39. If a manufacturer that is the major employer in a small city moves its operations to another city, it is reasonable to expect

a. a fall in housing demand, but no other changes in the real estate market.
b. a decline in demand for all types of real estate in the real estate market.
c. an immediate fall in the demand for industrial real estate, but no other changes in the real estate market.
d. an immediate decline in the prices for industrial and office real estate, but no impact on the residential market.

S 40. If a commercial real estate market is undersupplied, it is likely that

a. rental prices in that market will fall.
b. rental prices in that market will rise.
c. rental prices will remain stable until equilibrium is reached.
d. construction will increase to the point of equilibrium.

S 41. The amount of available property that becomes occupied over a period of time is called

a. vacancy.
b. absorption.
c. equilibrium.
d. occupation.

S 42 The roof of a property cost $20,000. The economic life of the roof is 20 years. Assuming the straight-line method of depreciation, what is the depreciated value of the roof after 3 years?

a. $20,000.
b. $17,000.
c. $14,000.
d. $3,000.

S 43. The income capitalization approach to appraising value is most applicable for which of the following property types?

a. Single family homes.
b. Apartment buildings.
c. Undeveloped land.
d. Churches.

S 44. In the income capitalization approach, an appraiser

    a. estimates gross income and multiplies times the gross income multiplier.
    b. estimates effective income, subtracts tax, and applies a capitalization rate.
    c. estimates net income and applies a capitalization rate to it.
    d. estimates potential income and applies a capitalization rate to it.

S 45. Net operating income is equal to

    a. potential income minus expenses minus debt service.
    b. effective gross income minus potential income.
    c. potential gross income minus vacancy and credit loss minus expenses.
    d. effective gross income minus vacancy and credit loss.

S 46. If net income on a property is $40,000 and the cap rate is 10%, the value of the property using the income capitalization method is

    a. $100,000.
    b. $400,000.
    c. $1,000,000.
    d. $4,000,000.

S 47. The key feature of an adjustable mortgage loan is that

    a. the interest rate may vary.
    b. the monthly payment increases over the life of the loan.
    c. the principal balance does not amortize.
    d. the loan term can be shortened or lengthened.

S 48. Why is a wraparound mortgage loan potentially interesting to a home seller as an investment?

    a. It is a senior loan that can be easily subordinated for additional debt.
    b. A wraparound lender can profit when the interest rate of the wraparound exceeds that of the underlying mortgage.
    c. The underlying loan is retired early.
    d. The second mortgage borrower may make payments directly to the first mortgage lender.

S 49. A builder is required to secure a loan with mortgages on three properties. This is an example of

    a. a participation mortgage loan.
    b. a blanket mortgage loan.
    c. a permanent mortgage loan.
    d. a bridge loan.

S 50. Which of the following is true of a loan with negative amortization?

    a. The interest rate on the loan increases as the principal balance decreases.
    b. Payments are not sufficient to retire the loan.
    c. The loan balance is diminishing, or going negative.
    d. Additional interest is being added to the monthly payment.

S 51. The loan-to-value ratio is used as an underwriting mechanism because

    a. the LTV determines the profitability of the loan.
    b. the loan amount needs to be less than the property's value.
    c. borrowers tend to inflate the true value of the property.
    d. a full-price loan overfinances the borrower.

S 52. In the past, borrowers were often surprised by unexpected or undisclosed borrowing fees and expenses at closing. This phenomenon has been largely corrected through disclosure requirements mandated by which of the following laws?

   a. Equal Credit Opportunity Act
   b. Truth-in-Lending laws
   c. National Disclosure Procedures Act
   d. Federal Fair Housing Laws

S 53. Which of the following is an important function of the secondary mortgage market?

   a. Participants borrow funds from banks so the banks can make more loans.
   b. Participants issue tax certificates and sell them to primary lenders.
   c. Participants purchase pools of defaulted loans from lenders to keep them solvent.
   d. Participants sell mortgage-backed securities in order to buy pools of loans.

S 54. Cash flow is a measure of how much pre-tax or after-tax cash an investment property generates. To derive cash flow it is therefore necessary to exclude

   a. cost recovery expense.
   b. interest expense.
   c. loan principal payments.
   d. net operating income.

S 55. The method for deriving an investor's return on investment, or ROI, is by

   a. dividing net operating income by cash flow.
   b. multiplying the required yield times after-tax cash flow.
   c. dividing net income by the price paid for the property.
   d. multiplying cash flow times the price paid for the property.

S 56. Which of the following items would affect a homeowner's adjusted basis?

   a. Installing a higher capacity air conditioning and purifying system.
   b. Replacing a washing machine.
   c. Stripping and staining hardwood floors.
   d. Replacing a broken picture window.

S 57. Which of the following is true with respect to real property taxation by the federal government?

   a. It imposes ad valorem property taxes and capital gain tax.
   b. It may not impose property taxes or tax liens.
   c. There are no federal ad valorem taxes on real property.
   d. It imposes ad valorem tax, but not capital gain tax.

S 58. Ad valorem taxes are based on

   a. the replacement value of property.
   b. the assessed value of property.
   c. the millage value of property.
   d. the broker's estimate of value.

S 59. A retirement facility prohibits ownership of any unit by persons under 55 years of age. The association claims it has made the prohibition properly. Which of the following is true?

   a. They are violating the Civil Rights Act of 1866.
   b. They are violating the Fair Housing Amendments Act of 1988.
   c. They are guilty of age discrimination.
   d. The prohibition may be legal if performed correctly.

S 60. An agent receives a full-price offer from a minority party. The agent presents the offer to the seller and discloses the buyer's minority status. The seller at that point instructs the agent to inform the buyer that the property has just gone under contract. The agent duly complies, telling the offeror that the home has just been temporarily removed from the market and is unavailable – but may be available soon if the contract falls through. Which party or parties, if any, have violated fair housing laws?

    a. The agent only.
    b. The owner only.
    c. The agent and the owner.
    d. Neither agent nor owner.

S 61. Which of the following are examples of closing items not prorated between buyer and seller?

    a. Taxes.
    b. Inspection fees.
    c. Utilities.
    d. Condominium assessments.

S 62. Which of the following activities is not allowed under the Real Estate Settlements and Procedures Act?

    a. A broker having any business relationship with an insurance company that is involved in the broker's transaction.
    b. A broker pre-qualifying a buyer for a mortgage loan.
    c. A lender requiring a deposit from a borrower for a tax and insurance escrow account.
    d. A lender paying a fee to a broker for referring a borrower to the lender.

S 63. Which of the following communication records must (as opposed to should) be kept?

    a. Notes on every conversation.
    b. Copies of required communications to principals.
    c. Notes from company training sessions.
    d. Business cards of licensees one meets at open houses.

S 64. To minimize the risk of violating fair housing laws, a licensee should

    a. refuse to use terms that refer to or describe any of the classes of persons protected by the laws.
    b. avoid working in neighborhoods that are predominantly occupied by a single ethnic group.
    c. make discriminatory or derogatory remarks in conversation only, never in writing.
    d. give better service to members of a protected class than is standard for other clients or customers.

S 65. What are "tenant improvements?"

    a. Modifications to a rental suite to conform to a tenant's usage specifications
    b. Marketing programs that yield a higher quality of tenant
    c. Increased revenue resulting from a rise in rental rates
    d. Increased occupancy resulting from a population increase in the market area

S 66. For the proper handling of client and owner monies, a property manager is generally required to

    a. deposit all funds every month in the management firm's central operating account.
    b. employ a notary to witness and record every deposit or payment received.
    c. maintain a special trust account in a qualified financial depository.
    d. disburse all funds to their legal owners on a weekly basis.

S 67. Jennifer advised her clients they needed to paint their living room before showing the property. The walls of these rooms were all 8' high. The wall lengths were 14', 18', 16', and 18'. If a gallon of paint covers 200 SF, how many whole gallons would the homesellers have to buy?

    a.   1
    b.   2
    c.   3
    d.   6

S 68. An investor just purchased a rectangular 2-acre retail lot for $250 a frontage foot. If she paid $100,000 total, what was the depth of the lot?

    a.   400'
    b.   250
    c.   871'
    d.   218'

S 69. Andra can afford to spend $5,000 in closing costs to refinance her home. The lender quotes closing costs of $800 plus 2 points. The house appraised out at $240,000, and she can get an 80% loan. Can Annika afford to refinance?

    a.   No, she is short by $64.
    b.   No, she is short by $1,600.
    c.   Yes, with $360 left over.
    d.   Yes, she in fact breaks even.

S 70. A lender offers an investor a maximum 70% LTV loan on the appraised value of a property. If the investor pays $230,000 for the property, and this is 15% more than the appraised value, how much will the investor have to pay as a down payment?

    a. $93,150
    b. $79,350
    c. $90,000
    d. $69,000

S 71. A house is being appraised using the sales comparison approach. The house has three bedrooms, two bathrooms, and a patio. The appraiser selects a comparable house that has three bedrooms, 2.5 bathrooms, and no patio. The comparable house just sold for $100,000. A half-bath is valued at $5,000, and a patio at $1,000. Assuming all else is equal, what is the adjusted value of the comparable?

    a. $100,000
    b. $104,000
    c. $96,000
    d. $106,000

S 72. A family purchased a $90,000 lot to build a custom home. At the date of closing, the lot was assessed at $84,550 and the tax rate was $1.91 / $100 assessed valuation. When they completed the home, the assessment increased by $235,000 to include the new construction. If the monthly tax escrow is based on the assessed value, what will the monthly tax escrow be?

    a. $517
    b. $6096
    c. $508
    d. $367

S 73. The James family purchased a home for $180,000 five years ago and obtained an 80% LTV loan. Now the property has appreciated 25%. In addition, the loan has been paid down $11,000. What is the James's current equity in the home?

    a. $47,000
    b. $81,000
    c. $45,000
    d. $92,000

S 74. George and Mary have owned a rental house for 10 years. They bought it for $240,000 and estimated the land value @ 25%. If the property is depreciated on a 39-year schedule, and appreciation totals 50% over the period, what is their gain if they sell the property today?

    a. $159,230
    b. $166,150
    c. $181,538
    d. $120,000

S 75. Adelpha's home is valued at $250,000. She has insurance coverage of $160,000 with an 80% co-insurance clause. If Adelpha has a damage claim amounting to $100,000, how much will she receive from her policy?

    a. $32,000
    b. $60,000
    c. $80,000
    d. $100,000

S 76. The Georgia Fair Housing Code prohibits which of the following acts?

    a.   Refusing to show a property to a buyer who does not qualify financially
    b.   Indicating that a property is not available for sale or rent when it is available
    c.   Advertising a property by emphasizing its amenities
    d.   Refusing to rent to tenants that are a threat to other tenants

S 77. Which of the following statements is true regarding advertising?

    a.   An owner of residential property is exempt from fair housing advertising requirements if the property is sold without the aid of a licensee.
    b.   A licensee discovering a client has used misleading advertising must immediately take steps to stop the advertising until in compliance.
    c.   A licensee who uses misleading advertising can be immediately disciplined by the Commission.
    d.   Affiliated licensees can advertise property without the brokerage name if placed in a real estate publication.

S 78. Licensees are required to remove "for sale" signs from expired listings within _____ of expiration.

    a.   72 hours
    b.   5 days
    c.   10 days
    d.   48 hours

S 79. Which of the following statements is true regarding taxes?

    a.   Transfer tax is based on the sale price, and the intangible recording tax is based on the loan amount.
    b.   Transfer tax is based on the loan amount, and the intangible recording tax is based on the sale price.
    c.   The transfer tax is paid at loan application, and the intangible recording fee is paid at closing.
    d.   Real estate taxes must be paid no later than ten days after recording of the deed.

S 80. Which of the following statements is FALSE regarding support personnel working with affiliated licensees?

    a. The brokerage firm must have a written agreement with the support personnel.
    b. The affiliated licensee and the support personnel must have a separate written agreement specifying duties permitted and prohibited by the support personnel.
    c. Unlicensed support personnel are prohibited from performing any licensing activity.
    d. An individual actively licensed with one firm may not work as support personnel for a different firm.

S 81. Brokers are required to do which of the following?

    a. Have affiliated licensees as independent contractors
    b. Review all client contracts within 30 days for compliance with rules and regulations
    c. Offer designated agency as an option for potential clients
    d. Have affiliated licensees sign the written employment agreement form provided by the Commission

S 82. John, a licensee affiliated with Broker Bob, is selling an unlisted investment property he owns. John must do all the following EXCEPT

    a. disclose to the buyer that he is a real estate licensee.
    b. put the fact that he is a licensee in the purchase contract.
    c. deposit the earnest money into his personal account.
    d. advise Broker Bob in writing that he is selling the property.

S 83. Regarding environmental issues, licensees

    a. must investigate properties to discover any potential issues.
    b. must disclose known environmental hazards only if asked.
    c. may not disclose environmental issues when representing the seller.
    d. must disclose environmental issues of which they are aware.

S 84. Which of the following is true regarding ministerial acts?

    a. A broker engaged by a client does not violate the brokerage engagement by providing assistance to the other party in the transaction by performing ministerial acts.
    b. Support personnel may perform ministerial duties or brokerage activities.
    c. Ministerial acts are acts performed by a licensee on behalf of the client.
    d. Broker acting as transaction broker may not provide assistance to consumers by performing ministerial acts.

S 85. While on vacation in Hawaii, Broker Jane met Donna who is wanting to buy her first home. If Jane provides Donna's contact information to a Hawaii broker for a referral fee, what, if anything, is Jane required to disclose to Donna?

    a. Nothing, because the referral is not in Georgia
    b. Jane is prohibited from referring a potential buyer to a broker in another state.
    c. Jane must obtain Donna's written permission for the referral and disclose the fact that Jane will receive a referral fee.
    d. Jane must disclose to Donna the amount of the referral fee.

S 86. Which of the following individuals must have a real estate license when representing an owner in a real estate transaction?
    a. An administrator
    b. An executor
    c. An auctioneer selling real estate
    d. An attorney-in-fact under a power of attorney

S 87. A broker may be held responsible for license law violations of affiliated licensees unless the broker

    a. had errors and omissions insurance.
    b. informed the Commission upon learning of the violation.
    c. has a written policy prohibiting the activity.
    d. had reasonable procedures in place for supervising affiliates' actions and did not participate in or ratify the violation.

S 88. Licensees are required to disclose which of the following?

    a. The fact that one of the owners died of AIDS
    b. The fact that a homicide recently took place on the property
    c. The fact that a suicide recently took place on the property
    d. A homicide or suicide on the property, if asked by a potential buyer

S 89. Which of the following would be an unfair trade practice?

    a. Assisting a buyer customer in writing an offer
    b. Representing or attempting to represent a broker, other than broker holding license, without knowledge and consent of broker holding license
    c. Assisting a seller customer in locating an inspector
    d. Placing for sale or rent sign with written consent of owner or owner's authorized agent

S 90. If a licensee has been found guilty of a violation as a result of a hearing and has exhausted all administrative remedies, he has the option of

    a. requesting judicial review in the county of the Commission's domicile.
    b. requesting a rehearing.
    c. applying to the court of appeals.
    d. asking for a review by a panel of peers.

S 91. An associate broker

    a. is a broker-in-training.
    b. acts on behalf of and performs brokerage activity on behalf of the broker.
    c. may not serve as broker or qualifying broker.
    d. has a licensing requirement of a 40-hour course.

S 92. The Commission will resolve compensation disputes

    a. between cooperating brokers.
    b. between brokers and affiliated licensed.
    c. between brokers involved with referral of clients.
    d. under no circumstances.

S 93. Commission citations may result in all the following EXCEPT

    a. requirement for the licensee to complete a course in brokerage.
    b. requirement for the licensee to make periodic reports of the broker's trust account by an independent accountant.
    c. imposing a fine of up to $1,000 for each offense.
    d. revoking a license.

S 94. The statute of limitations for collection from the Real Estate Education, Research and Recovery fund is _____ years.

    a. two
    b. five
    c. three
    d. ten

S 95. Which of the following statements is true regarding leases?

    a. Tenants' right to their security deposit may be waived in the lease.
    b. The landlord's duty to make repairs may be waived in the lease.
    c. If the tenant does not give up possession as required in the lease, a dispossessory affidavit can be filed in court.
    d. In a tenancy at will, the landlord may evict the tenant with 30 days' notice.

S 96. Regarding mortgage law, Georgia is a

    a. lien theory state.
    b. title theory state.
    c. intermediate theory state.
    d. loan theory state.

S 97. In Georgia, the _____ is the type of deed that is commonly referred to in other states as the special warranty deed.

    a. quitclaim deed
    b. escrow deed
    c. limited warranty deed
    d. security deed

S98. In Georgia, which of the following covenants is not included in general warranty deeds?

    a. Covenant of title
    b. Covenant of further assurance
    c. Covenant against encumbrances
    d. Covenant of quiet enjoyment

S 99. Typically, the title search period in Georgia is

    a. 50 years.
    b. 40 years.
    c. 75 years.
    d. 30 years.

S 100. Which category of appraiser may appraise any type of property without regard to purpose?

    a. State Registered Appraiser
    b. State Licensed Appraiser
    c. State Certified General Appraiser
    d. State Certified Residential Appraiser

Section VII: Answer Key

NATIONAL TEST 1: Rights; Interests and Estates; Ownership

1.1 (a) Wells, driveways, and signs on a parcel of land.
The legal concept of real estate encompasses land and all man-made structures that are "permanently" attached to the land. The phrase "permanently attached" refers primarily to one's intention in attaching the item. Obviously, very few if any man-made structures can be permanently attached to the land in the literal sense. But if a person constructs a house with the intention of creating a permanent dwelling, the house is considered real estate. By contrast, if a camper affixes a tent to the land with the intention of moving it to another camp in a week, the tent would not be considered real estate.

1.2 (c) A chicken coop permanently attached to land.
Improvements to real estate include such things as fences, streets, buildings, wells, sewers, sidewalks and piers. Modifications to land or a developer's preparations of a parcel of land can include such activities as grading or clearing, neither of which are considered to be "improvements" in this sense of the word.

1.3 (b) The center of the earth and infinite space above the earth.
The legal concept of land encompasses the surface area of the earth; everything beneath the surface of the earth extending downward to its center; all natural things permanently attached to the earth; and the air above the surface of the earth extending outward to infinity. Land, therefore, includes minerals beneath the earth's surface, water on or below the earth's surface, and the air above the surface.

1.4 (a) enjoyed by the owner of a property.
This group of rights includes the right to Possess, Use, Transfer, Encumber, and Exclude others from using the property. (Remember: "PUTEE") Transfer rights include the right to sell, rent, donate, assign, or bequeath. The owner may also encumber the item by mortgaging it as collateral for debt.

1.5 (b) Any item of property that is not definable as real property.
Personal property is any owned item which is not real estate, and the rights associated with owning the personal property item. Items of personal property are also called chattels or personalty.

1.6 (b) pledge the property as collateral for debt..
The right to encumber the property essentially means the right to mortgage the property as collateral for debt. There may be restrictions to this right, such as a spouse's right to limit the degree to which a homestead may be mortgaged.

1.7 (a) transfer of a portion of the bundle of rights.
An ordinary lease is a common example of the transfer of a portion of one's bundle of rights. The owner relinquishes the right to possess portions of the surface, perhaps a building, in return for rent. The tenant enjoys the rights to possess and use the building over the term of the lease, after which these rights revert to the landlord. During the lease term, the tenant has no rights to the property's subsurface or airspace other than what the building occupies. Further, the tenant does not enjoy any of the other rights in the bundle of rights: he or she cannot encumber the property or transfer it. To a limited degree, the tenant may exclude persons other than the legal owner from the property.

1.8 (d) Yes. The drones infringe on his air rights.
Air rights apply to the space above the surface boundaries of the parcel, as delineated by imaginary vertical lines extended to infinity. Since the advent of aviation, property owners' air rights have been curtailed to allow aircraft to fly over one's property provided the overflights do not interfere with the owner's use and enjoyment of the property. The issue of violation of air rights for the benefit of air transportation is an ongoing battle between aircraft owners, airlines, airports, and nearby property owners.

1.9 (c) Navigable lakes, seas, and oceans.
Littoral rights concern properties abutting bodies of water that are not moving, such as lakes and seas. Owners of properties abutting a navigable, non-moving body of water enjoy the littoral right of use, but do not own the water nor the land beneath the water. The legal premise underlying the definition of littoral

rights is that a lake or sea is a navigable body of water, therefore, public property owned by the state. By contrast, a body of water entirely contained within the boundaries of an owner's property is not navigable. In such a case, the owner would own the water as well as unrestricted rights of usage.

1.10 (a) the high water mark of the body of water at the shoreline.
Ownership extends to the high-water mark of the body of water. The low water mark would imply that the owner owned the water itself at times of high water levels!

1.11 (d) They transfer with the property when the property is sold.
Littoral rights attach to the property. When the property is sold, the littoral rights transfer with the property to the new owner.

1.12 (c) Streams and rivers.
Riparian rights concern properties abutting moving water such as streams and rivers. If a property abuts a stream or river, the owner's riparian rights are determined by whether the water is navigable or not navigable. If the property abuts a non-navigable stream, the owner enjoys unrestricted use of the water and owns the land beneath the stream to the stream's midpoint. If the waterway in question is navigable, the waterway is considered to be a public easement. In such a case, the owner's property extends t the water's edge as opposed to the midpoint of the waterway.

1.13 (b) An item of personal property that has been converted to real property.
A personal property item that has been converted to real property by attachment to real estate is called a fixture. Typical examples are chandeliers, toilets, water pumps, septic tanks, and window shutters. The owner of real property inherently owns all fixtures belonging to the real property. When the owner sells the real property, the buyer acquires rights to all fixtures.

1.14 (a) the owner originally intended to remove it after a period of time.
One's original intention can override the test of movability in determining whether an item is a fixture or not. If someone attached an item to real property, yet intended to remove it after a period of time, the article may be deemed personal property. If a person intended an article to be a fixture, even though the item is easily removable, the article may be deemed a fixture. For example, an apartment renter installs an alarm system, fully intending to remove the system upon lease expiration. Here, the alarm system would be considered personal property.

1.15 (c) Fifty percent of the estate consisting of the indivisible whole of the real property.
An undivided interest is an owner's fractional interest in an entire (undivided) estate, but not in a physical portion of the real property itself. An owner who has an undivided equal interest with another cannot exercise exclusive rights over a portion of the real estate, which is an indivisible whole.

1.16 (a) an estate in land.
Interests are principally distinguished by whether they include possession. If the interest-holder enjoys the right of possession, the party is considered to have an estate in land, or, familiarly an estate. Freehold and leasehold estates in land are further distinguished by whether the duration of the owner's rights can be determined.

1.17 (a) a public interest.
Public entities may own or lease real estate, in which case they enjoy an estate in land. However, government entities also have non-possessory interests in real estate which act to control land use for the public good within the entity's jurisdiction. The prime example of public interest is police power, or the right of the local or county government to zone. Another example of public interest is the right to acquire ownership through the power of eminent domain.

1.18 (c) a freehold estate.
In a freehold estate, the duration of the owner's rights cannot be determined: the rights may endure for a lifetime, for less than a lifetime, or for generations beyond the owner's lifetime. By contrast, leasehold estates have expirations.

1.19 (d) that the estate is limited by a lease term.
A leasehold estate is distinguished by its specific duration, as represented by the lease term. Further, leasehold tenants only enjoy limited property rights: use; temporary possession, and limited exclusion.

1.20 (d) Fee simple defeasible.

The defeasible fee estate is perpetual, provided the usage conforms to stated conditions. Essential characteristics are that the property must be used for a certain purpose or under certain conditions, and, if the use changes or if prohibited conditions are present, the estate reverts to the previous grantor of the estate.

1.21 (c) An ordinary life estate.

A life estate is limited in duration to the life of the owner or other named person. Upon the death of the owner (ordinary life estate) or other named individual (pur autre vie life estate), the estate passes to the original owner (a reversionary interest) or another named party (a remainder interest). Thus with the life estate, the owner enjoys full ownership rights during the estate period, and holders of the future interest own either a reversionary or a remainder interest.

1.22 (b) a legal life estate.

Homestead, dower, and curtesy are legal life estates. A legal life estate is created by state law as opposed to being created by a property owner's agreement. The focus of a legal life estate is defining and protecting the property rights of surviving family members upon the death of the husband or wife.

1.23 (b) The boat, house, and motorcycle.

Separate property consists of: property owned by either spouse at the time of the marriage; property acquired by either spouse through inheritance or gift during the marriage; property acquired with separate-property funds; and income from separate property. Community property consists of all other property earned or acquired by either party during the marriage. A spouse owns separate property free and clear of claims by the other spouse. He or she can transfer it without the other spouse's signature. Upon the death of the separate property owner, the property passes to heirs by will or laws of descent. Community property cannot be transferred or encumbered without the signatures of both spouses. Upon the death of either spouse, half of the deceased's community property passes to the surviving spouse, and the other half passes to the decedent's heirs.

1.24 (d) The right to possess and use the premises.

Leasehold tenants are entitled to possess and use the leased premises during the lease term in the manner prescribed in the lease. They also have restricted rights to exclusion.

1.25 (a) the tenant makes, and landlord accepts, regular rent payments.

In an estate from period-to-period, also called a periodic tenancy, the tenancy period automatically renews as long as the tenant pays rent in a timely manner and the landlord accepts it. At the end of a tenancy period, if the landlord accepts another regular payment of rent, the leasehold is considered to be renewed for another period. A conveyance of leased property does not cancel a leasehold interest.

1.26 (c) terminates on the death of lessor or lessee.

The estate at will, also called a tenancy at will, has no definite expiration date and hence no "renewal" cycle. The landlord and tenant agree that the tenancy will have no specified termination date, provided rent is paid on time and other lease conditions are met. For example, a son leases a house to his father and mother "forever," or until they want to move. The estate at will is terminated by proper notice, or by the death of either party.

1.27 (a) an estate at sufferance.

In an estate at sufferance, a tenant occupies the premises without consent of the landlord or other legal agreement with the landlord. Usually such an estate involves a tenant who fails to vacate at the expiration of the lease, continuing occupancy without any right to do so. For example, a tenant violates the provisions of a lease and is evicted. The tenant protests and refuses to leave despite the eviction order.

1.28 (b) Estate from period to period.

In an estate from period-to-period, also called a periodic tenancy, the tenancy period automatically renews for an indefinite period of time, subject to timely payment of rent. At the end of a tenancy period, if the landlord accepts another regular payment of rent, the leasehold is considered to be renewed for another period.

1.29 (a) tenancy in severalty.
If a single party owns the fee or life estate, the ownership is a tenancy in severalty. Synonyms are sole ownership, ownership in severalty, and estate in severalty.

1.30 (c) tenancy in common.
The tenancy in common, also known as the estate in common, is the most common form of co-ownership when the owners are not married (though tenants in common can be married). The defining characteristics are: two or more owners; identical rights; interests individually owned; electable ownership shares; no survivorship; and no unity of time. With "identical rights", co-tenants share an indivisible interest in the estate, i.e., all have equal rights to possess and use the property subject to the rights of the other co-tenants.

1.31 (a) Parties must acquire respective interests at the same time.
To create a joint tenancy, all owners must acquire the property at the same time, use the same deed, acquire equal interests, and share in equal rights of possession. These are referred to as the four unities.

1.32 (b) cannot will their interest to a party outside the tenancy. The survivorship feature of joint tenancy presents an advantage to tenancy in common, in that interests pass without probate proceedings. On the other hand, joint tenants relinquish any ability to will their interest to parties outside of the tenancy.

1.33 (c) Legal life estate.
A legal life estate is created by state law as opposed to being created by a property owner's agreement. The focus of a legal life estate is defining and protecting the property rights of surviving family members upon the death of the husband or wife.

1.34 (a) A homestead interest cannot be conveyed by one spouse.
A homestead is one's principal residence. Homestead laws protect family members against losing their homes to general creditors attempting to collect on debts. Homestead laws generally provide that: the homestead interest cannot be conveyed by one spouse; both spouses must sign the deed conveying homestead property.

1.35 (a) sell or transfer his interest without the consent of the other tenants in common.
All tenants in common have distinct and separable ownership of their respective interests. Co-tenants may sell, encumber, or transfer their interests without obstruction or consent from the other owners. A co-tenant may not, however, encumber the entire property.

1.36 (c) Income derived from community property
If an income-producing property has been defined as community property, the revenue accruing from the investment is likewise community property.

1.37 (c) The beneficiary
A land trust allows the trustor to convey the fee estate to the trustee and to name himself or herself the beneficiary. The land trust applies only to real property, not to personal property. The agreement, or deed in trust, grants the beneficiary the rights to possess and use the property, and to exercise control over the actions of the trustee.

1.38 (c) The Buick and the second property
Community property laws define property rights of legal spouses before, during, and after their marriage, as well as after the death of either spouse. Community property law distinguishes real and personal property into categories of separate and community property. Separate property belongs to one spouse; community property belongs to both spouses equally. Separate property is that property which is acquired prior to the marriage, by gift or inheritance during the marriage, property acquired by separate-property funds, or income from separate property.

1.39 (a) A cooperative may hold an owner liable for the unpaid operating expenses of other tenants.
Since the corporation owns an undivided interest in the cooperative property, debts and financial obligations apply to the property as a whole, not to individual units as in a condominium.

1.40 (b) The owners enjoy an indivisible interest.
The tenancy in common, also known as the estate in common, is the most common form of co-ownership when the owners are not married (though tenants in common can be married). The defining characteristics are: two or more owners; identical rights; interests individually owned; electable ownership shares; no

survivorship; and no unity of time. With "identical rights," co-tenants share an indivisible interest in the estate, i.e., all have equal rights to possess and use the property subject to the rights of the other co-tenants.

1.41 (a) sell her interest to a third party without the consent of Robert

All tenants in common have distinct and separable ownership of their respective interests. Co-tenants may sell, encumber, or transfer their interests without obstruction or consent from the other owners. A co-tenant may not, however, encumber the entire property.

1.42 (d) It passes by probate to the deceased tenant's heirs.

A deceased co-tenant's estate passes by probate to the decedent's heirs and devisees rather than to the other tenants in common. Any number of heirs can share in the ownership of the willed tenancy.

1.43 (c) The tenants have an equal and indivisible ownership interest.

In a joint tenancy, two or more persons collectively own a property as if they were a single person. Rights and interests are indivisible and equal: each has a shared interest in the whole property which cannot be divided up. Joint tenants may only convey their interests to outside parties as tenant-in-common interests. One can not convey a joint tenant interest.

1.44 (a) there is a single title to the property.

Whereas tenants in common hold separate title to their individual interests, joint tenants together hold a single title to the property. This is referred to as unity of ownership.

1.45 (a) the new owner becomes a tenant in common with the other owners, who continue to hold a joint tenancy with each other and a tenancy in common with the new owner.

A joint tenant may transfer his or her interest in the property to an outside party, but only as a tenancy in common interest. Whoever acquires the interest co-owns the property as a tenant in common with the other joint tenants. The remaining joint tenants continue to own an undivided interest in the property, less the new co-tenant's share.

1.46 (d) It passes to the surviving joint tenants.

In most states, joint tenants enjoy rights of survivorship: if a joint tenant dies, all interests and rights pass to the surviving joint tenants free from any claims of creditors or heirs. When only one joint tenant survives, the survivor's interest becomes an estate in severalty, and the joint tenancy is terminated.

1.47 (c) If they are married.

Tenancy by the entireties is a form of ownership reserved exclusively for husband and wife. It features survivorship, equal interests, and limited exposure to foreclosure. In some states it now applies to same-sex couples.

1.48 (c) The trustee.

In an estate in trust, a fee owner-- the grantor or trustor-- transfers legal title to a fiduciary-- the trustee-- who holds and manages the estate for the benefit of another party, the beneficiary. The trust may be created by a deed, will, or trust agreement.

1.49 (a) sell or mortgage the unit without impediment from individual owners of neighboring units.

Condominium units can be individually sold, mortgaged, or otherwise encumbered without interference from other unit owners. An owner may not sell interests in the apartment separately from the interest in the common elements. Unit owners exclusively possess their apartment space, but must share common areas with other owners.

1.50 (b) the unit's pro rata share of the property value as defined in the declaration.

The unit's pro rata share of the property's ownership as defined in the declaration determines the amount of a unit owner's assessment. For example, if a unit represents a 2% share of the property value, that unit owner's assessment will be 2% of the property's common area expenses.

1.51 (a) shares in a corporation or association and a proprietary lease in a physical unit.

In a cooperative, or co-op, one owns shares in a non-profit corporation or cooperative association, which in turn acquires and owns an apartment building as its principal asset. Along with this stock, the shareholder acquires a proprietary lease to occupy one of the apartment units.

1.52 (d) the corporate entity of the cooperative association.
The corporate entity of the cooperative association is the only party in the cooperative with a real property interest. The association's interest is an undivided interest in the entire property. There is no ownership interest in individual units, as with a condominium.

1.53 (a) undivided interests in the property as tenants in common.
In a freehold time-share, or interval ownership estate, tenants in common own undivided interests in the property. Expense prorations and rules governing interval usage are established by separate agreement when the estate is acquired.

1.54 (c) As soon as it is affixed to the ground.
Mobile home units and manufactured homes are personal property until they are secured to the foundation of the lot in whatever form. Prior to affixing these items are personal property.

NATIONAL TEST 2: Encumbrances; Liens; Title Transfer and Recording; Leases

2.1 (c) A third party's interest in a real property that limits the interests of the freehold property owner.
An encumbrance is an interest in and right to real property that limits the legal owner's freehold interest. In effect, an encumbrance is another's right to use or take possession of a legal owner's property, or to prevent the legal owner from enjoying the full bundle of rights in the estate.

2.2 (a) They involve the property that contains the easement and a non-owning party. An easement is an interest in real property that gives the holder the right to use portions of the legal owner's real property in a defined way. One cannot own an easement over one's own property. Easement rights may apply to a property's surface, subsurface, or airspace, but the affected area must be defined. An easement may be affirmative, allowing a use, such as a right-of-way, or negative, prohibiting a use, such as an airspace easement that prohibits one property owner from obstructing another's ocean view.

2.3 (d) An easement appurtenant.
An easement appurtenant gives a property owner a right of usage to portions of an adjoining property owned by another party. The property enjoying the usage right is called the dominant tenement, or dominant estate. The property containing the physical easement itself is the servient tenement, since it must serve the easement use.

2.4 (c) easement by necessity.
An easement by necessity is an easement appurtenant granted by a court of law to a property owner because of a circumstance of necessity, most commonly the need for access to a property. Since property cannot be legally landlocked, or without legal access to a public thoroughfare, a court will grant an owner of a landlocked property an easement by necessity over an adjoining property that has access to a thoroughfare.

2.5 (b) an unauthorized physical intrusion of one property into another.
An encroachment is the unauthorized, physical intrusion of one owner's real property into that of another. Examples of encroachments are: a tree limb extending into the neighbor's property, violating his or her airspace; a driveway extending beyond the lot line onto the neighbor's land; and a fence built beyond the property line.

2.6 (c) a trespasser has been using an owner's property for a certain period with the owner's knowledge but without permission.
If someone uses another's property as an easement without permission for a statutory period of time and under certain conditions, a court order may give the user the easement right by prescription, regardless of the owner's desires. For a prescriptive easement order to be granted, the following circumstances must be true: the use has been occurring without permission or license; the owner knows or is presumed to have known of the use; and the use has been generally uninterrupted over the statutory prescriptive period.

2.7 (d) how a property may be used and what improvements may be built on it.
A deed restriction is a limitation imposed on a buyer's use of a property by stipulation in the deed of

conveyance or recorded subdivision plat. A deed restriction may apply to a single property or to an entire subdivision. A developer may place restrictions on all properties within a recorded subdivision plat. Subsequent re-sales of properties within the subdivision are thereby subject to the plat's covenants and conditions.

2.8 (c) the creditor's claim against the property as collateral security for the loan.
A lien is a creditor's claim against personal or real property as security for a debt of the property owner. If the owner defaults, the lien gives the creditor the right to force the sale of the property to satisfy the debt. For example, a homeowner borrows $5,000 to pay for a new roof. The lender funds the loan in exchange for the borrower's promissory note to repay the loan. At the same time, the lender places a lien on the property for $5,000 as security for the debt. If the borrower defaults, the lien allows the lender to force the sale of the house to satisfy the debt.

2.9 (d) An equitable interest.
A lienor generally has an equitable interest in the property, but not legal ownership. The exception is a mortgage lien on a property in a title-theory state. In these states, the mortgage transaction conveys legal title to the lender, who holds it until the mortgage obligations are satisfied. During the mortgage loan period, the borrower has equitable title to the property.

2.10 (a) Payment of the debt that is the subject of the lien and recording of the satisfaction.
A lien terminates on payment of the debt and recording of documents. Payment of the debt and recording of the appropriate satisfaction documents ordinarily terminate a lien. If a default occurs, a suit for judgment or foreclosure enforces the lien. These actions force the sale of the property.

2.11 (d) involuntary general lien.
A general lien is one placed against any and all real and personal property owned by a particular debtor. An example is an inheritance tax lien placed against all property owned by the heir. A specific lien attaches to a single item of real or personal property and does not affect other property owned by the debtor. In addition, judgment liens are junior, involuntary liens.

2.12 (a) Real estate tax lien.
The category of superior, or senior, liens ranks above the category of inferior, or junior, liens, meaning that superior liens receive first payment from the proceeds of a foreclosure. The superior category includes liens for real estate tax, special assessments, and inheritance tax. Other liens, including income tax liens, mortgage liens and judgment liens, are inferior.

2.13 (d) subordinate the lien.
A lienor can change the priority of a junior lien by voluntarily agreeing to subordinate, or lower, the lien's position in the hierarchy. This change is often necessary when working with a mortgage lender who will not originate a mortgage loan unless it is senior to all other junior liens on the property. The lender may require the borrower to obtain agreements from other lien holders to subordinate their liens to the new mortgage.

2.14 (c) A proceeding to enforce a lien by forcing the sale or transfer of a secured property.
All liens can be enforced by the sale or other transfer of title of the secured property, whether by court action, operation of law, or through powers granted in the original loan agreement. The enforcement proceedings are referred to as foreclosure. Note that lienors already possess equitable title, so they do not need to undertake a legal proceeding to establish this.

2.15 (b) file a foreclosure suit.
Judicial foreclosure occurs in states that use a two-party mortgage document (borrower and lender) that does not contain a "power of sale" provision. Lacking this provision, a lender must file a foreclosure suit and undertake a court proceeding to enforce the lien.

2.16 (a) strict foreclosure. Strict foreclosure is a court proceeding that gives the lender title directly, by court order, instead of giving cash proceeds from a public sale. On default, the lender gives the borrower official notice. After a prescribed period, the lender files suit in court, whereupon the court establishes a period within which the defaulting party must repay the amounts owed. If the defaulter does not repay the funds, the court orders transfer of full, legal title to the lender.

2.17 (d) A license, which terminates upon the owner's death.
A license is a personal right that a property owner grants to another to use the property for a specific purpose (to reach the kindergarten school bus). Unlike a personal easement in gross, which terminates only on the death of the grantee (Betty Luanne, in this instance), a license is revocable at any moment, is not transferable and does not attach to the land. It ceases on the death of either party, or on the sale of the property.

2.18 (d) Dominant tenement.
An easement appurtenant gives a property owner a right of usage to portions of an adjoining property owned by another party. The property enjoying the usage right is called the dominant tenement, or dominant estate. The property containing the physical easement itself is the servient tenement, since it must serve the easement use.

2.19 (b) a deed restriction.
A private party who wants to control the quality and standards of a property can establish a deed restriction. Deed restrictions take precedence over zoning ordinances if they are more restrictive.

2.20 (a) It involves a monetary claim against the value of a property.
A lien is a creditor's claim against personal or real property as security for a debt of the property owner. If the owner defaults, the lien gives the creditor the right to force the sale of the property to satisfy the debt. Liens do not necessarily alter the property value. Liens can be involuntary as well as voluntary. Finally, liens attach to the property, but so do other encumbrances.

2.21 (d) It is knowledge received or imparted through direct experience.
The term "notice" is synonymous with "knowledge." A person who has received actual notice has actual knowledge of something. Receiving actual notice means learning of something through direct experience or communication. Thus, a document in itself cannot be actual notice. It is the seeing of the document that makes it actual notice.

2.22 (b) It is knowledge one could have or should have obtained. Constructive notice, or legal notice, is knowledge of a fact that a person could have or should have obtained. The foremost method of imparting constructive notice is by recordation of ownership documents in public records, specifically, title records. Since public records are open to everyone, the law generally presumes that when evidence of ownership is recorded, the public at large has received constructive notice of ownership.

2.23 (a) grant, deed, and will.
Voluntary transfer, or voluntary alienation, is an unforced transfer of title by sale or gift from an owner to another party. If the transferor is a government entity and the recipient is a private party, the conveyance is a public grant. If the transferor is a private party, the conveyance is a private grant. A living owner makes a private grant by means of a deed of conveyance, or deed. A private grant that occurs when the owner dies is a transfer by will.

2.24 (c) It gives constructive notice of ownership.
Recording is not necessary to make a deed valid. However, it is in the grantee's best interests to do so. Recording the deed gives the public constructive notice of the grantee's ownership.

2.25 (b) granting clause.
The granting, or premises, clause is the only required clause. It contains the conveyance intentions; names the parties; describes the property; and indicates a nominal consideration.

2.26 (a) general warranty deed.
The general warranty deed, or warranty deed for short, contains the fullest possible assurances of good title and protection for the grantee. The deed is technically a bargain and sale deed in which the grantor promises to defend against any and all claims to the title. The overall general warranty covenant is: "I own and will defend."

2.27 (d) To have an encumbrance removed if the lienholder cannot prove its validity.
Where there is a possibility that prior errors in deeds or other recorded documents might cloud (encumber) the title, the relevant parties execute a quitclaim deed to convey "any and all" interest to the grantee. If a

party responsible for encumbering title refuses to quitclaim the interest, the owner may file a quiet title suit. This requires the lienor to prove the validity of an interest. If the defendant is unable to do so, the court removes the cloud by decree.

2.28 (a) A transfer tax based on the price of the property being conveyed.
State law usually requires payment of a documentary stamp tax on a conveyance of real property. The tax is based on the actual price of the property conveyed, thus enabling taxing authorities to ascertain current market value for ad valorem tax purposes. Payment of the tax is evidenced on the deed.

2.29 (b) probate.
A court proceeding called probate generally settles a decedent's estate, whether the person has died testate (having left a valid will) or intestate (having failed to do so).

2.30 (a) It will escheat to the state or county.
If an intestate decedent has no heirs, the estate escheats, or reverts, to the state or county after all claims and debts have been validated and settled.

2.31 (d) Eminent domain.
Various government and public entities can transfer private property to the public sphere by the power of eminent domain. The transfer is involuntary, even though the owner receives compensation. For example, a city government wants to widen a highway to accommodate growth. The government uses eminent domain to condemn and purchase all properties abutting the thoroughfare in order to complete the construction project.

2.32 (a) openly possessing and claiming the property without the owner's consent.
To claim legal title, the adverse possessor must be able to show a claim of right or color of title as reason for the possession; have notorious possession, which is possession without concealment; maintain a consistent claim of hostile possession, which is a claim to ownership and possession regardless of the owner's claims or consent; occupy the property continuously for a statutory period of time; in some states, pay taxes.

2.33 (c) The buyer.
Title records protect the buyer by revealing whether a property has marketable title, one free of undesirable encumbrances. The buyer is legally responsible for knowing the condition of title, since it is a matter of public record.

2.34 (a) a clouded title.
Chain of title refers to the succession of property owners of record dating back to the original grant of title from the state to a private party. If there is a missing link in the chronology of owners, or if there was a defective conveyance, the chain is said to be broken, resulting in a clouded title to the property.

2.35 (b) standard owner's title insurance policy.
An owner's policy may have standard coverage or extended coverage. Standard coverage protects against title defects such as incompetent grantors, invalid deeds, fraudulent transaction documents, and defects in the chain of title. Extended coverage protects against liabilities that may not be of public record, including fraud, unrecorded ownership claims, unintentional recording errors, and unrecorded liens.

2.36 (a) voluntary alienation.
Voluntary alienation is an unforced transfer of title by sale or gift from an owner to another party.

2.37 (d) A quitclaim deed.
A quitclaim deed transfers real and potential interests in a property, whether an interest is known to exist or not. The grantor makes no claim to any interest in the property being conveyed and offers no warrants to protect the grantee. Where there is a possibility that prior errors in deeds or other recorded documents might cloud (encumber) the title, the relevant parties execute a quitclaim deed to convey "any and all" interest to the grantee.

2.38 (a) pass to the heirs by the laws of descent and distribution.
In this circumstance, the estate, including real property, will pass to lawful heirs according to the state's laws of descent and succession or distribution. These laws apportion the estate without regard to the wishes

of the heirs or the intentions of the decedent. Escheat, by which the state takes the property, applies only if there are no legal heirs.

2.39 (d) declined because possession was secretive.
One of the preconditions for a claim of ownership based on adverse possession is notorious possession, or possession without concealment. Even if the length of possession in this case meets the statutory requirement, the drifter's secretiveness would invalidate the claim.

2.40 (b) free of undisclosed defects and encumbrances.
Marketable title is, by definition, one that is free and clear of undesirable and unknown encumbrances, claims, clouds, or other defects. Attorney's abstracts and title certificates do not guarantee that a title is marketable.

2.41 (c) Estate at will.
Three of the four principal types of leasehold estate are: the estate for years, which has a specific lease term; the estate from period-to-period, where the lease term of a specific period automatically renews; and the estate at will, which has no specified lease term. The fourth principal type, the estate at sufferance, is a tenancy without consent that therefore also has no specific term.

2.42 (b) for specified reasonable purposes.
A tenant has the sole right to occupy and use the premises without interference from outside parties, including the landlord. The landlord may enter the premises for specified purposes such as inspections, but the interference must be reasonable and limited. In addition, the landlord can do nothing outside of the lease's express provisions that would impair the tenant's enjoyment of income deriving from use of the premises.

2.43 (a) compliance with the rules and regulations of the building.
The lease defines the tenant's obligations, which principally are to pay the rent on time; maintain the property's condition; and comply with the rules and regulations of the building.

2.44 (b) providing required building support and services.
The lease defines the landlord's obligations, which principally are to provide the necessary building support and services, and maintain the condition of the property. It is the tenant's responsibility to obtain insurance and to determine the fairness of the rent.

2.45 (d) the tenant's estate is still obligated under the lease.
A valid lease creates obligations that survive the death of the landlord or tenant, with certain exceptions. A tenant's estate remains liable for payment of rent if the tenant dies; the landlord's estate remains bound to provide occupancy despite the landlord's death.

2.46 (a) The remaining tenant is responsible for the full rent obligation.
Multiple tenants who sign a single lease are jointly and severally responsible for fulfilling lease obligations. Thus, if one renter abandons an apartment, the other renters remain liable for rent.

2.47 (c) sublease.
Subletting (subleasing) is the transfer by a tenant, the sublessor, of a portion of the leasehold interest to another party, the sublessee, through the execution of a sublease. The sublease spells out all of the rights and obligations of the sublessor and sublessee, including the payment of rent to the sublessor. The sublessor remains primarily liable for the original lease with the landlord. The subtenant is liable only to the sublessor.

2.48 (d) net lease.
A net lease requires a tenant to pay for utilities, internal repairs, and a proportionate share of taxes, insurance, and operating expenses in addition to rent. In effect, the landlord "passes through" actual property expenses to the tenant rather than charging a higher rent level. Net leases vary as to exactly what expenses the tenant is responsible for. The purest form of net lease requires tenants to cover all expenses, including major repairs and property taxes.

2.49 (a) gross lease.
A gross lease, or full service lease, requires the landlord to pay the property's operating expenses, including

utilities, repairs, and maintenance, while the tenant pays only rent. Rent levels under a gross lease are higher than under a net lease, since the landlord recoups expense outlays in the form of added rent.

2.50 (b) An owner-developer wants to retain ownership of the land portion of the improved real property.

Ground leases are primarily used when an owner wishes to lease raw land to an agricultural or mining interest; when unimproved property is to be developed and the owner wants to retain ownership of the land; when the developer or future users of the property do not want to own the land; or when the owner of an improved property wishes to sell an interest in the improvements while retaining ownership of the underlying land.

2.51 (a) either party giving proper notice.

In the absence of an explicit term with beginning and ending date, a court will generally construe the lease to be a tenancy at will, cancelable upon proper notice.

2.52 (b) a tenancy from period-to-period.

URLTA sets standards for improving oral, vague, or unbalanced lease agreements. In the case of an unclear lease expiration date, the lease is generally deemed to be a periodic tenancy.

2.53 (a) a hotel.

State laws based on URLTA generally do not apply to transient occupancies, such as hotel and motel rentals, proprietary leases in cooperatives, or to occupancy in a residence that is under a contract for deed.

2.54 (c) a temporary possessory interest.

A lease is both an instrument of conveyance and a contract between principal parties to uphold certain covenants and obligations. As a conveyance, a lease conveys an interest, called the leasehold estate, but does not convey legal title to the property. For this reason, a leasehold is also called a less-than-freehold estate.

2.55 (d) A leased fee estate.

In conveying the leasehold estate, the landlord acquires a leased fee estate, which entails the rights to: receive rent; re-possess the property following the lease term; and monitor the tenant's obligations to maintain the premises.

2.56 (c) occupy the property.

The legal essence of a valid lease is that it conveys an exclusive right to use and occupy a property for a limited period of time in exchange for rent and the return of the property after the lease term is over.

2.57 (a) The buyer acquires title subject to the lease, which remains in effect.

The landlord may sell, assign, or mortgage the leased fee interest. However, transferring and encumbering the leased property do not extinguish the obligations and covenants of a lease. Buyers and creditors, therefore, must take their respective interests subject to the terms of the lease.

2.58 (c) When either party gives proper notice.

In the absence of an explicit term with beginning and ending date, a court will generally construe the lease to be a tenancy at will, cancelable upon proper notice.

2.59 (c) a five-year lease must be in writing to be enforceable.

Generally, a lease for a period exceeding one year cannot be oral but must be in writing to be enforceable because of the statute of frauds.

2.60 (b) The original tenant retains primary responsibility for performance of the original lease contract.

In a sublease-- a transfer of a portion of the leasehold-- the sublessor (original tenant) remains primarily liable for the original lease with the landlord. The subtenant is liable only to the sublessor.

2.61 (d) deficiency judgment.

Whenever there are insufficient funds to retire a defaulted and foreclosed mortgage loan, a deficiency judgment may be ordered – if allowed by law – to make up the difference. To comply with the judgment, the borrower must raise additional funds from other sources to make up the difference between the outstanding loan balance and the proceeds from the foreclosure sale.

2.62 (b) The possession must have been unconcealed, for the necessary length of time, and without permission

Adverse possession is only possible if the possession is open, continuous for the statutory period, and the possessor claims ownership.

2.63 (a) Recording instruments establishes the title's marketability.

When deeds, tax stamps, and liens are recorded, the public is given notice of the property's indebtedness and encumbrances. In turn, any future buyer can visualize what must be done to clear title and convey marketable title.

NATIONAL TEST 3: Land Use Regulation & Control; Legal Descriptions; Contract Law

3.1 (d) Zoning ordinances are a primary means of keeping land use in harmony with the master plan.

The master plan fuses state and regional land use laws with local land use objectives that correspond to the municipality's social and economic conditions. The completed plan becomes the overall guideline for creating and enforcing zones, building codes, and development requirements.

3.2 (c) specify usage for every parcel within the zoning authority's jurisdiction.

The intent of zoning ordinances is to specify land usage for every parcel within the jurisdiction. In some areas, state laws permit zoning ordinances to apply to areas immediately beyond the legal boundaries of the city or county.

3.3 (b) To separate land uses so that they do not interfere with each other.

One of the primary applications of zoning power is the separation of residential properties from commercial and industrial uses. Proper design of land use in this manner preserves the aesthetics and value of neighborhoods and promotes the success of commercial enterprises through intelligently located zones. Six common types of zone are: residential; commercial; industrial; agricultural; public; and planned unit development (PUD).

3.4 (c) The public interest

The principal forms of exceptions to a conforming use is legal nonconforming use (grandfathered in); variance based on hardship; and special exception based on the public interest.

3.5 (d) The area of a commercial or industrial facility in relation to the size of the site.

Commercial zoning regulates intensity of usage by limiting the area of store or office per site area. Intensity regulation is further achieved by minimum parking requirements, setbacks, and building height restrictions.

3.6 (c) It requires that multiple tracts of land be developed according to a single design.

Planned unit development zoning restricts use to development of whole tracts that are designed to use space efficiently and maximize open space. A PUD zone may be for residential, commercial, or industrial uses, or combinations thereof.

3.7 (a) A homeowner in a residential zone converts her residence to a private school.

A legal nonconforming use can be illustrated as follows. A motel is situated in a residential area that no longer allows commercial activity. The zoning board rules that the motel may continue to operate until it is sold, destroyed or used for any other commercial purpose. An illegal nonconforming use is one that conflicts with ordinances that were in place before the use commenced. For instance, if the motel in the previous example is sold, and the new owner continues to operate the property as a motel, the motel is now an illegal, nonconforming use.

3.8 (b) A variance is granted by the zoning board if the owner has a justifiable reason.

A nonconforming use is one that clearly differs from current zoning and is subject to change upon conveyance. A zoning variance allows a use that differs from the applicable ordinance for a variety of justifiable reasons.

3.9 (c) certificate of occupancy.
Building inspectors inspect a new development or improvement for code compliance. If the work complies, the municipality or county issues a certificate of occupancy which officially clears the property for occupation and use.

3.10 (c) It conveys legal title to the acquiring entity.
Eminent domain allows a government entity to purchase a fee, leasehold, or easement interest in privately owned real property for the public good, regardless of the owner's desire to sell or otherwise transfer any interest. In exchange for the interest, the government pays the owner a "just" compensation. To acquire a property, the public entity initiates a condemnation suit. Transfer of title extinguishes all existing leases, liens, and other encumbrances on the property.

3.11 (d) parties responsible for improper disposal of hazardous waste could be charged for the cleanup costs.
Under CERCLA and the Superfund Amendment of 1986, current landowners as well as previous owners of a property may be held liable for environmental violations, even if "innocent" of a violation. Sellers often carry the greatest exposure, and real estate licensees may be held liable for improper disclosure.

3.12 (a) Individual property rights and the public's interest.
The optimum management of real property usage must take into account both the interests of the individual and the interests of the surrounding community. While maintaining the value of an individual estate is important, the owner of an estate must realize that unregulated use and development can jeopardize the value not only of the owner's estate but of neighboring properties.

3.13 (c) police power.
At the local level, county and city governments control land use through the authority known as police power. The most common expressions of police power are county and municipal zoning.

3.14 (d) The owner must sell the property in exchange for market-value compensation.
Eminent domain allows a government entity to purchase a fee, leasehold, or easement interest in privately owned real property for the public good, regardless of the owner's desire to sell or otherwise transfer any interest. In exchange for the interest, the government pays the owner a "just" compensation.

3.15 (a) reasonably promote community health, safety and welfare.
Local planners do not have unlimited authority to do whatever they want. Their zoning ordinances must be clear in import, apply to all parties equally, and promote health, safety, and welfare of the community in a reasonable manner.

3.16 (d) To ensure that improvements comply with codes.
Local governments enforce zoning ordinances by issuing building permits to those who want to improve, repair, or refurbish a property. To receive a permit, the project must comply with all relevant ordinances and codes.

3.17 (b) To regulate the density of dwellings in the residential zone.
Residential zoning regulates density, by limiting the number and size of dwelling units and lots in an area.

3.18 (a) a special exception.
A special exception grant authorizes a use that is not consistent with the zoning ordinance in a literal sense, yet is clearly beneficial or essential to the public welfare and does not materially impair other uses in the zone.

3.19 (c) a legal nonconforming use.
An illegal nonconforming use is one that conflicts with ordinances that were in place before the use commenced. For instance, if a motel that was allowed as a legal nonconforming use is sold, and the new owner continues to operate the property as a motel, the motel is now an illegal, nonconforming use.

3.20 (b) a plat of subdivision.
In addition to complying with zoning ordinances, a developer of multiple properties in a subdivision must

meet requirements for subdivisions, including submission of a plat of subdivision.

3.21 (a) accurately identifies the boundaries of the property as distinct from all other properties.
A legal description of real property is one which accurately locates and identifies the boundaries of the subject parcel to a degree acceptable by courts of law in the state where the property is located. The general criterion for a legal description is that it alone provides sufficient data for a surveyor to locate the parcel. A legal description identifies the property as unique and distinct from all other properties.

3.22 (c) reference points, angles, and distances.
A metes and bounds description identifies the boundaries of a parcel of real estate using reference points, distances, and angles. The description always identifies an enclosed area by starting at an origination point, called point of beginning, or POB, and returning to the POB at the end of the description.

3.23 (b) two consecutive common meridians.
The "vertical" area between consecutive meridians is called a range. A range is identified by its relationship to the principal meridian. All ranges are six miles wide.

3.24 (c) two consecutive parallels.
The "horizontal" area between two parallels is called a tier, or a township strip. A tier is identified by its relationship to the base parallel. All tiers are six miles wide.

3.25 (b) Six miles by six miles, or 6 miles square.
A township is the area enclosed by the intersection of two consecutive meridians and two consecutive parallels. Since the parallels and meridians are six miles apart, a township is a square with six miles on each side. Its area is therefore 36 square miles. Remember to differentiate square miles from miles square: 4 square miles is a measure of area (2 miles x 2 miles); 4 miles square is a representation of the sides of a square (4 miles by 4 miles).

3.26 (d) 1/64.
The size in acres of a subsection of a township is a fraction of 640 acres, since there are 640 acres in a section. Thus ten acres is 10/640, or 1/64th of a section.

3.27 (d) properties in a subdivision.
The recorded plat method, also called the lot and block system, is used to describe properties in residential, commercial, and industrial subdivisions. Under this system, tracts of land are subdivided into lots. The entire group of lots comprises the subdivision. In a large subdivision, lots may be grouped together into blocks for ease of reference.

3.28 (c) Metes and bounds.
A metes and bounds description identifies the point of beginning and describes the distance and direction from that point to the first monument, and thence to subsequent monuments and back to the beginning to define the property's enclosed perimeter.

3.29 (d) Thirty-six.
The rectangular survey system divides a township into thirty-six sections.

3.30 (a) 640.
Each side of a section is one mile in length. Thus the area of a section is one square mile, or 640 acres.

3.31 (c) something of value traded in exchange for something of value.
A contract must contain a two-way exchange of valuable consideration as compensation for performance by the other party. The contract is not valid or enforceable if just one party provides consideration. Valuable consideration may be something of tangible value, such as money, or something the party promises to do. It may also be something intangible that a party must give up.

3.32 (a) contain a legal description of the property.
In addition to satisfying the requirements of a valid contract in general, a contract that conveys an interest in real estate must be in writing, contain a legal description of the property, and be signed by one or more of the parties.

3.33 (d) A reasonable time, or until the expiration date on the offer.

If an offer contains an expiration date and the phrase "time is of the essence," the offer expires at exactly the time specified. In the absence of a stated time period, the offeree has a "reasonable" time to accept an offer.

3.34 (b) The buyer's death terminated the offer.

Any of the following actions or circumstances can terminate an offer: acceptance; rejection; revocation; lapse of time; counteroffer; or death or insanity of either party.

3.35 (c) A contract for the sale of undeveloped land.

A real estate contract that is not a personal contract for services can be assigned to another party unless the terms of the agreement specifically prohibit assignment. Listing agreements, for example, are not assignable, since they are personal service agreements between agent and principal. Sales contracts, however, are assignable, because they involve the purchase of real property rather than a personal service.

3.36 (b) the parties act is if there is a contract.

An implied contract is an unstated or unintentional agreement that may be deemed to exist when the actions of any of the parties suggest the existence of an agreement.

3.37 (b) A sale contract before closing.

An executory contract is one in which performance is yet to be completed. A sales contract prior to closing is executory: while the parties have agreed to buy and sell, the buyer has yet to pay the seller and the seller has yet to deed the property to the buyer.

3.38 (a) both parties promise to do something in exchange for the other party's performance.

A bilateral contract is one in which both parties promise to perform their respective parts of an agreement in exchange for performance by the other party. An example of a bilateral contract is an exclusive listing: the broker promises to exercise due diligence in the efforts to sell a property, and the seller promises to compensate the broker when and if the property sells.

3.39 (c) The broker may have a claim for marketing expenses expended during the listing term.

The damaged party may elect the following legal remedies: rescission; forfeiture; suit for damages; or suit for specific performance. However, the broker must show that the seller has breached the contract.

3.40 (d) the failure of a party to perform according to the terms of the contract.

A breach of contract is a failure to perform according to the terms of the agreement.

3.41 (b) The act of declaring that a contract is no longer in effect for a given party.

Parties to a contract may rescind a contract by mutual consent, or a damaged party may rescind the contract unilaterally. This act of rescission cancels the contract and returns the parties to their pre-contract condition, including the refunding of any monies already transferred.

3.42 (a) reflect a mutual understanding or agreement.

Mutual consent, also known as offer and acceptance and meeting of the minds, requires that a contract involve a clear and definite offer and an intentional, unqualified acceptance of the offer.

3.43 (c) unenforceable.

A valid contract that is in writing is enforceable within a statutory time period. A valid contract that is made orally is also generally enforceable within a statutory period, with the exception that some contracts are enforceable only if they are in writing. These laws apply in particular to the transfer of interests in real estate. A void or voidable contract was not a truly valid contract.

3.44 (b) is possibly valid and enforceable.

Incompetent parties, or parties of "unsound mind," may not enter into enforceable contracts. However, during the period of one's incompetency, a court may appoint a guardian who may act on the incompetent party's behalf with court approval.

3.45 (c) a counteroffer.

By changing any of the terms of an offer, the offeree creates a counteroffer, and the original offer is void. At this point, the offeree becomes the offeror, and the new offeree gains the right of acceptance. If accepted, the counteroffer becomes a valid contract provided all other requirements are met.

3.46 (d) valuable consideration.
Valuable consideration can be something of tangible value, such as money, or something a party promises to do or not do. For example, a home builder may promise to build a house for a party as consideration for receiving money from the home buyer.

3.47 (c) is void.
The content, promise, or intent of a contract must be lawful. A contract that proposes an illegal act is void.

3.48 (a) must act within a statutory period.
The statute of limitations restricts the time period for which an injured party in a contract has the right to rescind or disaffirm the contract. A party to a voidable contract must act within the statutory period.

3.49 (b) require certain conveyance-related contracts to be in writing.
The statute of frauds requires that certain contracts must be in writing to be enforceable. Real estate contracts that convey an interest in real property fall in this category, with the exception that a lease of one year's duration or less may be oral.

3.50 (b) The buyer has no obligations to the seller whatsoever.
The mutual consent required for a valid contract is reached through the process of offer and acceptance. If the offeree accepts all terms without amendment, the offer becomes a contract. The exact point at which the offer becomes a contract is when the offeree gives the offeror notice of the acceptance. If an offer contains an expiration date and the phrase "time is of the essence," the offer expires at exactly the time specified.

NATIONAL TEST 4: Agency; Listing Agreements

4.1 (b) the laws of agency, or in some states, by statute.
In every state, a body of law, generally called the law of agency, defines and regulates the legal roles of this relationship. While the relationship is subject to contract law, agency law dictates how the relationship will achieve its purposes, regardless of what the listing contract states.

4.2 (c) The relationship is independent of any compensation arrangement.
It is important to understand that the agency relationship does not require compensation or any form of consideration. Nor does compensation define an agency relationship: a party other than the principal may compensate the agent.

4.3 (c) The defaulting party may have a financial consequence.
Involuntary termination of the relationship may create legal and financial liability for a party who defaults or cancels. For example, a client may renounce an agreement but then be held liable for the agent's expenses or commission.

4.4 (b) present all offers to the principal regardless of their amount.
A conventional listing agreement does not authorize an agent to obligate the client to contracts, and it does not allow the agent to conceal offers to buy, sell, or lease coming from a customer or another agent. Further, since a client relies on a broker's representations, a broker must exercise care not to offer advice outside of his or her field of expertise.

4.5 (c) confidentiality.
The confidentiality standard is one of the duties that extends beyond the termination of the listing: at no time in the future may the agent disclose confidential information.

4.6 (d) comparable to that of other practitioners in the area.
The agent is hired to do a job, and is therefore expected to do it with diligence and reasonable competence. Competence is generally defined as a "standard of practice" equal to the level of real estate marketing skills and knowledge of other practitioners in the area.

4.7 (c) disclose the information to the seller.
An agent has the duty to inform the client of all material facts, reports, and rumors that might affect the client's interests in the property transaction. This includes: the agent's opinion of the property's condition; information about the buyer's motivations and financial qualifications; discussions between agent and buyer regarding the possibility of the agent's representing the buyer in another transaction.

4.8 (a) the Andersons.
Since Gerry executed an agency agreement with the Andersons, they become the client and the Lincolns the customer, regardless of who pays the commission.

4.9 (c) a broker who has an agency relationship with a client.
In a subagency, a broker or licensed salesperson works as the agent of a broker who is the agent of a client. Subagents might include a cooperating licensed broker, that broker's licensed salespeople, and the listing broker's licensed salespeople, all of whom agree to work for the listing broker on behalf of the client.

4.10 (b) One agent represents both sides in a transaction.
Dual agency means representing both principal parties to a transaction. The agent represents both buyer and seller or tenant and owner.

4.11 (c) disclosing material facts that affect the value of the property to both parties.
In the role of facilitator, the broker's only fiduciary duties and standards of conduct are those of accounting; skill, care, and diligence; honesty and fair dealing; and disclosure to both parties of all material facts in residential sale transactions affecting the property's value. Some states do not allow for this form of relationship in a real estate transaction.

4.12 (a) The agent is showing the client's property to a prospective buyer.
Agency disclosure must occur upon "substantive contact" between the listing agent and a customer. Examples of substantive contact include: showing the prospect a property; eliciting confidential information from a prospect regarding needs, motivation, or financial qualification; and executing a contractual offer to sell or lease.

4.13 (d) trust, confidence, and good faith.
The essence of the agency relationship is trust, confidence, and mutual good faith. The principal trusts the agent to exercise the utmost skill and care in fulfilling the authorized activity, and to promote the principal's best interests. The agent undertakes to strive in good faith to achieve the desired objective, and to fulfill the fiduciary duties.

4.14 (b) general.
In a general agency, the principal delegates to the agent ongoing tasks and duties within a particular business or enterprise. Such delegation may include the authority to enter into contracts.

4.15 (b) special.
Under a special agency agreement, the principal delegates authority to conduct a specific activity, after which the agency relationship terminates. In most cases, the special agent may not bind the principal to a contract. Real estate brokerage is commonly based on a special agency.

4.16 (c) a party creates an agency relationship outside of an express agreement.
An agency relationship can arise by implication, intentionally or unintentionally. Implication means that the parties act as if there were an agreement. For example, if an agent promises a buyer to do everything possible to find a property at the lowest possible price, and the buyer accepts the proposition, there may be an implied agency relationship even though there is no specific agreement.

4.17 (a) Condemnation of the property
An agency relationship may terminate contrary to the wishes of the parties by reason of: death or incapacity of either party; abandonment by the agent; condemnation or destruction of the property; renunciation; breach; bankruptcy; or revocation of the agent's license.

4.18 (a) The agent has violated the duty of confidentiality.
An agent may not disclose any information that would harm the client's interests or bargaining position, or anything else the client wishes to keep secret. The confidentiality standard is one of the duties that extends

beyond the termination of the listing: at no time in the future may the agent disclose confidential information.

4.19 (b) the agent has not violated fiduciary duty.
Since it is illegal to refuse to show buyers the property based on where the buyers live, the agent has not violated fiduciary duty. The duty of obedience only applies to legal activities.

4.20 (d) inform the seller.
An agent has the duty to inform the client of all material facts, reports, and rumors that might affect the client's interests in the property transaction.

4.21 (a) prior to completing a listing agreement.
An agent who intends to represent a seller or owner must disclose the import of the proposed agency relationship in writing before the listing agreement is executed.

4.22 (c) Whenever substantive communication is made beyond casual conversation.
A listing agent must disclose in writing to a buyer or tenant that the agent represents the owner in the transaction. This disclosure must occur before or at the first "substantive contact" with the customer prospect. In some states, buyer representatives must disclose the agency relationship to sellers or their agents upon initial contact.

4.23 (b) upon initial contact.
A buyer agent must disclose the agency relationship to the seller or seller's agent on first contact. Substantive contact is assumed to occur immediately in this circumstance.

4.24 (a) may not represent one party's interests to the detriment of the other.
A dual agent's first duty is to disclose the agency relationship to both principal parties or to withdraw from one side of the duality. After disclosing, the agent must obtain the written consent of both parties. If both parties accept the dual agency, the agent owes all the fiduciary duties to both parties except full disclosure, undivided loyalty, and exclusive representation of one principal's interests.

4.25 (d) practicing law without a license.
An agent should not act or speak outside the agent's area of expertise. A customer may rely on anything an agent says, and the agent will be held accountable. For example, an agent represents that a property will appreciate. The buyer interprets this as expert investment advice and buys the property. If the property does not appreciate, the buyer may hold the agent liable.

4.26 (a) Fiduciary and contractual obligations with the client.
A listing agreement establishes an agency relationship between agent and client that commits the agent to the full complement of fiduciary duties to the client in fulfilling the agreement.

4.27 (d) market, sell and show the property.
Special agency limits the scope of the broker's authority to specific activities, generally those which generate customers and catalyze the transaction. A special agency agreement usually does not authorize a broker to obligate the client to a contract as a principal party. Normally, principals do not delegate the authority to negotiate price to an agent in a residential transaction.

4.28 (b) An implied agency may have been created, with obligations to perform for both seller and agent.
Clients and agents may also create an implied agency listing based on substantive actions rather than on an express agreement. For example, if a seller allows a broker to undertake certain activities toward effecting a transaction without a specific authorization, but with full knowledge and consent, an implied agency may have been created.

4.29 (a) The agent cannot assign the listing agreement.
Since a listing agreement is a personal service contract, it is not assignable. In particular, a broker cannot assign a listing to another broker.

4.30 (b) exclusive right to sell.
The exclusive right to sell listing, or "exclusive," gives the agent the most control over the property and the

greatest likelihood of being compensated for his or her marketing efforts.

4.31 (c) A listing that is entered in a multiple listing service to enable cooperation with member brokers.
Though not a distinct type of listing agreement, multiple listing is a significant feature of brokerage practice. Multiple listing is an authorization to enter a listing in a multiple listing service.

4.32 (b) The customer must be legally competent to undertake the transaction.
Effecting a completed transaction means finding a customer who is not only ready, willing, and able, but one who makes an acceptable offer. A ready, willing, and able customer is one who is: amenable to the terms of the transaction (ready and willing), and is financially capable of paying the price and legally capable of completing the transaction (able).

4.33 (a) obtain and distribute compensation.
In the normal course of business, a listing broker delegates marketing responsibilities to salespeople. A salesperson may not, however, seek compensation directly from a client. Only the broker can obtain and disburse the compensation.

4.34 (c) Perry, since he found the customer.
The two principal determinants of procuring cause are being first to find the customer, and being the one who induces the customer to complete the transaction.

4.35 (d) It may be terminated against the agent's will.
A listing may terminate on grounds of: performance; infeasibility; mutual agreement; revocation; abandonment; breach; lapse of time; invalidity of the contract; incapacitation of either party; destruction of the property; or, in this case; involuntary title transfer.

4.36 (b) Sue the broker for money damages.
If the broker cancels the listing or otherwise defaults, the client may sue the broker for money damages.

4.37 (b) exclusive agency agreement.
An exclusive agency listing authorizes a single broker to sell the property and earn a commission, but leaves the owner the right to sell the property without the broker's assistance, in which case no commission is owed.

4.38 (c) open listing.
An open listing is a non-exclusive authorization to sell or lease a property. The owner may offer such agreements to any number of brokers in the marketplace. With an open listing, the broker who is the first to perform under the terms of the listing is the sole party entitled to a commission.

4.39 (d) net listing.
A net listing is one in which an owner sets a minimum acceptable amount to be received from the transaction and allows the broker to have any amount received in excess as a commission, assuming the broker has earned a commission according to the other terms of the agreement.

4.40 (a) the client.
Generally, buyer and tenant representation agreements are subject to the same laws and regulations as those applying to owner listings. The only difference is the client and his or her transaction expectations.

4.41 (a) To list the owner's property in a multiple listing service.
A multiple listing is not a distinct listing contract but rather a provision in an exclusive listing authorizing the broker to place the listing into a multiple listing service. A multiple listing service is an organization of member brokers who agree to cooperate in the sale of properties listed by other brokers in exchange for a share of the broker's resulting commission.

NATIONAL TEST 5: Brokerage Business; Sale Contracts

5.1 (d) Non-profit corporation.
A non-profit corporation is a corporate entity which is not legally entitled to generate profit. A non-profit

organization may not broker real estate.

5.2 (c) are properly licensed.
A joint venture is a partnership formed to complete a specific business endeavor, such as a real estate development. Individuals, general and limited partnerships, and corporations may participate. A joint venture may broker real estate, provided the co-venturers are duly licensed.

5.3 (b) a single employing broker who has an active broker's license.
Only a broker with an active broker's license can hire and employ a licensed salesperson. A licensed salesperson may work only for the employing broker and may not work for or receive direct compensation from any other broker.

5.4 (c) Offer a property for lease on behalf of the employing broker.
A sales agent is only authorized to represent a broker and carry out such duties as the broker may legitimately delegate. Thus a sales agent does not directly represent the client in a transaction but is rather the agent of the broker and subagent of the client.

5.5 (d) The employing broker.
Agents can only receive compensation from their employing brokers. Co-op commissions, referral fees, and other compensations always flow through the broker to the sales agent.

5.6 (d) $4,940.
First calculate the total commission, then the co-brokerage splits, then the agent-broker split. Thus: $380,000 x 6.5% = $24,700 total commission. ($24,700 x 50%) = $12,350 total listing broker share. ($12,350 x 40% = $4,940 agent's share.

5.7 (c) $4,278.
The total commission is ($245,000 x 3%) = $7,350. The agent gets (65% x $7,350) - $500, which equals $4,278.

5.8 (c) complete the signing of the listing.
Once the seller signs the listing, the next critical task is to get it signed, thereby making the listing a contract. Some states allow a salesperson to do this and in other states, the listing must be given to the broker for signing. This result will set in motion the process of marketing the property. The agency disclosures must take place prior to the execution of the agreement.

5.9 (b) Present the offer to the seller at the earliest possible moment.
When a buyer or tenant makes an offer, the agent must present it to the seller or landlord at the earliest possible moment. If the terms of the offer are unacceptable, the agent may assist the seller in developing a counteroffer.

5.10 (c) The broker has illegally converted security funds for business use.
Conversion is the act of misappropriating escrow funds for the broker's business or personal use. Conversion carries serious consequences, including license revocation.

5.11 (d) Never.
All advertising must reveal the identity of the broker; licensed brokers and agents may not use blind ads that conceal their identities.

5.12 (a) fair trade and anti-trust laws.
Brokerage companies, like other businesses, are subject to anti-trust laws designed to prevent monopolies and unfair trade practices. In real estate brokerage, the primary manifestations of unfair trade practice are collusion, price fixing and market allocation. In this instance the brokers are price fixing.

5.13 (b) Outside brokers assist a listing agent in procuring a buyer.
Most listing agreements provide for brokerage cooperation in the multiple listing clause. A transaction involving a cooperating subagent is called co-brokerage. In a co-brokered transaction, the listing broker splits the commission with the "co-broker," typically on a 50-50 basis.

5.14 (d) Only members of the National Association of Realtors®.
The term Realtor® is a protected trade name of the National Association of Realtors®. Only members of this organization may use the term to refer to themselves.

5.15 (a) represent their employing broker in procuring clients and customers.
Agents may only act on behalf of their broker. They may not assume responsibilities for other listings since listings are not transferable.

5.16 (a) The IC is responsible for his or her own taxes; the broker does not withhold.
Generally, a broker has limited control over the actions of a contractor. Specifically: a broker can require performance results, but is limited in demanding how a contractor performs the work; and the broker does not take responsibility for a contractor's income and social security taxes.

5.17 (b) competitive conditions.
Commission structures are negotiated between the agent and employing broker as a function of competitive market conditions.

5.18 (c) avoid disclosing what price the owner will accept.
An agent must be extremely careful at this point to abide by fiduciary obligations to the client, whoever that party may be. Discussions of price are particularly delicate: whether the client is buyer or seller, the agent's duty is to uphold the client's best interests. Thus it is not acceptable to suggest to a customer what price the client will or will not accept.

5.19 (d) mixing escrow funds with the broker's operating funds.
Commingling, a prohibited activity, is the act of mixing the broker's personal or business funds with escrow funds.

5.20 (a) There is insufficient evidence of anything other than a normal business practice.
Charging identical commission rates in itself is legitimate. Price-fixing occurs when competitors have in fact colluded together to set prices.

5.21 (c) all the obligations and promises are performed and the transaction is closed.
An executory contract is one for which the signatories have yet to perform their respective obligations and promises. Upon closing, the sale contract is fully performed and no longer exists as a binding agreement.

5.22 (a) Use a standard contract promulgated by a state agency or a real estate board.
It is advisable, and legally required in most states, for a broker to use a standard contract form promulgated by state agencies or real estate boards, as such forms contain generally accepted language. This relieves the broker of the dangers of creating new contract language, which can be construed as a practice of law for which the broker is not licensed.

5.23 (b) be written.
A contract for the sale of real estate is enforceable only if it is in writing. A buyer or seller cannot sue to force the other to comply with an oral contract for sale, even if the contract is valid.

5.24 (a) The contract has been legitimately cancelled and is null and void.
To be valid, a contract must meet the criteria of: competent parties, voluntary act of good faith, mutual consent, legal purpose, and valuable consideration. The buyer broke the mutual consent requirement by opting out before being told of the seller's acceptance. Thus, there is no valid contract.

5.25 (c) An offer and acceptance.
A contract of sale is created by full and unequivocal acceptance of an offer. Offer and acceptance satisfy the mutual consent requirement for a valid contract. The offeree must accept the offer without making any changes whatsoever.

5.26 (d) Equitable title.
A sale contract gives the buyer an interest in the property that is called equitable title, or ownership in equity. If the seller defaults and the buyer can show good faith performance, the buyer can sue for specific performance, that is, to compel the seller to transfer legal title upon payment of the contract price.

5.27 (b) a condition that, if unmet, renders the contract unenforceable.
A contingency is a condition that must be met before the contract is enforceable. If one party cannot meet a contingency condition by a specified deadline, the other party may cancel the contract.

5.28 (c) The buyer may be able to have the contract canceled.
The termite inspection clause is a contingency clause. If one party cannot meet a contingency condition by a specified deadline, the other party may cancel the contract. Did the clause state that the inspector had to be properly licensed? If so, the buyer has a good case for cancellation.

5.29 (a) Until the seller communicates acceptance of the offer.
An offeror may revoke an offer for any reason prior to communication of acceptance by the offeree.

5.30 (b) Fred has entered into contracts with both Jack and Sally to sell the same property.
Jack's acceptance of Fred's offer creates a valid contract, just as Fred's acceptance of Sally's offer creates a valid contract. Fred should have revoked his offer to Jack before accepting Sally's offer.

5.31 (d) agency relationships and property condition.
It is common for the seller to disclose the property condition requiring the buyer to acknowledge receipt of the disclosure. The broker discloses the applicable agency relationships in the transaction and names the party who must pay the brokerage commission.

5.32 (b) valuable consideration and a right to buy.
An option-to-buy is an enforceable contract in which a potential seller, the optionor, grants a potential buyer, the optionee, the right to purchase a property before a stated time for a stated price and terms. In exchange for the right of option, the optionee pays the optionor valuable consideration.

5.33 (a) Schmidt must sell to Carboy for $10,000.
Mary's option-to-buy contract is enforceable, assuming she paid a consideration for it.

5.34 (d) It is always assignable unless the contract prohibits assignment.
A real estate contract that is not a personal service contract can be assigned to another party unless the terms of the agreement specifically prohibit assignment. An option-to-buy is therefore assignable in the absence of such a prohibiting clause.

5.35 (c) At the end of the contract period, the vendor conveys legal title, provided the vendee has fulfilled all obligations.
A contract for deed is a bilateral agreement between a seller, the vendor, and a buyer, the vendee, in which the vendor defers receipt of some or all of the purchase price of a property over a specified period of time. At the end of the period, the buyer completes payment to the vendor of the full purchase price and the vendor deeds legal title to the vendee.

5.36 (b) the parties have completed a verbal, executory contract.
As a sale contract created by an offer and acceptance, the parties have an executory contract: the parties have yet to perform their respective obligations and promises. However, as a contract for the sale of real estate, this verbal contract is not enforceable. An enforceable real estate sale contract must be in writing.

5.37 (c) The assignor has completed a legal action.
Either party to a sale transaction can assign the sale contract to another party, subject to the provisions and conditions contained in the agreement.

5.38 (d) any conveyance may trigger an acceleration of any loans secured by the property.
The mortgage agreement may or may not state that the seller's loan will be accelerated by the lender and called due on sale. The due-on-sale clause in the sale contract merely stipulates that the buyer and seller recognize the possibility that loans that survive the closing may be called due.

5.39 (d) The option is expired, and the tenant has no rightful claim to money paid for the option.
The option automatically expires at the end of the option period. The landlord has no obligation, either to sell the property or to return the consideration, after the expiration date.

5.40 (c) the seller retains legal title while the buyer makes partial payments until the contract is fully executed.

In a contract for deed, the seller, or vendor, defers receipt of some or all of the purchase price of a property over a specified period of time. During the period, the vendor retains legal title and the vendee acquires equitable title. At the end of the period, the buyer pays the vendor the full purchase price and the vendor deeds legal title to the vendee.

5.41 (d) Telephone Consumer Protection Act

The TCPA was enacted to rein in invasive telemarketing practices by requiring certain identification procedures, compliance with do-not-call requests, and a Do-Not-Call list registry.

5.42 (a) the CAN-SPAM Act.

The CAN-SPAM Act bans unwanted commercial messages sent to wireless devices, requires prior authorization to transmit certain messages, and requires and opt-out provision where the receiver can shut off the advertiser from sending future messages.

NATIONAL TEST 6: Economics; Appraisal

6.1 (b) demand for the item is increasing in relation to supply of the item.

In a market economy, the primary interactions between supply, demand and price are: if supply increases relative to demand, price decreases; if supply decreases relative to demand, price increases; if demand increases relative to supply, price increases; and if demand decreases relative to supply, price decreases.

6.2 (d) Supply and demand are equal, and price and value are equal.

A market tends toward a state of equilibrium in which supply equals demand, and price, cost, and value are identical. According to this principle, market demand moves to meet supply, and supply moves to meet demand. If there is an extreme shortage of an item for which there is normally a strong demand, suppliers will rush to increase production to close the gap. If inventories of an item are very high, suppliers will stop production until the oversupply has been depleted.

6.3 (c) the uniqueness of every parcel.

In comparison with other economic products and services, real estate has certain unique traits. Traits of real estate include: inherent product value; uniqueness of every property; demand must come to the supply; illiquidity; slow to respond to changes; and a decentralized local market.

6.4 (d) Prices rise.

If demand is increasing and a moratorium slows supply, demand will begin to outpace supply, forcing prices to rise as the product becomes scarcer in relation to demand.

6.5 (b) an increase in demand for all types of real estate.

New businesses will arise to support the new company. They will hire new employees, some from out of town. The new employees will need housing. Hence the demand for residential real estate, as well as for commercial and industrial, will intensify, and it will also stimulate new construction.

6.6 (d) The number of available units that become occupied over a period of time.

Absorption is the amount of available property that becomes occupied over a period of time.

6.7 (a) rising prices.

Within the business cycle of real estate, declining vacancy indicates a combination of increasing demand which "fills up" supply which in turn decreases. As space becomes scarcer, rents for available space increase.

6.8 (b) desire, utility, scarcity, and purchasing power.

The value of something is based on the answers to four questions: how much do I desire it; how useful is it; how scarce is it; and am I able to pay for it.

6.9 (b) will increase.

If there is no longer a supply to meet the increasing demand of a growing population, prices for existing supply will rise.

6.10 (d) the market tending toward equilibrium.
A market tends toward a state of equilibrium in which supply equals demand, and price, cost, and value are identical. Thus if supply is scarce, construction will increase to stabilize the imbalance.

6.11 (c) the market is over-supplied.
Falling prices indicate an oversupply of commercial properties in relation to demand. In this case, construction of new supply will also slow down.

6.12 (a) have been increasing.
A rise in prices is a market signal that there is an undersupply of product in relation to demand. As the market moves toward equilibrium, builders construct more buildings to meet the unmet demand.

6.13 (c) It is often difficult to convert to cash.
Since real estate is often a large, long-term investment that has no exact duplicate, the process of a buyer's evaluating and choosing the right property is long and complex; hence, finding a buyer at a desired price can take a long time.

6.14 (b) The number of persons employed in base industries in an area
Base employment is the number of persons employed in the base industries that represent the economic foundation of an area. It is the driving component of total employment, which includes secondary and support industries, and which creates demand for all types of real estate.

6.15 (d) The total existing space of a certain type that is unoccupied at a given time
Vacancy is the amount of total real estate inventory of a certain type that is unoccupied at a given time. It is often stated as a percentage of total inventory, the vacancy rate for that property type.

6.16 (a) local government influencing the real estate market, regardless of demand.
Local governments sometimes declare a moratorium on new construction because of present or projected inadequacies of the infrastructure—water, sewer, power, roads, etc.—or because of the desire to conform to a master plan. The result may be to drive up prices, as supply cannot freely increase to meet demand.

6.17 (c) In- and out-migrations of major employers
Changes in employment numbers in a local market area, especially in major industries, have a direct impact on real estate demand in the area. Money supply, interest rates, and trade imbalances also have an impact, but they are regional or national factors rather than strictly local.

6.18 (b) Vacancy rises and prices fall.
New construction generally occurs to meet an excess of demand. By adding supply, it tends to increase vacancy and lower prices until supply-demand equilibrium is achieved.

6.19 (d) Residential
While all types of users may have these needs, they are most prominent for residential users because of concerns for family comfort and safety. Retail users are more concerned with competitive features of the trade area; office users care more about occupancy costs and suitability for the business; industrial users care more about such features as functionality, accessibility, and the labor pool.

6.20 (c) its susceptibility to swings in the local economy.
Because a real property cannot be transferred to a large, central real estate marketplace, its marketability is closely tied to local conditions. Investors and users must come to the product, unlike other types of economic product that can be moved to a place in search of greater demand.

6.21 (b) anticipation.
Anticipation is the value principle that a buyer will pay a price based on the benefits the buyer expects to derive from a property over a holding period. For example, if an investor anticipates an annual rental income from a leased property to be one million dollars, this expected sum has a direct bearing on what the investor will pay for the property.

6.22 (b) A homeowner adds a third bathroom to a house and thereby increases the appraised value by $10,000.

The principle of contribution focuses on the degree to which a particular improvement affects market value of the overall property. In essence, the contribution of the improvement is equal to the change in market value that the addition of the improvement causes. For example, adding a bathroom to a house may contribute an additional $15,000 to the appraised value. Thus the contribution of the bathroom is $15,000.

6.23 (a) assemblage.

Assemblage, or the conjoining of adjacent properties, sometimes creates a combined value that is greater than the values of the unassembled properties. The excess value created by assemblage is called plottage value.

6.24 (d) Market value is an estimate; market price is the price at which a property sold.

Market value is an estimate of the price at which a property will sell at a particular time. The market price, as opposed to market value, is what a property actually sells for. Market price should theoretically be the same as market value if all the conditions essential for market value are present. Market price, however, may not reflect the analysis of comparables and of investment value that an estimate of market value includes.

6.25 (d) define the appraisal problem and the purpose of the appraisal.

The first step in the process is to define the appraisal problem and the purpose of the appraisal. This involves identifying the subject property by legal description; specifying the interest to be appraised; specifying the purpose of the appraisal; specifying the date for which the appraisal is valid; and identifying the type of value to be estimated.

6.26 (c) weighing the applicability of the approaches and considering the quality of data supporting each approach.

The final step in the appraisal process is to reconcile the value estimates produced by the three approaches to value into a final value estimate. To do this, an appraiser must weigh the appropriateness of a particular approach to the type of property being appraised and take into account the quality and quantity of data obtained in each method.

6.27 (b) Make dollar adjustments to the sale prices of comparable properties to account for competitive differences with the subject. The sales comparison approach consists of comparing sale prices of recently sold properties that are comparable with the subject, and making dollar adjustments to the price of each comparable to account for competitive differences with the subject. After identifying the adjusted value of each comparable, the appraiser weights the reliability of each comparable and the factors underlying how the adjustments were made. The weighting yields a final value range based on the most reliable factors in the analysis.

6.28 (d) takes into account the competitive value of specific amenities of the subject property.

The sales comparison approach is widely used because it takes into account the subject property's specific amenities in relation to competing properties. In addition, because of the currency of its data, the approach incorporates present market realities.

6.29 (a) adds value to a comparable that is inferior to the subject property.

If the comparable is inferior to the subject in some characteristic, an amount is added to the price of the comparable. If the comparable is better than the subject in some characteristic, an amount is deducted from the sale price of the comparable. This neutralizes the comparable's competitive advantage or disadvantage in an adjustment category. For example, a comparable has a swimming pool and the subject does not. To equalize the difference, the appraiser deducts an amount, say $6,000, from the sale price of the comparable.

6.30 (b) requires the fewest and smallest adjustments.

As a rule, the fewer the total number of adjustments, the smaller the adjustment amounts, and the less the total adjustment amount, the more reliable the comparable.

6.31 (c) $195,000.

Since the comparable has an extra bath, it is adjusted downward to equalize with the subject. Conversely, since it has no patio, the appraiser adds value to the comparable. Thus, $200,000 minus $7,000 plus $2,000 equals $195,000.

6.32 (d) Add the estimated land value and cost of improvements and subtract the accrued depreciation of the improvements.
The cost approach consists of estimating the value of the land "as if vacant;" estimating the cost of improvements; estimating and deducting accrued depreciation; and adding the estimated land value to the estimated depreciated cost of the improvements.

6.33 (b) is very accurate for a property with new improvements that represent the highest and best use.
The strengths of the cost approach are that it: provides an upper limit for the subject's value based on the undepreciated cost of reproducing the improvements. It is also very accurate for valuing a property with new improvements which are the highest and best use of the property.

6.34 (c) a property loses the same increment of value each year over the economic life of the property.
All property improvements have an economic life, which becomes incrementally shorter year after year as physical deterioration takes its toll. The property as a whole does not lose value, since land itself does not depreciate. Similarly, an improvement can regain value if it is repaired or updated. Finally, not all properties lose value from economic obsolescence.

6.35 (d) $115,000.
To appraise value using the cost approach, add the land value to the value of the depreciated improvement. Thus you have $30,000 + ($95,000 - 10,000), or $115,000.

6.36 (b) Divide the income a property generates by a rate of return.
An appraiser obtains an indication of value from the income capitalization method by dividing the estimated net operating income for the subject by the rate of return, or capitalization rate. The formula is: NOI / Cap rate = Value.

6.37 (c) uses a method that is also used by investors to determine how much they should pay for an investment property.
The strength of the income approach is that it is used by investors themselves to determine how much they should pay for a property. Thus, in the right circumstances, it provides a good basis for estimating market value. The approach, however, does not project what an income property's future income will be. Moreover, it is not an applicable method for estimating value if the subject is a non-income producing property.

6.38 (a) $370,000.
First, identify net income by subtracting out vacancy and expenses. Then divide by the capitalization rate. Thus, ($60,000 –3,000 – 20,000) ÷ 10% = $370,000.

6.39 (d) 150.
The monthly gross rent multiplier for a property is equal to the price divided by the monthly rent. Thus, ($450,000 ÷ $3,000) = 150.

6.40 (c) $203,000.
Multiply the monthly gross income times 12 to derive annual income. Multiply annual income times the gross income multiplier to derive the estimate of price. Thus, $1,200 times 12 equals $14,400. This times 14.1 equals $203,040, or $203,000 rounded.

6.41 (c) the state in which the appraiser operates.
A state-certified appraiser is one who has passed the necessary examinations and competency standards as established by each state in conformance with the federal standards.

6.42 (a) The Financial Institutions Reform, Recovery and Enforcement Act (FIRREA).
Title XI of FIRREA requires that competent individuals whose professional conduct is properly supervised perform all appraisals used in federally-related transactions. As of January 1, 1993, such federally-related appraisals must be performed only by state-certified appraisers.

6.43 (a) if two similar properties are for sale, a buyer will purchase the cheaper of the two.
According to the principle of substitution, a buyer will pay no more for a property than the buyer would

have to pay for an equally desirable and available substitute property. For example, if three houses for sale are essentially similar in size, quality and location, a potential buyer is unlikely to choose the one that is priced significantly higher than the other two.

6.44 (a) is physically and financially feasible, legal, and the most productive.
This valuation principle holds that there is, theoretically, a single use for a property that produces the greatest income and return. A property achieves its maximum value when it is put to this use. The use must however be legal.

6.45 (d) $200,000. Market value is an opinion of the price that a willing seller and willing buyer would probably agree on for a property at a given time if: the transaction is for cash; the property is exposed on the open market for a reasonable period; buyer and seller have full information about market conditions ; there is no abnormal pressure on either party; it is an "arm's length" transaction; title is marketable; and the price does not include hidden influences such as special financing deals. The amount Lynne actually paid is the market price. The previous listing price and Ken's offer might be interesting data for the appraiser, but the appraisal must also consider other market data, such as comparable sales.

6.46 (a) there may be no recent sale price data in the market.
The sales comparison approach is limited in that every property is unique. As a result, it is difficult to find good comparables, especially for special-purpose properties. In addition, the market must be active; otherwise, sale prices lack currency and reliability.

6.47 (c) selects comparable properties, adjusts the comparables, and estimates the value.
The steps are to first identify comparable sales; then compare comparables to the subject and make adjustments to comparables; then, finally, weigh values indicated by adjusted comparables for the final value estimate of the subject.

6.48 (b) the seller offers below-market seller financing.
The principal factors for comparison and adjustment are time of sale, location, physical characteristics, and transaction characteristics. An adjustment may be made for such differences as mortgage loan terms, mortgage assumability, and owner financing.

6.49 (b) weights the comparables.
The last step in the approach is to perform a weighted analysis of the indicated values of each comparable. The appraiser, in other words, must identify which comparable values are more indicative of the subject and which are less indicative. However, all comparables are taken into account, not simply the nearest comparable.

6.50 (b) market value is not always the same as what the property cost.
The limitations of the cost approach are that: the cost to create improvements is not necessarily the same as market value; and depreciation is difficult to measure, especially for older buildings.

6.51 (b) replacement cost.
Reproduction cost is the cost of constructing, at current prices, a precise duplicate of the subject improvements. Replacement cost is the cost of constructing, at current prices and using current materials and methods, a functional equivalent of the subject improvements.

6.52 (d) functional obsolescence.
Functional obsolescence occurs when a property has outmoded physical or design features which are no longer desirable or acceptable to current users.

6.53 (b) incurable economic obsolescence.
Economic (or external) obsolescence is the loss of value due to adverse changes in the surroundings of the subject property that make the subject less desirable. Since such changes are usually beyond the control of the property owner, economic obsolescence is considered an incurable value loss.

6.54 (c) depreciation.
Depreciation is the loss of value in an improvement over time. The loss of an improvement's value can come from any cause, such as deterioration, obsolescence, or changes in the neighborhood.

6.55 (a) estimates depreciation, subtracts depreciation from cost, and adds back the land value.
The steps in the costs approach are: (1) estimate land value; (2) estimate reproduction or replacement cost of improvements; (3) estimate accrued depreciation; (4) subtract accrued depreciation from reproduction or replacement cost; and (5) add land value to depreciated reproduction or replacement cost.

6.56 (b) Uniform Standards of Professional Appraisal Practice (USPAP)
USPAP is the professional code of conduct established by the Appraisal Qualifications Board that regulates appraisal practice in the USA. Standards relate to reporting requirements, methodologies, and proper disclosures to clients and the public.

NATIONAL TEST 7: Finance

7.1 (b) A state in which a mortgagee has equitable title to a secured property.
States differ in their interpretation of who owns mortgaged property. Those that regard the mortgage as a lien held by the mortgagee (lender) against the property owned by the mortgagor (borrower) are called lien-theory states. Those that regard the mortgage document as a conveyance of ownership from the mortgagor to the mortgagee are called title-theory states.

7.2 (d) It is evidence of the borrower's debt to the lender.
A valid mortgage or trust deed financing arrangement requires a note as evidence of the debt.

7.3 (a) trust deed or mortgage.
The mortgage or trust deed is evidence of the collateral pledge of the purchased property as security for the loan.

7.4 (b) mortgagor.
The mortgagor is the borrower and the mortgagee is the lender. As a memory aid, notice that "lender" and "mortgagee" both have two "e"s. "Mortgagor" and "borrower" both have two "o"s.

7.5 (d) $1,000.
Multiply the rate times the loan amount and divide by 12 to calculate monthly interest. Thus, ($200,000 x 6%) ÷ 12 = $1,000.

7.6 (b) $100,000.
The equation for the loan amount is (annual interest divided by the interest rate) = loan amount. Thus, ($500 x 12) ÷ .06 = $100,000.

7.7 (a) 7.5%.
The equation for the interest rate is (annual payment / loan amount) = interest rate. Thus ($3750 / $50,000) = 7.5%.

7.8 (b) $2,000.
A discount point is one percent of the loan amount. Thus, one point on a $100,000 loan equals ($100,000 x 2%) or ($100,000 x .02), or $2,000.

7.9 (b) Part of each periodic payment is applied to repayment of the loan balance in advance and part is applied to payment of interest in arrears.
In an amortizing loan, part of the principal is repaid periodically along with interest, so that the principal balance decreases over the life of the loan. The annual interest is never the same, since the principal balance to which the interest rate applies changes every year. Interest on a loan is always paid in arrears, not in advance.

7.10 (b) private mortgage insurance.
Mortgage insurance protects the lender against loss of a portion of the loan (typically 20-25%) in case of borrower default. Private mortgage insurance generally applies to loans that are not backed by the Federal Housing Administration (FHA) or Veterans Administration (VA) and that have a down payment of less than 20% of the property value. The FHA has its own insurance requirement for loans with a down payment of less than 20%.

7.11 (d) The fraction of the appraised value of the property offered as collateral which the lender is willing to lend.

The relationship of the loan amount to the property value, expressed as a percentage, is called the loan-to-value ratio, or LTV. If the lender's loan to value ratio is 80%, the lender will lend only $80,000 on a home appraised at $100,000. The difference between what the lender will lend and what the borrower must pay for the property is the amount the borrower must provide in cash as a down payment.

7.12 (c) buyer's down payment.

Price less loan is the down payment. This is also the buyer's initial equity.

7.13 (a) refusing a loan because the borrower does not match the lender's target market.

The Equal Credit Opportunity Act (ECOA) requires a lender to evaluate a loan applicant on the basis of that applicant's own income and credit rating, unless the applicant requests the inclusion of another's income and credit rating in the application. In addition, ECOA has prohibited a number of practices in mortgage loan underwriting, including refusing a loan based on an applicant's demographic characteristics.

7.14 (b) $1680.

Monthly income qualification is derived by multiplying monthly income by the income ratio. Thus (72,000 / 12) x .28 = $1680. Remember to first derive the monthly income.

7.15 (b) adjust the applicant's debt ratio calculation and lower the loan amount.

Since a lender lends only part of the purchase price of a property according to the lender's loan-to-value ratio, a lender will verify that a borrower has the cash resources to make the required down payment. If someone is lending an applicant a portion of the down payment with a provision for repayment, a lender will consider this another debt obligation and adjust the debt ratio accordingly. This can lower the amount a lender is willing to lend.

7.16 (c) All loans secured by a residence.

Regulation Z applies to all loans secured by a residence. It does not apply to commercial loans or to agricultural loans over $25,000. Its provisions cover the disclosure of costs, the right to rescind the credit transaction, advertising credit offers, and penalties for non-compliance with the act.

7.17 (d) the borrower has a limited right to cancel the transaction within a certain period.

A borrower has a limited right to cancel the credit transaction, usually within three days of completion of the transaction. The right of rescission does not apply to "residential mortgage transactions," that is, to mortgage loans used to finance the purchase or construction of the borrower's primary residence. It does, however, apply to refinancing of mortgage loans, and to home equity loans. State law may require a rescission period and notice on first mortgage loan transactions as well.

7.18 (b) ask the buyer/borrower about his/her religion or national origin.

ECOA prohibits discrimination in extending credit based on race, color, religion, national origin, sex, marital status, age, or dependency upon public assistance. A creditor may not make any statements to discourage an applicant on the basis of such discrimination or ask any questions of an applicant concerning these discriminatory items. A real estate licensee who assists a seller in qualifying a potential buyer may fall within the reach of this prohibition.

7.19 (d) not FHA-insured or VA-guaranteed.

A conventional mortgage loan is a permanent long-term loan that is not FHA-insured or VA-guaranteed. FNMA does not "back" loans; FHA only insures FHA loans; and the VA, not GNMA guarantees loans.

7.20 (b) limited by when the loan was originated.

Rules for assumability vary according to when the FHA-insured loan was originated and whether the original loan was for an investment property or an owner-occupied principal residence. Loans originated before December 1, 1986, are generally assumable without restriction. Loans originated after December 1, 1986, require that the assumer show creditworthiness. Some mortgages executed from 1986 through 1989 contain language that is not enforced as a result of later Congressional action. Mortgages from that period are now freely assumable, despite any restrictions stated in the mortgage.

7.21 (c) how much of a loan the VA will guarantee.
A veteran must apply for a Certificate of Eligibility to find out how much the VA will guarantee in a particular situation.

7.22 (d) Zero.
If a loan is fully amortizing, its loan balance is zero at the end of the loan term.

7.23 (b) The buyer gives the seller a mortgage and note as part of the purchase price of the property.
With a purchase money mortgage, the borrower gives a mortgage and note to the seller to finance some or all of the purchase price of the property. The seller in this case is said to "take back" a note, or to "carry paper," on the property.

7.24 (c) hypothecation.
The process of securing a loan by pledging a property without giving up ownership of the property is called hypothecation.

7.25 (a) The borrower gives the lender a note and a mortgage in exchange for loan funds.
When a borrower gives a note promising to repay the borrowed money and executes a mortgage on the real estate for which the money is being borrowed as security, the financing method is called mortgage financing.

7.26 (c) The trustor conveys title to a trustee in exchange for loan funds from the beneficiary.
A deed of trust conveys title to the property in question from the borrower (trustor) to a trustee as security for the loan. The trustee is a third party fiduciary to the trust. While the loan is in place, the trustee holds the title on behalf of the lender, who is the beneficiary of the trust.

7.27 (a) title-theory state.
States that regard the mortgage document as a conveyance of ownership from the mortgagor to the mortgagee are called title-theory states.

7.28 (b) usury.
Many states have laws against usury, which is the charging of excessive interest rates on loans. Such states have a maximum rate that is either a flat rate or a variable rate tied to an index such as the prime lending rate.

7.29 (c) $1,200.
A point is one percentage point of a loan amount. Thus, 2 points on a $60,000 loan equal (.02 x $60,000), or $1,200.

7.30 (a) an amortized loan is paid off over the loan period.
Amortized loans retire the principal balance over the loan period. If a loan does not do this, one must make a balloon payment at the end of the loan term to complete the loan payoff.

7.31 (c) it is a negotiable instrument.
A promissory note is a negotiable instrument, which means the payee may assign it to a third party. The assignee would then have the right to receive the borrower's periodic payments.

7.32 (d) may be required to execute a release of mortgage document.
Lenders may be required to release the mortgage or trust document to the borrower when the borrower has paid off the loan and all other sums secured by the document. The release clause, also known as a defeasance clause, may specify that the mortgagee will execute a satisfaction of mortgage (also known as release of mortgage and mortgage discharge) to the mortgagor.

7.33 (a) an appraisal report.
Loan underwriting is the process of assessing the lender's risk in giving a loan. Mortgage underwriting includes: evaluating the borrower's ability to repay the loan; appraising the value of the property offered as security; and determining the terms of the loan.

7.34 (c) the ability to re-pay, the value of the collateral, and the profitability of the loan.
A lender assesses risks by examining, or qualifying, both borrower and property. In qualifying a borrower,

an underwriter weighs the ability of the borrower to repay the loan. In qualifying a property, an underwriter assesses the ability of the property value to cover potential losses. In this evaluation, a lender requires that the appraised value of the property be more than adequate to cover the contemplated loan and costs. Finally, the loan must make money for the lending organization as a basic business precept.

7.35 (b) they want to ensure there is more than enough collateral to cover the loan amount.
Without an ample difference between the property value and the loan amount, a drop in property values could cause the loan balance to exceed the collateral itself. This greatly increases the risk of a loan loss should the borrower default since the balance could not be completely recovered in a foreclosure sale.

7.36 (b) consider the income of a spouse in evaluating a family's creditworthiness.
The Equal Credit Opportunity Act (ECOA) requires a lender to evaluate a loan applicant on the basis of that applicant's own income and credit rating, unless the applicant requests the inclusion of another's income and credit rating in the application. In such a case, a lender may not discount or disregard income from part-time work, a spouse, child support, alimony, or separate maintenance.

7.37 (a) insure the buyer has the earning power to make the loan payments.
Both the income and debt ratios in borrower qualification quantify how much a borrower can safely afford to pay on a mortgage loan. The income ratio focuses on the borrower's earning power.

7.38 (d) debt payments divided by gross income.
The debt ratio formula is (debt obligations) ÷ (income).

7.39 (c) the parties complete all loan origination documents and the loan is funded.
Closing of a mortgage loan normally occurs with the closing of the real estate transaction. At the real estate closing, the lender typically has deposited the funded amount with an escrow agent, along with instructions for disbursing the funds. The borrower deposits necessary funds with the escrow agent, executes final documents, and receives signed copies of all relevant documents.

7.40 (b) Truth-in-Lending laws and Regulation Z.
Regulation Z, which implements the Truth-in-Lending Act, applies to all loans secured by a residence. It does not apply to commercial loans or to agricultural loans over $25,000. It prescribes requirements to lenders regarding the disclosure of costs, the right to rescind the credit transaction, advertising credit offers, and penalties for non-compliance with the Truth-in-Lending Act.

7.41 (a) The Equal Credit Opportunity Act.
ECOA prohibits discrimination in extending credit based on race, color, religion, national origin, sex, marital status, age, or dependency upon public assistance.

7.42 (c) the Real Estate Settlement and Procedures Act.
RESPA is a federal law which aims to standardize settlement practices and ensure that buyers understand settlement costs. RESPA applies to purchases of residential real estate (one- to four-family homes) to be financed by "federally related" first mortgage loans. In addition to imposing settlement procedures, RESPA provisions prohibit lenders from paying kickbacks and unearned fees to parties who may have helped the lender obtain the borrower's business.

7.43 (b) Buying securities, changing the discount rate, and controlling banking reserves.
The Federal Reserve System regulates the money supply by means of three methods: selling or re-purchasing government securities, primarily Treasury bills, changing the reserve requirement for member banks; changing the interest rate, or discount rate, the system charges member institutions for borrowing funds from the Federal Reserve System.

7.44 (a) It cycles funds back to primary lenders so they can make more loans.
Secondary mortgage market organizations buy pools of mortgages from primary lenders and sell securities backed by these pooled mortgages to investors. By purchasing loans from primary lenders, the secondary market returns funds to the primary lenders, thereby enabling the primary lender to originate more mortgage loans.

7.45 (a) Fannie Mae, Freddie Mac, and Ginnie Mae.
As major players in the secondary market, the Federal National Mortgage Association (FNMA, "Fannie

Mae"), Government National Mortgage Association (GNMA, "Ginnie Mae), and Federal Home Loan Mortgage Corporation (FHLMC, "Freddie Mac") tend to set the standards for the primary market. FHA, VA, and the Federal Reserve are not organizations in the secondary mortgage market.

7.46 (c) It purchases FHA-backed and VA-backed loans.
Fannie Mae buys conventional, FHA-backed and VA-backed loans; gives banks mortgage-backed securities in exchange for blocks of mortgages; and sells bonds and mortgage-backed securities. It does not guarantee, insure, or originate loans.

7.47 (b) It insures loans made by approved lenders.
The Federal Housing Administration (FHA) does not lend money, but insures permanent long-term loans made by others. The lender must be approved by the FHA, and the borrower must meet certain FHA qualifications.

7.48 (a) It guarantees loans made by approved lenders.
The Veterans Administration (VA) offers loan guarantees to qualified veterans. The VA partially guarantees permanent long-term loans originated by VA-approved lenders on properties that meet VA standards. The VA's guarantee enables lenders to issue loans with higher loan-to-value ratios than would otherwise be possible.

7.49 (c) the loan payments gradually increase.
Graduated payment mortgages allow for smaller initial monthly payments which gradually increase. The interest rate remains fixed as does the loan term.

7.50 (b) the borrower pays additional interest at the onset in order to obtain a lower interest rate.
A buydown loan entails a prepayment of interest on a loan. The prepayment effectively lowers the interest rate and the periodic payments for the borrower. Buydowns typically occur in a circumstance where a builder wants to market a new development to a buyer who cannot quite qualify for the necessary loan at market rates.

NATIONAL TEST 8: Investments; Taxation; Professional Practices

8.1 (b) negative leverage.
Leveraging is borrowing funds in order to make an investment that is larger than your own resource permits you to do directly. In negative leverage situations, your cost of borrowing funds to make the investment becomes greater than the income the investment returns to you.

8.2 (b) income properties.
Cost recovery, or depreciation, allows the owner of income property to deduct a portion of the property's value from gross income each year over the life of the asset. Principal residences cannot be depreciated (unless portions are treated as a home office.) Further, land cannot be depreciated.

8.3 (c) 19.5 %.
Appreciation amount is the current value of the property minus the original cost. The total appreciation rate is derived by dividing the appreciation amount by the original cost. Subtract the estimated current market value from the price originally paid (239,000 - 200,000 = 39,000) and then divide the result by the original price (39,000 / 200,000 = . 195 or 19.5%).

8.4 (d) a deduction for mortgage interest.
Deducting mortgage interest is a significant tax advantage of owning one's residence. Depreciation and cost-deductions do not apply to a non-income producing residence. Appreciation is a benefit, but not a tax benefit.

8.5 (d) $232,900.
The figure for net proceeds from sale is expressed by the formula: sale price - costs of sale = net proceeds. Thus $250,000 - (6% x 250,000) – 600 – 1,500 = $232,900.

8.6 (b) $157,000.

The beginning basis is the cost of acquiring a property. Basis is increased by capital improvements and decreased by depreciation. The basic formula for adjusted basis is Beginning basis ($150,000) + capital improvements ($3,000 + $4,000) - depreciation ($0) = adjusted basis ($157,000).

8.7 (c) $34,000.

The gain on sale (capital gain) of a primary residence is represented by the basic formula: amount realized (net sales proceeds, $210,000) - adjusted basis ($176,000) = gain on sale ($34,000). Note the purchase price of the second house is irrelevant.

8.8 (a) There is no taxable gain.

There is no taxable gain because the gain falls under the exclusion limit of $250,000. As of August 5, 1997, tax law provides an exclusion of $250,000 for an individual taxpayer and $500,000 for married taxpayers filing jointly on the gain from sale of a principal residence. The seller must have owned the property for at least two years during the five years preceding the date of sale; used the property as principal residence for a total of two years during that five-year period; and have waited two years since the last use of the exclusion for any sale.

8.9 (c) direct investment.

Individuals, corporations, or other investor entities may invest as active investors in a property by buying it directly and taking responsibility for managing and operating the property. This investment mode is called direct investment.

8.10 (a) $2,100.

Annual gross operating income ($1,500 x 12 = $18,000) - annual operating expenses ($500 x 12 = $6,000) = annual net operating income ($12,000); annual net operating income ($12,000) - cost recovery expense ($5,000) = taxable income ($7,000); taxable income ($7,000) x tax rate (30%) = tax liability ($2,100).

8.11 (b) the more the investor stands to gain, the greater the risk that the investor may lose.

The general rule in investments is that the safer the investment, the more slowly it gains in value. The more you want it to gain, and the more quickly, the more you must risk losing it. Reward in investing corresponds directly to the degree of risk.

8.12 (a) income and tax benefits.

The basic financial rewards of an investment include income, appreciation in asset value, positive borrowing leverage, and tax benefits.

8.13 (d) relatively illiquid.

Real estate is by nature more difficult to convert to cash than many other types of investment. Compare the selling of a home with the ease of drawing money out of a bank account or selling a stock.

8.14 (b) a more management-intensive investment.

Real estate tends to require a high degree of investor involvement in management of the investment. Even raw land requires some degree of maintenance to preserve its value. Improved properties often require extensive management, including repairs, maintenance, onsite leasing, tenant relations, security, and fiscal management.

8.15 (a) a general partnership.

A general partnership is a syndicate in which all members participate equally in managing the investment and in the profits or losses it generates.

8.16 (d) gross income minus expenses minus building depreciation.

Taxable income from investment real estate is the gross income received minus any expenses, deductions or exclusions that current tax law allows. Depreciation of land is not allowed.

8.17 (c) deduct interest payments from income.

Taxable income is net operating income minus all allowable deductions. The interest portion of debt service is allowed and is deducted from Net Operating Income as interest expense. Principal repayment is not an allowable deduction on investment properties. Capital gain derivation does not involve interest or principal payments.

8.18 (d) The owner may be able to avoid capital gain tax when the property is sold.

Provided the owner meets certain ownership and use tests, there is no capital gain tax on sale of the property unless the gain exceeds $250,000 for a single taxpayer or $500,000 for married taxpayers who file jointly. Since the property is not used for business, deductions for expenses against income are not allowed.

8.19 (c) may be deducted from the sale price for gains tax purposes.

Selling costs include such expenses as brokerage commissions, relevant advertising, legal fees, seller-paid points and other closing costs. These costs are deducted from the selling price to get the amount realized, which is reduced by the adjusted basis to calculate gain on sale for gains tax purposes.

8.20 (b) the difference between amount realized and adjusted basis.

The formula for gain tax is Taxable Gain on Sale x the owner's marginal tax bracket. The formula for gain on sale is: Amount Realized - Adjusted Basis = Gain on Sale. The formula for Amount Realized is: Selling Price - Selling costs = Amount Realized. Therefore, the gain tax = (Amount Realized - Adjusted Basis) x tax rate.

8.21 (c) A tax district.

Real estate property taxes are imposed by "taxing entities" or "taxing districts" at county and local levels of government. States may legally levy taxes on real property, but most delegate this power to counties, cities, townships and local taxing districts. The federal government does, however, tax income derived from real property and gains realized on the sale of real property.

8.22 (b) properties owned by a government agency.

Certain types of property are exempt from property taxes. Certain classes of property owner may also be exempted or have a reduced liability. Exemptions include government-owned properties, real properties owned by churches, and properties owned by other non-profit organizations.

8.23 (c) It adjusts assessments in a locality to make them more consistent with an average level for the state or other higher level jurisdiction.

Equalization factors level out the unevenness of valuations for groups of properties. For instance, if assessed values of properties in one county are consistently ten percent below the average for other counties, an equalization board may multiply each assessed value in that county by a factor of 110% to raise them to the average level for the state.

8.24 (c) $2,000,000,000.

The mill rate = (tax requirement / the tax base). A mill is one one-thousandth of a dollar ($.001). To solve for the tax base, reconfigure this formula to be: Base = Tax Requirement / Mill Rate. Thus the Base = $20,000,000 / .010, or $2,000,000,000.

8.25 (d) $441.

The library tax is ($1.00 x 147) and the fire district tax is ($2.00 x 147). Thus the tax is $441.

8.26 (b) $5,700.

Special assessments are based on the cost of the improvement and apportioned on a pro rata basis among benefiting properties according to the value that each parcel will receive from the improvement. Here, Mary's share is 38 / 200, or 19%. 19% x $30,000 = $5,700.

8.27 (a) A conveyance instrument for a property that is sold to enforce a tax lien.

A tax deed is a legal instrument for conveying title when a property is sold for non-payment of taxes. The application for a tax deed causes the taxing agency to institute a tax sale or tax foreclosure.

8.28 (d) a statutory right of redemption.

If the taxpayer can redeem the property after the tax sale, this right is known as a statutory right of redemption. In this case, the taxpayer must pay the amount paid by the winning bidder at the tax sale, plus any charges, additional taxes, or interest that may have accumulated.

8.29 (b) the total of all assessed values of properties minus exemptions.

The tax base of an area is the total of the appraised or assessed values of all real property within the area's boundaries, excluding partially or totally exempt properties such as those owned by the government or non-profit organizations.

8.30 (c) multiplying each district's tax rate times the taxable value of the property.

Each property owner's tax bill is determined by multiplying the tax rate for each taxing district times the taxable value of the property. Taxable value is the assessed value after all exemptions and adjustments have been taken into account.

8.31 (a) Civil Rights Act of 1866.

The original fair housing statute, the Civil Rights Act of 1866, prohibits discrimination in housing based on race. The prohibition relates to selling, renting, inheriting, and conveying real estate.

8.32 (c) race, color, religion, and national origin.

Title VIII of the Civil Rights Act of 1968, known today as the Fair Housing Act, prohibits discrimination in housing based on race, color, religion, or national origin.

8.33 (c) Advertising a property as available to individuals of a particular race.

The prohibition against discriminatory advertising states that an agent may not advertise residential properties in such a way as to restrict their availability to any prospective buyer or tenant.

8.34 (c) An agent persuades a family to put their house on the market because ethnic minority families are beginning to move into the neighborhood.

Blockbusting, a prohibited activity, is the practice of inducing owners in an area to sell or rent to avoid an impending change in the ethnic or social makeup of the neighborhood that will cause values to go down.

8.35 (a) The Home Mortgage Disclosure Act.

The Home Mortgage Disclosure Act requires lenders involved with federally guaranteed or insured loans to exercise impartiality and non-discrimination in the geographical distribution of their loan portfolio. In other words, the act is designed to prohibit redlining, the practice of restricting loans by geographical are(a)

8.36 (c) privately owned single-family residences listed with a broker.

Among the circumstances where the Fair Housing Act might allow for an exemption is: a privately owned single-family home where no broker is used, with certain additional conditions. In other words, as soon as a broker is used in the sale, the law applies.

8.37 (a) illegal, because the agent changed the terms of the sale to discourage this particular couple.

The Fair Housing Act prohibition against discriminatory misrepresentation states that an agent may not conceal available properties, represent that they are not for sale or rent, or change the sale terms for the purpose of discriminating.

8.38 (d) The owner of a duplex who resides in one of the units refuses to rent the other unit to a non-Christian.

The Fair Housing Act would exempt the owner in this situation because it involves rental of an apartment in a 1-4 unit building where the owner is also an occupant and there is no discriminatory advertising.

8.39 (b) File a complaint with HUD and/or file suit against the offending parties in a state or federal court within the prescribed time period.

The Fair Housing Amendments Act of 1988 prohibits discrimination based on sex. If May feels she has been discriminated against in this way, she may file a complaint with the Office of Fair Housing and Equal Opportunity (OFHEO) in HUD within one year or file suit in a federal or state court within two years of the alleged violation.

8.40 (a) Inform Scott that the condition is illegal and that she cannot comply with it.

Scott is not allowed to discriminate based on race, color, religion, national origin, sex, family status, or handicap. If an agent goes along with a client's discriminatory act, the agent is equally liable for violation of fair housing laws. It is thus imperative to avoid complicity with client discrimination. Further, an agent should withdraw from any relationship where client discrimination occurs.

8.41 (c) require families without children to pay the same security deposit that families with children must pay.

Fair housing laws prohibit discriminatory advertising, discrimination on the basis of national origin, discrimination based on age in dwellings of more than four units, and discrimination against families with children. The fact that the owner is requiring the same deposit from tenants with and without children does not discriminate against families with children but actually favors them.

8.42 (d) It is a single-family house, and the owner owns only one other rental home in addition to his own residence.

Federal fair housing laws do not prohibit age and family status discrimination in residential dwellings of four units or less and in single family houses if sold or rented by owners who have no more than three houses.

8.43 (c) the Fair Housing Amendments Act of 1988.

The Fair Housing Amendments Act of 1988 prohibited discrimination based on sex and discrimination against handicapped persons and families with children. Executive Order 11063 concerned racial discrimination in housing where federal funding was involved; the Civil Rights Act of 1968 concerned discrimination based on race, color, religion, and national origin; Jones v Mayer concerned racial discrimination.

8.44 (c) steering.

Steering is the illegal practice of limiting customers' choices by encouraging or discouraging them about the suitability of an area and directing them only to areas the agent deems suitable for them.

8.45 (a) providing unequal services.

The agent may be illegally providing unequal services by altering the nature or quality of brokerage services to a party based on race, color, sex, national origin, or religion.

8.46 (a) discriminatory misrepresentation by omission.

Discriminatory misrepresentation is the concealing of available properties, representing that they are not for sale or rent, or changing the sale terms for the purpose of discriminating.

8.47 (c) Prior to the sale of an occupied 1-4 unit dwelling

The Seller's Property Condition Disclosure form must be completed by the seller prior to the closing of any resale of a 1-4-unit residential dwelling. New homes are exempted, as are commercial properties. In some jurisdictions, the property disclosure form must be completed when an offer is completed.

8.48 (d) must still be completed according to local requirements

Whether the seller lists or sells by-owner, he or she must still fulfill the obligation to complete the Property Condition form in a timely fashion. Similarly, the licensee is required to disclose all known material facts regardless of the seller's disclosures.

8.49 (c) A previous occupant died in the house

Sellers are not required to disclose fact that do not materially impact the value or condition of the property including suicides, AIDS-related illness, and other property stigmas. Licensees, however are required to disclose known material facts.

NATIONAL TEST 9: Closings; Risk Management; Property Management

9.1 (c) returns funds to the buyer.

If for any reason the transaction cannot be completed, the escrow instructions usually provide a mechanism for reconveying title to the seller and funds to the buyer. In such a case, both parties return to their original status as if no sale had occurred.

9.2 (d) disclose in writing any business relationships they have with other parties involved in the transaction.

Business relationships and affiliations among real estate firms, mortgage brokers, title insurance firms and other such companies that are involved in a transaction are permitted, provided the relationships are disclosed in writing to the consumer, the consumer is free to go elsewhere for the relevant service, and the companies do not exchange fees for referrals.

9.3 (a) The item must be prorated and recorded as a debit to one party and a credit to the other party for the same amount.

An income or expense item that affects both parties is apportioned, or prorated, to each party to reflect the proper amount that each owes or should receive. A prorated item is treated as a debit to one party and a credit to the other party for the same amount.

9.4 (b) at some time after the expense is incurred.

Items paid in arrears are paid after the expense has been incurred.

9.5 (d) A debit to the seller and credit to the buyer for $580.

For income the seller received in advance, the buyer receives a credit and the seller receives a debit. In effect, the seller has received some of the buyer's income, and the seller must pay this share to the buyer. Therefore the seller is debited and the buyer is credited the $580 the buyer is entitled to earn as the new owner.

9.6 (b) A debit to the seller and credit to the buyer for $43.

For an item the buyer will pay in arrears, the buyer receives a credit and the seller receives a debit. In effect, the seller has incurred some of the expenses that the buyer will be paying for after closing. Thus the seller must pay the buyer the used portion of the expense, or $43.

9.7 (b) $546.00.

The daily tax expense, first, is ($2,190 ÷ 365) or $6.00. Since the buyer will pay the taxes after closing, the seller will owe the buyer his or her portion of the tax bill, which is the 91 days from the beginning of the year through closing. Therefore, credit the buyer and debit the seller ($6.00 x 91), or $546.00.

9.8 (d) $191.67.

This method assumes all months are 30 days and the year is 360 days. The daily proration is therefore $375 ÷ 360, or $1.04. The closing occurs on the 184th day of the year. Thus, ($1.04 x 184) = $191.67. Note that if the day of closing is the buyer's, there would be 183 day's worth of prorated expense.

9.9 (d) $735.34.

Assuming a 365 day year, the daily tax expense is ($1,100 ÷ 365), or $3.013. As taxes are paid in arrears, the buyer will be paying the annual bill. Thus, he will be owed a credit for the seller's share of the bill, which is $3.013 x 244 days, or $735.34.

9.10 (a) $116.03.

The buyer's share is the unused portion, or (365 days – 244 days), or 121 days. The daily expense is ($350 ÷ 365), or $.9589. ($.9589 x 121) = $116.03. The seller receives this amount as a credit and the buyer a debit.

9.11 (a) $507.50.

If the buyer pays $525 interest for 30 days, the daily expense is ($525 ÷ 30), or $17.50. If there are 29 days of pre-paid expense, the buyer's charge is ($17.50 x 29), or $507.50.

9.12 (c) $1,775.

$88,750 x .02 = $1,775. Remember, one point = 1% of the loan amount.

9.13 (d) $11,250.

$187,500 x 6% = $187,500 x .06 = $11,250.

9.14 (d) the buyer must pay the expense.

Explicit agreements in the sale contract supercede traditional expense-payment responsibilities which can vary from state to state.

9.15 (a) the excess of the buyer's debits over the buyer's credits.
To determine how much money the buyer owes at closing, the buyer's debits are totaled and compared with the total of the buyer's credits. The excess of debits over credits is the amount the buyer must bring to the closing.

9.16 (d) negligence, error or omission in carrying out professional services.
A standard E&O policy provides coverage for "damages resulting from any negligent act, error or omission arising out of Professional Services." It does not cover dishonest or illegal acts, including environmental violations and mishandling of funds.

9.17 (a) Failing to inform and disclose properly.
Agency risks commonly concern the requirement to inform and disclose. Most states require agency relationships to be in writing and to be disclosed to all parties to a transaction. In states that do not use agency, there is still the obligation to explain and disclose the nature of the relationship.

9.18 (b) failing to disclose known adverse facts.
Depending on the state, the licensee may have no further duty to disclose property condition after properly informing parties of their rights and obligations. However, the licensee may still be subject to legal action for failing to disclose adverse facts the licensee knew about or should have known about.

9.19 (d) avoid creating a false impression that the licensee is a certified appraiser.
Misuse of such terms as "appraisal" and "value" could lead to a charge of misrepresenting oneself as an appraiser.

9.20 (b) exceeding the authority of the agreement.
Licensees must stay within the bounds of the authority granted by the agency agreement and avoid doing anything requiring permission without first getting that permission in writing.

9.21 (a) use a checklist of all items, contingencies, dates and responsibilities that must be met.
One way to reduce risk in the contracting process is to use a checklist that covers all the contract items, such as inclusions and exclusions, contingency periods, documents, forms, data checking, and milestone dates.

9.22 (d) the principals may make changes as long as they sign or initial each change.
Real estate professionals who are not attorneys are usually limited to filling in blanks or making deletions on a preprinted contract form prepared by a lawyer. While a licensee may make deletions, additions to a form should be drafted by an attorney. The principals themselves can make changes as long as each change is signed or initialed by all signers.

9.23 (b) obtain education in the content and intent of the laws.
The risk of violating fair housing laws can be minimized through ongoing education that addresses both the intent of the laws and their current content..

9.24 (a) being present at a conversation where the setting of commission rates is discussed.
Antitrust laws forbid brokers to band together to set a price on their services in listing and selling property. Even being overheard discussing commission rates or being present at such a conversation can lead to charges of *price fixing*.

9.25 (a) License discipline, fines, and possible incarceration.
Intentional misrepresentation, as a type of fraud, is a criminal act that may result in fines and incarceration, in addition to discipline from state regulators and professional organizations.

9.26 (c) stating that a client should seek legal counsel.
Unintentional misrepresentation occurs when a licensee *unknowingly* gives a consumer inaccurate information concerning a property, financing or agency service. Information that the licensee, as a professional, should have known to be false or inaccurate may be included in the definition. Telling a client that legal counsel would be advisable is not misrepresentation and, in fact, is often an important risk management technique.

9.27 (d) avoid speculative statements in all reports.
Progress reports should be accurate, timely, in writing, and free of speculation. Speculation may encourage the consumer to believe the agent has expertise that in fact is non-existent. If a consumer has a question about the meaning of something in an inspection report, the licensee should refer the consumer to the person who wrote the report rather than trying to explain it.

9.28 (b) It reduces the chance of presenting an offer from an unqualified buyer.
Using a lender to qualify the buyer protects the agent against leading a seller to believe a purchaser is fully qualified when this may not be the case. Also, lenders and loan agents are better able to look into the buyer's qualifications than a real estate licensee is. If it is necessary to show a property to a potential buyer who has not been qualified by a lender, the licensee can gain some protection by performing an informal qualification and documenting the fact that it was based on the information provided by the buyer.

9.29 (c) the agency relationship.
Maintaining the confidentiality of any information that would harm the client's interests or bargaining position or anything else the client wishes to keep secret, unless the law requires disclosure, is one of the primary duties of agency. The duty to maintain confidentiality generally survives the termination of a listing agreement into perpetuity.

9.30 (a) performing a comparative market analysis.
In preparing a Comparative Market Analysis, licensees should guard against using the terms "appraisal" and "value," which are reserved for the use of certified appraisers. Misuse of these terms could lead to a charge of misrepresenting oneself as an appraiser.

9.31 (d) make a substantial misrepresentation.
The license laws of most states list as illegal advertising activities subject to discipline such actions as making any substantial and intentional misrepresentation, making false promises, and making misleading or untruthful statements in any advertising.

9.32 (c) fiduciary
The management agreement creates an agency relationship between the manager and the principal. This is a fiduciary relationship and, in general, the agent is charged with producing the greatest possible net return on the owner's investment while safeguarding the value of the investment for the owner/investor.

9.33 (b) financial reporting to the principal.
Financial reporting to the principal is a fundamental responsibility of the property manager. Reports may be required monthly, quarterly, and annually. Required reports typically include operating budget, cash flow, profit and loss, and budget comparison statements.

9.34 (d) revenue from all sources minus losses from uncollected rents, vacancies, and evictions.
The total of scheduled rents plus revenues from such sources as vending services, storage charges, late fees, utilities, and contracts is the potential gross income. Subtracting losses caused by uncollected rents, vacancies and evictions gives effective gross income.

9.35 (a) cost per tenant prospect generated per lease.
The efficiency of marketing activities can be judged in terms of how many prospects per completed lease they generate. The lower the cost per prospect per lease, the more effective and efficient the program.

9.36 (b) raise rental rates.
Vacancy rates are directly related to demand and competitive supply in the market. If vacancy rates in the managed property are too high, the manager may have to lower rates or identify problems in the property or its management that are contributing to vacancy level. On the other hand, if the property's vacancy rate is significantly lower than market rates, the manager may conclude that higher rental rates are called for.

9.37 (b) Routine, preventive, and corrective
The foremost maintenance objective is generally to preserve the value of the physical asset for the owner over the long term. Three general types of maintenance are required to keep a property in serviceable condition: routine (day-to-day), preventive (scheduled), and corrective (repairs and replacements).

9.38 (a) ensure that disabled employees have the same level of access to facilities that all employees have.

Employers with at least fifteen employees must follow nondiscriminatory employment and hiring practices and make reasonable accommodations to enable disabled employees to perform essential functions of their jobs. Modifications to the physical components of the building may be necessary to provide the required access to tenants and their customers. Existing barriers must be removed when the removal is "readily achievable," that is, when cost is not prohibitive.

9.39 (a) replacement value.

The amount of coverage provided by certain types of policies may be based on whether the property is insured at depreciated value or current replacement value. Depreciated value is original value minus the loss in value over time. Current replacement value, which is more expensive, is the amount it would cost to rebuild or replace the property at current rates. Commercial policies include coinsurance clauses requiring the insured to bear a portion of the loss. Fire and hazard policies usually require the coverage to be in an amount equal to at least 80 percent of the replacement value.

9.40 (b) cash for the management firm's operating expenses.

Managers are responsible for proper handling of monies belonging to other parties (trust funds) that come into the manager's hands in the course of doing business. For property managers, such trust funds include rents collected from tenants, security deposits, and capital contributions from the property owner. Funds belonging to the management firm must not be commingled with those of the client

9.41 (c) General

Property managers are usually considered to be general agents empowered to perform some or all of the ongoing tasks and duties of operating the property, including the authority to enter into contracts.

9.42 (b) The tenant pays a fixed rent, and the landlord pays all operating expenses.

In a gross lease, the tenant pays an established, fixed rent, and the landlord pays all property operating expenses, such as taxes, insurance, utilities, and other services. This is the arrangement commonly used in residential leases. If the tenant pays some of the operating expenses, the lease is a form of net lease.

9.43 (d) the property manager does not have to maintain it.

The lease should set forth items that are excluded or included in the leased property. For instance, a residential lease may include built-in appliances such as dishwashers but exclude freestanding ones, such as refrigerators. At issue for the landlord is the cost of maintenance. If a refrigerator is not included, it does not have to be maintained by the property manager.

9.44 (b) deliver a habitable property.

The landlord (by way of the property manager), is expected to deliver a property that is habitable. This means keeping heating, plumbing, cooling, and electrical systems in good repair as well as maintaining serviceability of floors, stairways, railings, roofs, and windows.

9.45 (c) A tenant declares a landlord in default and vacates the leased premises.

A constructive eviction occurs when a tenant vacates the leased premises and declares the lease void, claiming that the landlord's actions have made the premises unfit for the purpose described in the lease. The tenant must prove that it was the landlord's actions that were responsible and may be able to recover damages.

9.46 (a) the competitive market for the property.

In preparing a management plan, a manager must consider the owner's objectives, including financial goals; the competitive market for the property, both local and regional, depending on the property type; and the features of the particular property. The plan will also include a budget and indications of what the manager intends to do with the property to meet the owner's objectives.

NATIONAL TEST 10: Real Estate Math

10.1 (a) $.023 / SF

5/6ths of an acre = (5 x 43,560 SF) / 6, or 36,300 SF. Her commission was (.06 x $28,000) x .50, or $840. $840 / 36,300 SF = $.023 / SF.

10.2 (b) $370,170

The land costs $.50 x 43,560 SF/ac. x 1.5 ac, or $32,670. The home will cost $135 / SF x 2,500, or $337,500. The total property will cost $370,170.

10.3 (a) 12%

The lot measures 43,560 / 4, or 10,890 SF. The tennis court will take up 9,600 SF, leaving 1,290 SF. This amount is 11.8% of the total lot area.

10.4 (c) 40

The total area available for lots is 11.2 acres (16 acres x 70% for houses), or 487,872 SF (11.2 x 43,560). Dividing this area by 12,000 SF / lot = 40.66. Thus he can have a 40-lot subdivision.

10.5 (a) 6

First, the requirement = 2(13'x 9') +2 (18'x 9') =558 SF. Each roll is 2'x 50', or 100 SF. Thus she will need 6 rolls.

10.6 (d) 1,376 SF

First figure the area to be mulched. If the home is 40 x 30, the flower area adds 8' to each side of the house. Thus the outside perimeter of the flowered area is (40+8+8) by (30+8+8), or 46' by 56'. The area of the flowered area is (46' x 56') minus the house area of 1,200 SF. This is 1,376 SF.

10.7 (b) 40 acres

First, remember that a section contains 640 acres. The area in question is a forth of a half of a half of the total section. So divide 640 by (4 x 2 x 2). 4 x 2 x 2 is 16 and 640/16= 40 acres.

10.8 (c) 10 acres

This key to this question is to recall that a section has 640 acres. Theresa's property only is a ¼ of a ¼ of a ¼ of the entire section. Multiply 4 x 4 x 4 which equals 64. Savannah owns 1/64 of the section. Divide 640 by 64 and you get the answer of 10 acres.

10.9 (a) $38,955

Their fixed rent is (1,800 SF x $1.40/SF) x 12 months, or $30,240. The percentage rent is ($41,500 x .0175) x 12, or $8,715. Total rent is ($30,240 + 8,715), or $38,955.

10.10 (a) 5.04%

First, convert to decimals: 2 2/3 % = 2.67%; 5 1/5% = 5.2%; 7 1/4% = 7.25%. Thus total appreciation = (2.67% + 5.2% + 7.25%), or 15.12%. Divide by 3 to derive the average: 15.12% / 3 = 5.04%

10.11 (c) 29 %.

Appreciation as a per cent can be estimated by (1) subtracting the estimated current market value from the price originally paid (239,000 - 185,000 = 54,000) and (2) dividing the result by the original price (54,000 / 185,000 = . 29 or 29%).

10.12 (c) 94%

To find the percent of listing price the offer is, divide the offer by the listing price. In this question the offer is $290,000 and the listing price is $308,000. $\dfrac{\$290,000}{\$308,000} = 94\%$

10.13 (a) $206,000.

Remember the formula V = I / R where V is value, I is annual income, and R is the cap rate. Variations of this are: R = I / V in solving for the cap rate, and I = V x R in solving for income. Here, first identify net income by subtracting out vacancy and expenses. Then divide by the capitalization rate. Thus, ($30,000 – 1,500 – 10,000) / 9% = $205,555, or $206,000 rounded.

10.14 (b) $375,000.
Value = Income / Cap rate. Thus, V= $30,000 / .08 = $375,000.

10.15 (b) $13,600.
First derive the annual depreciation which is the cost divided by the economic life. Then multiply annual depreciation times the number of years to identify total depreciation. Remember to subtract depreciation from the original cost if the question asks for the ending value. Thus, ($16,000 / 20 years x 3 years) = $2,400 total depreciation. The ending value is $16,000 –2,400, or $13,600.

10.16 (a) $1,077
First, Lee's depreciable basis, without the land, is $280,000 x 75%, or $210,000. The annual depreciation for the entire home is ($210,000 / 39 years), or $5,384.61. Second, his office is 20% of the house (500 sf / 2,500 sf). Therefore Lee can take annual depreciation of ($5,384.61 x 20%), or $1,076.92.

10.17 (d) $188,000.
Cost Approach formula: Land + (Cost of Improvements + Capital Additions – Depreciation) = Value.
Thus you have $40,000 + ($175,000 - 27,000), or $188,000.

10.18 (c) $475,000
Use the same Cost Approach formula: Land + (Cost of Improvements + Capital Additions – Depreciation) = Value. The land is worth (100,000 x 125%), or $125,000. Remember, you cannot depreciate the land, only the cost of the improvements. Therefore, annual depreciation is ($400,000 / 40), or $10,000. Total depreciation is ($10,000 x 5 years), or $50,000. Thus the value is ($125,000 + 400,000 – 50,000), or $475,000.

10.19 (d) 125.
Use the formula: GRM = Price / Monthly Rent. Thus, $400,000 / $3,200 = 125.

10.20 (c) $194,000.
Use the formula: GIM = Price / Annual Income. To solve for price convert the formula to Price = GIM x Annual Income. Thus, ($1,100 x 12) equals $13,200 annual income. ($13,200 x 14.7 GIM) = $194,040, or $194,000 rounded.

10.21 (d) $750
The loan amount is $200,000 x .75, or $150,000. The first month interest equals ($150,000 x 6%) / 12 months, or $750.

10.22 (b) $179,000.
The equation for the loan amount is (annual interest divided by the interest rate) = loan amount. Thus, ($790 x 12) / .053 = $178,868 or $179,000 rounded.

10.23 (a) 4.82%.
The equation for the interest rate is (annual payment / loan amount) = interest rate. Thus ($1,000 x 12) / $249,000 = 4.82%.

10.24 (b) $1,456.95
In the first month they pay interest of ($280,000 x 6.25%) / 12, or $1,458. If their fixed payment is $1,724, they paid down the principal by $266 ($1,724 - 1,458). Now they must pay 6.25% interest on the new principal balance of $279,734. This equals (279,734 x .0625) / 12, or $1,456.95.

10.25 (b) The second option, by 150.
The first option's interest total is (6.5% x $60,000) x 5 years, or $19,500. The second option will charge (6.25% x $60,000) x 5 years, plus $600, or a total of $19,350. The 2nd option is $150 cheaper.

10.26 (b) 1.67 points
A discount point is one percent of the loan amount. Jose's loan is ($410,000 x 90%), or $369,000. If he paid $6,150, he paid 1.67% of the loan amount ($6,150 / 369,000), or 1.67 points.

10.27 (c) $4,875.
$325,000 x .015 = $4,875. Remember, one point = 1% of the loan amount.

10.28 (c) $162,500
Use the formula: Price x LTV Ratio = Loan. Then plug in the figures and calculate: Price x .80 = $130,000. Therefore, Price = $130,000 / .80 = $162,500.

10.29 (c) $379,259
First, the annual interest paid is $1,600 x 12, or $19,200. The interest rate is 6.75%. Using the formula (Loan = Interest / Rate), the loan amount is $19,200 / 6.75%, or $284,444. As this is 75% of the price, the price is ($284,444 / .75), or $379,259.

10.30 (b) $1,900.
Monthly income qualification is derived by multiplying monthly income by the income ratio. Thus (76,000 / 12) x .30 = $1,900. Remember to first derive the monthly income.

10.31 (a) $253,846
Total depreciation on this property = ($600,000 / 39 years) x 10 years, or $153,846. His adjusted basis is therefore ($680,000 original price – 153,846 depreciation taken), or $526,154. The gain is then ($780,000 – 526,154), or $253,846.

10.32 (b) $257,000.
Adjusted basis = beginning basis ($250,000) + capital improvements ($2,000 + $5,000) – depreciation (0) = adjusted basis ($257,000).

10.33 (c) $34,000.
Capital gain = amount realized (net sales proceeds, $265,000) - adjusted basis ($231,000) = ($34,000).

10.34 (d) $125,000.
The basic formula for adjusted basis is: Beginning Basis + Capital Improvements - Exclusions and Credits = Adjusted Basis. Debra's adjusted basis is therefore $120.000 + $5,000 = $125,000. The financing terms and subsequent selling price are not relevant.

10.35 (c) $15,000 overpriced.
Use the same formula V = I / R where V is the price and R is the rate of return. Then plug in the numbers to solve for V. The NOI of this property is ($60,000 - $22,000), or $38,000. The return is 11%. Therefore, the value to get this return must be $38,000 / .11, or $345,455. Since the price is $360,000, the price exceeds the amount needed for an 11% return by approximately $15,000 ($360,000 - $345,455 = $14,545).

10.36 (b) Yes, since he will yield 8.375%
Use the same formula R = I / V where V is the $2 million price, and R is the cap rate or rate of return. To identify income: (25,000 SF x $10/SF) = $250,000 gross income, minus 5% vacancy (.05 x $250,000), or $12,500, minus expenses of $70,000 = $167,500 net income. ($250,000 – 12,500 – 70,000) Now divide net income of $167,500 by $2,000,000 to derive the return of 8.375%.

10.37 (a) $1,680.
Annual gross operating income ($1,650 x 12 = $19,800) - annual operating expenses ($600 x 12 = $7,200) = annual net operating income ($12,600); annual net operating income ($12,600) - cost recovery expense ($7,000) = taxable income ($5,600); taxable income ($5,600) x tax rate (30%) = tax liability ($1,680).

10.38 (c) $10,640
The basic formula for tax liability is: Taxable Income x Tax Rate = Tax Liability. Taxable Income is Net Operating Income - Interest Expense - Cost Recovery Expense. Therefore, the annual tax is $150,000 (NOI) - $105,000 (Interest Expense) - $7,000 (Cost Recovery Expense) x 28% = $10,640. Note that the principal payment is not deductible in calculating taxable income.

10.39 (d) 31.4%
The formula for profit % is (profit / initial investment). The profit made was ($23,000 x 4) – 70,000 initial investment, or $22,000. Dividing this by the amount invested derives a profit percent of 31.4%.

269

10.40 (c) $1,000,000,000.
The mill rate = (tax requirement / the tax base). A mill is one one-thousandth of a dollar ($.001). To solve for the tax base, reconfigure this formula to be: Base = Tax Requirement / Mill Rate. Thus the Base = $10,000,000 / .010, or $1,000,000,000.

10.41 (a) $1,495
First, always use the assessed valuation, not the market value. Subtract out the homestead exemption to derive taxable value, or $140,000 – 25,000 = $115,000. As a shortcut to calculating the tax bill, simply add up all the mills, multiply them times .001 to convert mills to decimals, then multiply this number times the taxable value. Thus (7 + 3 + 2 + 1) x .001 x $115,000 = $1,495.

10.42 (b) 2.13%
The rate = budget / tax base. Thus, $8,000,000 / (400,000,000 – 25,000,000) = 2.13%

10.43 (d) $1,778.
First calculate the total commission, then the co-brokerage splits, then the agent-broker split. Thus: $127,000 x 7% = $8,890 total commission. ($8,890 x 50%) = $4,445 total listing broker share. ($4,445 x 40% = $1,778 agent's share.

10.44 (a) $6,866
Figure the total commission, then the co-brokerage splits, then the broker-agent splits. Thus, ($325,000 x 6.5%) = $21,125. ($21,125 x 50%) = $10,563. ($10,563 x .65) = $6,866.

10.45 (c) A credit to the buyer and debit to the seller for $785.34.
The daily tax expense, first, is ($3,150 / 365) or $8.63. Since the buyer will pay the taxes after closing, the seller must pay the buyer his or her portion of the tax bill at closing, which is the 91 days from the beginning of the year through closing. Therefore, credit the buyer and debit the seller ($8.63 x 91), or $785.34.

10.46 (a) $507.50.
If the buyer pays $525 interest for 30 days, the daily expense is ($525 / 30), or $17.50. If there are 29 days of pre-paid expense, the buyer's charge is ($17.50 x 29), or $507.50.

10.47 (d) Credit buyer $712.26.
For the monthly proration using the 365-day method, solve first for the daily rent amount: ($1,380 / 31), or $44.52. Since the landlord received the rent and owes the buyer portions of the rent, the buyer will be credited. The owed amount is for the 16th through the 31st, or 16 days, since the closing day belongs to the buyer. Therefore, credit the buyer and debit the seller ($44.52 x 16),or $712.26.

10.48 (d) $86,372
First calculate the transfer tax: ($322,600 / 500) = 645.2 units of $500. Round this up to 646, then multiply times $1.00 to get $646 transfer tax cost. Next figure the commission @ ($322,600 x .07), or $22,582. Next, the seller's real estate tax proration charge will be $2,000. Then, add up the expenses: ($646 transfer tax + 450 title + 550 attorney + 22,582 commission + 210,000 loan payoff + 2,000 tax proration) = $236,228. Subtracting this from the sale price = $86,372.

10.49 (d) $5,848.
Be careful here. Since the net price is $5,000, the taking price (TP) minus the commission must equal the net price. In other words, the net price is 90% of the taking price. Since TP x 90% = Net, TP = Net / 90%. So the taking price is $5,556 ($5,000 / .9). Apply the same logic to deriving the asking price: the taking price is 95% of the list price, therefore the list price = (taking price / 95%), or $5,848. Now work backwards to prove your answer: (5,848 x 95% margin x .90 net of commission) = $5,000

10.50 (d) $468,750
Use the formula: (Percent of insurable property value carried / 80% replacement cost) x claim = recovery, where the insurable property value variable excludes the land value and is valued at replacement cost. Here, the insurable portion of the property is ($740,000 - 25% land value), or $555,000. The Wildes are carrying insurance to cover 75% of the replacement cost of the entire property. Their recovery amount is therefore (75% / 80%) x $500,000, or $468,750.

10.51 (c) $140,000

Use the formula: (Percent of insurable property value carried / 80% replacement cost) x claim = recovery. Thus, (75% / 80% x $150,000) = $140,625. However, the face value of the policy is the maximum they can receive, which is $140,000

STATE TEST 11: Definitions; R.E. Commission; Licensing Regulation; Disciplinary Actions; Violations & Sanctions

11.1 (d) six members appointed by the Governor.
" There is created the Georgia Real Estate Commission, which shall be composed of six members, each of whom shall be appointed by the Governor and confirmed by the Senate for a term of five years" § 43-40-2 (a)

11.2 (c) five years and serve until a replacement is named.
" There is created the Georgia Real Estate Commission, which shall be composed of six members, each of whom shall be appointed by the Governor and confirmed by the Senate for a term of five years."
" Members of the commission shall serve until their successors are appointed and qualified. § 43-40-2 (a) and (b)

11.3 (a) Pass rules and regulations relating to the Real Estate Profession
The Commission does not set commissions or specify what is included in the brokerage agreement with affiliated licensees. "The commission is authorized to pass rules and regulations, not inconsistent with this chapter, relating to the professional conduct of licensees and the administration of this chapter." § 43-40-2 (e)

11.4 (c). If not completed within one year and licensee enrolled and paid for the course within one year, license is lapsed and licensee has an additional six months to comply.
"Any salesperson who has enrolled in any approved 25 instructional hour course within one year of the issuance of an original license, has paid all required fees for the course, and has not completed all in-class sessions, required exercises, or examinations for any reason may reinstate the license by completing the course within six months of the lapsing of the license;." § 43-40-8 (d)(1)

11.5 (b) The license will lapse.
"Failure to complete any of the educational requirements as provided in this Code section shall be grounds for denial of a license or denial of renewal of a license without further hearing." § 43-40-8 (g)

11.6 (c) A person who buys, sells, manages or exchanges real estate on behalf of others for compensation
" 'Broker' means any person who, for another, and who, for a fee, commission, or any other valuable consideration or with the intent or expectation of receiving the same from another:(A) Negotiates or attempts to negotiate, or assists in procuring prospects for the listing, sale, purchase, exchange, renting, lease, or option for any real estate or of the improvements thereon;..." § 43-40-1 (2)

11.7 (b) The qualifying broker must be a general partner of the partnership.
"The qualifying broker for a firm which operates as a partnership must be a partner."
§ 43-40-18 (e)

11.8 (c) on last day of her birth month, in the fourth year.
" (1) Whenever an individual applicant activates an original license, that applicant shall pay an activation fee and a renewal fee which shall cover all fees due the Commission until the applicant's month of birth in the fourth calendar year following the calendar year in which the license was activated." " (3) Renewals. Unless renewal fees are paid, all licenses issued under the provisions of paragraph (1) of this Rule will lapse: (a) in the case of the individual license, on the last day of the month of the birthday of the individual license." Rule 520-1-.05

11.9 (a) Wait ten years before reapplying for licensure
"...the commission may issue an associate broker's or a broker's license only if: (1) At least ten years have passed since the date that the applicant's occupational license was revoked or surrendered; (2) No criminal charges are pending against the applicant at the time of application; and(3) The applicant presents to the

commission satisfactory proof that the applicant now bears a good reputation for honesty, trustworthiness, integrity, and competence to transact the business of a licensee in such a manner as to safeguard the interest of the public." § 43-40-15 (h)

11.10 (a) is subject to license suspension, revocation, censure or reprimand by the Commission.
The Commission may not suspend a license without affording the licensee a hearing. License law violations are misdemeanors. The Commission may suspend, revoke, censure or otherwise reprimand the license of a licensee who is in violation of any of the provisions of license law. § 43-40-15

11.11 (a) not engage in any real estate activity requiring a license.
Licensees whose license has lapsed or who or on inactive status are prohibited to performing any real estate activity. Rule 520-1-.05, (4)(k)

11.12 (b) complete a renewal form regarding status of any trust accounts of broker or affiliated licensees.
When renewing a broker's license, a broker shall submit, along with the renewal application a summary of data on the broker's trust account(s) on a form prepared by or approved by the Commission or a report from a Certified Public Accountant. Rule 520-1.08(7)

11.13 (d) when the wall certificate of licensure is received by the broker.
" After making an original application for licensure to the Commission, a salesperson or a community association manager shall not commence work in real estate brokerage activities until the broker has received the licensee's wall certificate of licensure." Rule 520-1.05 (2) (b)

11.14 (a) issue a cease and desist order prohibiting a non-licensee from practicing without a license.
"Notwithstanding any other provisions of law to the contrary, the commission may issue a cease and desist order prohibiting any person from violating the provisions of this chapter by engaging in the practice of a real estate broker without a license." §43-40-30 (c)

11.15 (b) nine hours per year.
" In order to renew an active license, a licensee shall furnish to the Commission evidence of satisfactorily completing thirty-six (36) instructional hours of continuing education courses during the renewal period. The effective date of this requirement shall be July 1, 2015. Any licensee who renews an active license on or after this date must have completed thirty-six (36) hours of continuing education courses to renew." Rule 520-1-.05 (1)(d)

11.16 (b) $125 for all licensees.
https://www.grec.state.ga.us/renewinfo.html

11.17 (b) a licensee with a broker-type license who acts on behalf of the broker.
"Associate broker" means a person who acts on behalf of a real estate broker in performing any act authorized by this chapter to be performed by the broker." § 43-40-1(1)

11.18 (c) Auctioneer selling real estate
" It shall be unlawful for any licensed auctioneer to act in such capacity in the sale of real property unless such auctioneer shall also be licensed as a real estate broker, associate broker, or salesperson under Chapter 40 of this title; provided, however, that any auctioneer who was licensed as such by this state prior to July 1, 1978, and who, prior to December 31, 1984, submits proof to the commission that he or she has been auctioning real property for five years or more immediately prior to the date of application shall not be required to meet the provisions of this subsection but such person shall not thereby be construed to be a real estate broker, associate broker, or salesperson under Chapter 40 of this title." § 43-6-9(b)

11.19 (c) Performing community association management services if employed full-time by the association
"Except as otherwise provided, this chapter shall not apply to...Any person employed on a full-time basis by the owner of property for the purpose of providing property management services or community association management services, selling, buying, leasing, managing, auctioning, or otherwise dealing with such property;" § 43-40-29 (a)(8)

11.20 (d) Yes, if obtaining brokers' permission and if one of the brokers is in another state that permits affiliation in both states

Licensees cannot be licensed under more than one Georgia broker during the same period of time. The licensee may affiliate a license of another state with a broker in that state if that state's law allows it and the licensee has written permission of his Georgia broker with delineates duties that can be undertaken for each broker and indicating real estate activity in Georgia will be only on behalf of the Georgia broker. Rule 520-1-.05(2)(a)

11.21 (c) The licensee must complete an additional 27 hours of continuing education prior to renewal.

The 25-hour post license course will count as nine hours, leaving an additional 27 hours of continuing education required for renewal. https://www.grec.state.ga.us/grec/reconted.html

11.22 (a) Three months

" Any person who has taken the community association manager's examination and successfully passed the examination and any person who has taken the salesperson's examination and successfully passed the examination must make application for an active or inactive license within three months from the date of the examination taken, or after three months, must pay a fee equal to two times the original application fee." Rule 520-1-.04(5)(a)

11.23 (b) A company assisting individuals in exchanging property

" "Broker" means any person who, for another, and who, for a fee, commission, or any other valuable consideration or with the intent or expectation of receiving the same from another:(A) Negotiates or attempts to negotiate, or assists in procuring prospects for the listing, sale, purchase, exchange, renting, lease, or option for any real estate or of the improvements thereon;" § 43-40-1(2)(A)

11.24 (b) Having maintained an active license for the past five years

The broker applicant must have been actively licensed three of the past five years. "In order to qualify to become an applicant for a broker or associate broker's license, an individual shall…
have maintained a license in active status for at least three of the five years immediately preceding the filing of an application to become a broker;" §43-40-8(c)(4)

11.25 (a) Guaranteeing future profits on a property

"Licensees shall not engage in… guaranteeing or authorizing any person to guarantee future profits which may result from the resale of real property;" §43-40-25(b)(10)

11.26 (a) Failing to pay commission to a cooperating broker

Failing to pay a cooperating broker's commission and failing to pay commission to an affiliated licensee are actions that are not addressed in license law; therefore, they are not violations. Nonpayment could be addressed in court, but not through the Commission.

11.27 (b) A broker paying a commission to a broker in another state not licensed in Georgia for performing licensing activity in Georgia

The broker not licensed in Georgia would be practicing real estate in Georgia without a license. Listed under "Unfair Trade Practices": "Paying a commission or compensation to any person for performing the services of a real estate licensee who has not first secured the appropriate license under this chapter…." § 43-40-25(b)(17)

11.28 (a) including a specific expiration date in a listing agreement

Listings must contain a specific expiration date. Licensees may provide a price opinion but cannot provide appraisals unless also licensed as an appraiser. Inducing someone to break a current contract or agreement is a violation. Licensees must disclose their status as a licensee when buying or selling property. §43-42-25(b)

11.29 (c) A salesperson sharing a commission with another licensee affiliated with the same broker for assisting with a transaction.

Listed as an unfair practice is "Accepting a commission or other valuable consideration by a licensee from anyone other than the broker holding that licensee's license without the consent of that broker." § 43-40-25(b)(8)

11.30 (d) is exempt from licensure.
Brokerage activities (activities requiring a license) are listed in the definition of "broker". If the office manager performs none of the activities listed, she is exempt. § 43-40-1(2)(A-J)

11.31 (c) deposits earnest money into her personal account.
The Commission does not set interest rates. The broker can be the paid by a client or customer, and payment of compensation does not determine agency. "Each broker who accepts down payments, earnest money deposits, security deposits, rents, association fees, or other trust funds in a real estate brokerage transaction or whose affiliated licensees accept such trust funds shall maintain a separate, federally insured account at a financial institution in this state which shall be designated a trust or escrow account wherein all down payments, earnest money deposits, or other trust funds received by the broker or the broker's affiliated licensees, on behalf of a principal or any other person, shall be deposited." Rule 520-1-.08

11.32 (c) compensate individuals who have suffered financial loss due to licensees' violations of license law.
"The commission shall maintain a minimum balance of $1 million in the real estate education, research, and recovery fund from which any person, except bonding companies when they are not principals in a real estate transaction, aggrieved by an act, representation, transaction, or conduct of a licensee which is in violation of this chapter or of the rules and regulations of the commission…, may recover, by order of any court having competent jurisdiction, actual or compensatory damages…." § 43-40-22(b)

11.33 (a) They may complete information on contract forms as directed by a licensee.
"… the Commission has identified the following tasks that support personnel may perform:… type contract forms as directed by the firm or affiliated licensee of the firm." Unlicensed support personnel may not perform licensing activities. Rule 520-1-.07(e)

11.34 (b) They are illegal in Georgia.
"The Commission prohibits the acceptance by brokers of net brokerage engagements and hereby makes it obligatory upon the broker, when securing the brokerage engagement, to add the broker's fee thereby notifying the client of the gross price of the property and the broker's services." Rule 520-1-.06(1)(c)

11.35 (b) designated agents.
A broker may assign directly or through the adoption of a company policy different licensees affiliated with the broker as designated agents to exclusively represent different clients in the same transaction. § 10-6A-13(a)

11.36 (c) The Commission may on its own motion investigate a licensee.
"The commission may, upon its own motion, and shall, upon the sworn written request of any person, investigate the actions of any applicant for licensure, licensee, or real estate courses and instructors approved by the commission. § 43-40-27(a)

11.37 (c) A professional negotiator who assists clients in obtaining the best price for their properties
Listed in the definition of brokerage (licensing activities) is someone who "Negotiates or attempts to negotiate, or assists in procuring prospects for the listing, sale, purchase, exchange, renting, lease, or option for any real estate or of the improvements thereon;" § 43-40-1(2)(A)

11.38 (a) Disclosing in a timely manner to all parties in a real estate transaction any agency relationship that the licensee may have with any of the parties.
Failing to disclose in a timely manner would be a violation. § 43-40-25(b)(30)

11.39 (a) being at least 21 years old.
"In order to qualify to become an applicant for a community association manager's license, an individual shall have attained the age of 18 years;". The applicant must have a high school diploma or equivalent, complete a 25-hour course, and provide a criminal history report to the Commission. § 43-40-8(a)(1)

11.40 (d) If salesperson or community association manager applicant does not apply within three months of passing the licensing exam, the fee doubles.
"Any person who has taken the community association manager's examination and successfully passed the examination and any person who has taken the salesperson's examination and successfully passed the examination must make application for an active or inactive license within three months from the date of

the examination taken, or after three months, must pay a fee equal to two times the original application fee." Rule 520-1-.04(5)(a)

11.41 (b) when the fund pays on behalf of a licensee, the licensee has six months in which to repay the amount or the license will be revoked.

When the Commission pays from the fund any amount in settlement of a claim or toward satisfaction of a judgment against a licensee, the licensee's license is automatically revoked upon the issuance of a court order authorizing payment from the fund. Licensee is not eligible to receive a new license until licensee pays the amount in full, plus interest. Bankruptcy does not relieve the penalties. § 43-40-22(d)(6).

11.42 (b) three years.

"Except for investigations of applicants for licensure, investigations of allegations of fraudulent conduct or of mishandling of funds held in a fiduciary capacity, or investigations of possible violations of this chapter which have been litigated in the courts or arise from litigation in the courts, the commission shall not initiate an investigation on its own motion or investigate a licensee's activity as the result of a sworn written request for investigation unless the act or acts which may constitute a violation of this chapter occurred within three years of the initiation of the investigation." This is not to be confused with the two-year statute of limitations for an aggrieved party to collect from the Real Estate Education, Research, and Recovery Fund. § 43-40-7(a)

STATE TEST 12: Management Responsibilities; Trust Accounts; Advertising; Handling Transactions

12.1 (d) under no circumstances.

"When a licensee requests that a release form be signed, the releasing broker shall immediately sign the release and forward the wall certificate of licensure of the departing licensee to the Commission or notify the Commission in writing that the wall certificate of licensure has been forwarded to the new broker for whom the licensee will act." Further, "A dispute between licensees as to whether the terms of their agreement have been met shall not be grounds for the broker's refusal to sign a release and to forward the wall certificate of licensure to the Commission nor for either party to file a complaint with the Commission." Rule 520-1-.07(5)(b)

12.2 (c) all the parties in the transaction and any broker involved in the transaction.

"If any offer to purchase, sell, lease, or exchange is accepted and signed by all parties, copies of that document shall be properly distributed, one to each person signing the document and one to each brokerage firm involved in the transaction. Rule 520-1-.10(3)

12.3 (c) License number of each firm and licensee participating in the transaction

" A licensee preparing or signing a brokerage engagement or an offer to purchase, sell, lease, or exchange real property shall include the license number issued by the Commission of each firm and of each licensee participating in the transaction. The licensee shall include the six digit license number issued by the Commission." Rule 520-1-10(2)

12.4 (d) a complete record of transactions and funds handled during contract and not previously accounted for.

"Failure to deliver to a community association terminating a management contract within 30 days of the termination, or within such other time period as the management contract shall provide a complete and accurate record of all transactions and funds handled during the period of the contract and not previously accounted for;" § 43-40-25(b)(34)(A)

12.5 (c) inform the principal of the referral commission no later than closing of the transaction.

"In a transaction where a licensee refers a principal to another broker for brokerage or relocation services …, the payment of a commission, fee or other thing of value to the referring licensee by the broker working with the principal shall be disclosed in writing to the principal by the broker to whom the referral was made no later than at the closing…." Rule 520-1-.10(6)(b)

12.6 (b) within three business days.

"Failure of a licensee to deposit trust funds promptly where the deposit was made more than three business days after receipt unless the contract provides otherwise." 520-1-.14(3)(t). Fine is $600.00.

12.7 (d) Yes, if permission is granted by the listing broker and the ad discloses the property is listed with another company and the name of listing licensee
" ... a licensee advertising real estate that is listed with another firm shall clearly and conspicuously disclose that fact and the name of the listing firm unless the listing firm has expressly agreed in writing to waive those clear and conspicuous disclosures." Rule 520-1-.09(3)

12.8 (a) must retain records of this transaction for three years.
 "Failing to keep for a period of three years a true and correct copy of all sales contracts, closing statements, any offer or other document that resulted in the depositing of trust funds, accounting records related to the maintenance of any trust account required by this chapter, and other documents relating to real estate closings or transactions...." § 43-40-5(b)(27)

12.9 (a) 30 days
Brokers must notify the commission in writing within 30 days of the opening or closing of a designated trust account. § 43-40-12(m)(1).

12.10 (d) Patrick is guilty of illegally practicing law.
Licensees must advise clients to obtain expert advice as to material matters which are beyond the expertise of the licensee. License law specifically states that licensees may complete listing or sales contracts or leases whose form has been prepared by legal counsel and such conduct shall not constitute the unauthorized practice of law. § 43-40-25.1

12.11 (a) the principals approve of the account and agree in writing on who will receive the interest.
"If the broker elects to deposit any funds into an interest-bearing trust account, the broker shall obtain the written agreement of the parties indicating to whom the broker shall pay any interest earned on trust funds deposited into that interest-bearing checking account prior to depositing those funds into such an account." Rule 520-1-.08(1)(d)

12.12 (b) at the time of closing.
A broker must deliver to the seller a detailed closing statement in every real estate transaction, at the time said transaction is consummated. § 43-40-25

12.13 (d) if they handle the funds of others.
"Each broker who accepts down payments, earnest money deposits, security deposits, rents, association fees, or other trust funds in a real estate brokerage transaction or whose affiliated licensees accept such trust funds shall maintain a separate, federally insured account at a financial institution in this state...." § 43-40-20(a)

12.14 (c) Yes, if Jim's broker approves and provides the Commission with Jim's name and the bank account information
If the broker approves the affiliated licensee's holding a trust account owned by the licensee, the broker must assure that the bank designates the account as a trust account and notify the Commission of the name of the bank, account number, and the name of the licensee. § 43-40-20(h)

12.15 (a) obtaining a brokerage agreement knowing or having reason to believe that another broker has exclusive brokerage agreement, unless licensee has written permission from that broker.
Unfair trade practices include obtaining a brokerage agreement, a sales contract, or a lease from any owner, purchaser, or tenant while knowing or having reason to believe that another broker has an exclusive brokerage agreement with such owner, purchaser, or tenant, unless the licensee has written permission from the broker having the first exclusive brokerage agreement. § 43-40-25(b)(26)

12.16 (b) their employing/sponsoring broker.
Accepting a commission or other valuable consideration from anyone other than the broker holding that licensee's license is a violation. § 43-40-25(b)(8)

12.17 (b) Failing to notify the Commission within 30 days of an address change of the broker's place of business
"Should a broker change the address of the broker's place of business, the broker shall notify the

commission, in writing, within 30 days of such change." § 43-40-19(a)

12.18 (d) No, licensees must have written approval to advertise property.
"A licensee shall not advertise any real estate for sale, rent, lease, or exchange unless the licensee has first secured the written permission of the owner, the owner's authorized agent, or the owner of a leasehold estate." Rule 520-1.09(3)

12.19 (c) The broker's license number must be included in all ads.
The broker's license number is not required. The ad must identify the brokerage and the brokerage phone number, and all ads must be under the supervision of the broker. Outdated information must be removed within 30 days. An ad without the brokerage name is referred to as a "blind ad". Rule 520-1-.09

12.20 (b) misdemeanors.
"Any person acting as a real estate licensee within the meaning of this chapter without a license and any person who violates any other provision of this chapter shall be guilty of a misdemeanor." § 43-40-31

12.21 (a) No, the agreement must terminate at a specific time without prior notice by the seller.
Failure of a licensee to include a fixed date of expiration in a listing agreement or failure to leave a copy with the principal is a violation. Rule 520-1-.14(3)(z)

12.22 (c) An attorney
In Georgia, closings must be conducted by an attorney, per the Commission's Georgia Real Estate InfoBase Contents - Chapter 47, https://www.grec.state.ga.us/infobase/tableofcontents/chapter47.html .

12.23 (d) The Commission will examine brokers trust account during each renewal period, or accept a report of compliance or summary of data on the Commission's form.
The Commission may examine the broker's account at any time with reasonable cause. Nonresident brokers are permitted to maintain a trust count in their state of residence. The account must be federally insured. § 43-40-20 (a)&(c)&(g)

12.24 (d) Disclosing the client that the seller has AIDS
Not only does the federal Fair Housing Act prohibit disclosure, but Georgia law states that no cause of action shall arise against an owner, a real estate broker, or any affiliated licensee for the failure to disclose the fact or suspicion that a property is or was occupied by a person who was infected with a virus or any other disease which has been determined by medical evidence as being highly unlikely to be transmitted through the occupancy of a dwelling place. § 44-1-16(a)(1)(A)

12.25 (b) Yes, if both brokers agree in writing to details as specified in the law
If the brokers have a written agreement enumerating the transactions involved, stating that the form broker will assume responsibility for the licensee's actions in those transactions, and expressing terms under which the licensee will be compensated by the former broker. § 43-40-19(c)

12.26 (b) When the transaction has closed
In a sales transaction, if the transaction has closed or the date of closing specified in the sales agreement and any extensions of that date have passed, the broker may disburse the funds. Rule 520-1-.08(3)(d)(1)

12.27 (d) Assemble documents for closings
In order to provide reasonable guidelines for firms, licensees and support personnel, the Commission identified the certain tasks that support personnel may perform, including assembling documents for closings. Rule 520-1-.07(6)(e)

12.28 (c) may be either an independent contractor or employee.
Nothing in the Act establishes an employer-employee or broker-independent contractor relationship between licensees. Whether brokers and their affiliated licensees establish employer-employee or broker-independent contractor relationships is at the discretion of the licensees. § 43-40-30.1

12.29 (d) Brokers who do not collect, maintain, control, or disburse more than $60,000 at any time
"Any broker who provides community association management services and collects, maintains, controls, has access to, or disburses community association funds must be covered at all times under a fidelity bond

or fidelity insurance policy unless the broker at no time collects, maintains, controls, has access to, or disburses community association funds totaling more than $60,000.00." Rule 520-1-.06(3)

12.30 (c) failed to have the affiliated licensees enter into an employment agreement with the firm.
The broker must ensure that the firm and all licensed affiliates enter into a written agreement specifying the terms under which the licensee will be compensated how the licensee will be compensated for work begun but not completed prior to the termination of their affiliation. § 43-40-18(c)(9)

12.31 (d) a statement that the client must consent to dual agency.
There must be a statement indicating that the client is NOT required to consent to dual agency. § 10-6A-12

12.32 (d) Affiliated licensees who have trust accounts must provide their broker with a reconciliation statement at least quarterly.
On at least a quarterly basis a written reconciliation statement comparing the licensee's total trust liability with the reconciled bank balance of the licensee's trust account. Brokers may use electronic bookkeeping systems and may have more than one account. § 43-40-20(h)

12.33 (c) brokerage engagement.
"Brokerage engagement" means a written contract wherein the seller, buyer, landlord, or tenant becomes the client of the broker and promises to pay the broker a valuable consideration or agrees that the broker may receive a valuable consideration from another in consideration of the broker producing a seller, buyer, tenant, or landlord ready, able, and willing to sell, buy, or rent the property or performing other brokerage services." § 10-6A-3(4)

12.34 (c) licensee must request inactive status within 30 days of ceasing real estate activity.
"A reasonable fee, not to exceed the renewal fee charged broker licensees, may be imposed by the commission on a licensee who fails to notify the commission in writing within 30 days of a change of address, of the opening or closing of a designated trust account, of transferring to a new company, or of leaving a firm to go on inactive status;" § 43-40-12(m)(1)

12.35 (a) hold the license until the broker receives a transfer request from the new broker.
"When an affiliated licensee leaves a broker for whom such licensee is acting, the broker shall immediately cause the license of that licensee to be forwarded either to the commission or to the new broker for whom the licensee will act." § 43-40-19(b)

12.36 (b) the brokerage must secure a new qualifying broker within 60 days to continue licensure.
"Whenever the qualifying broker of a partnership, limited liability company, or corporation dies, resigns, or is discharged unexpectedly, the partnership, limited liability company, or corporation must secure a new qualifying broker within 60 days or cease all real estate brokerage activity until it does secure a new qualifying broker." Rule 520-1-07(3)(a)

12.37 (a) multiple listing service.
"Common source information companies" means any person, firm, or corporation that is a source, compiler, or supplier of information regarding real estate for sale or lease and other data and includes but is not limited to multiple listing services." § 10-6A-2(7)

12.38 (b) within three business days of acceptance of the offer.
Listed as a violation is "Failure of a licensee to deposit trust funds promptly where the deposit was made more than three business days after receipt unless the contract provides otherwise…." Fine of $600.00. Rule 520-1-.14

STATE TEST 13: Brokerage Relationships; Other Georgia-specific Laws

13.1 (d) To all parties, in a timely manner, but no later than when any party first makes an offer
A licensee must make or cause to be made a written disclosure to all parties revealing the party(ies) for whom the licensee's firm is acting and from whom the firm will receive compensation. The written disclosure must be made in a timely manner, but never later than when any party first makes an offer. Rule

13.2 (c) Discovering adverse material facts unknown to the licensee

Although licensees must disclose any known material facts, and licensees are prohibited from misleading consumers, they are not required to discover adverse material facts. "Nothing in this subsection shall be deemed to create any duty on the part of a broker to discover or seek to discover either adverse material facts pertaining to the physical condition of the property or existing adverse conditions in the immediate neighborhood." § 10-6A-5(b)(2)

13.3 (d) Undisclosed dual agency

"A broker may act as a dual agent only with the written consent of all clients. "§ 10-6A-12(a).

13.4 (d) Family status

Georgia law lists the seven same protected classes as those in the federal fair housing laws: race, color, religion, sex, handicap, family status, and national origin. Age, ancestry and marital status are not protected per Georgia law. Rule 520-1-.13

13.5 (b) disclosure of material facts.

Confidentiality, loyalty and obedience are owed only to clients. Disclosure of material facts is owed to all parties. § 10-6A.

13.6 (a) $563.90

"The real estate transfer tax is based upon the property's sale price at the rate of $1 for the first $1,000 or fractional part of $1,000 and at the rate of 10 cents for each additional $100 or fractional part of $100." https://dor.georgia.gov/real-estate-transfer-tax . $563,850 - $1,000 = $562,850 ÷ 100 = 5,628.5, rounded to $5,629 because .5 is a fractional part of $100. $5,629 x $.10 = $562.90; add $1 for the first $1,000 of sale price = $563.90.

13.7 (b) A transaction broker must disclose to buyers and tenants adverse material facts known to the broker pertaining to the property and neighborhood within one mile of the property.

Transaction brokers must disclose "All material facts pertaining to existing adverse physical conditions in the immediate neighborhood within one mile of the property which are actually known to the broker and which could not be discovered by the buyer upon a diligent inspection of the neighborhood or through the review of reasonably available governmental regulations, documents, records, maps, and statistics." Licensees are not held responsible for unknowingly providing false information if the licensee discloses the source of information. Buyers and tenants have a responsibility to inspect property for adverse conditions, regardless of whether represented by a licensee or not. § 10-6A-14(b)(3)(A)&(B)

13.8 (c) in a timely manner

A broker engaged by the seller must promote the best interests of the seller by, in addition to other duties, by "Timely presenting all offers to and from the seller, even when the property is subject to a contract of sale;" § 10-6A-5(a)(2)(B)

13.9 (c) a spouse's right to a year's support can supersede a will.

"The surviving spouse and minor children of a testate or intestate decedent are entitled to year's support in the form of property for their support and maintenance for the period of 12 months from the date of the decedent's death." § 53-3-1(c)

13.10 (a) Equitable right of redemption

Georgia does not recognize statutory right of redemption (after the sale) except for tax sales. Georgia does not recognize tenancy by the entirety or community property.
https://www.grec.state.ga.us/infobase/table%20of%20contents%20pdf/Chapter%2040.p
https://www.grec.state.ga.us/infobase/table%20of%20contents%20pdf/Chapter%2015.pdf

13.11 (a) 20 years with good title.

Period of time to establish adverse possession with good title is 20years; with color of title seven years. § 44-5-163&164

13.12 (a) BRRETA
§ 10-6A.

13.13 (d) Providing a buyer with information on properties for sale in the area
Negotiating, coaching or recommending a price are tasks that an agent performs. Providing a buyer with information on area properties is a ministerial act that can be performed for someone not represented by the licensee. § 10-6A-14

13.14 (b) A designated agent may share confidential information with his/her broker.
Disclosure of confidential information between a broker and any of the broker's affiliated licensees assisting the broker in representing the seller is not deemed to breach the duty of confidentiality. § 10-6A-5(a)(5)

13.15 (a) When the broker has obtained prior written consent of both parties
Broker must advise prospective clients of the types of agency relationship available through the broker prior to entering into brokerage engagement relationships. § 10-6A-10. Broker may act as a dual agent only with the written consent of all clients. § 10-6A-12.

13.16 (a) an agent appointed to represent either the buyer or seller in a transaction to the exclusion of other company licensees.
"Designated agent" means one or more licensees affiliated with a broker who are assigned by the broker to represent solely one client to the exclusion of all other clients in the same transaction and to the exclusion of all other licensees affiliated with the broker." § 10-6A-3(9)

13.17 (b) seven days following the execution of a contract.
The right of rescission when purchasing a timeshare is seven days following execution of the contract (Sundays and holidays excepted). § 44-3-174

13.18 (a) For written contracts not under seal, six years; if under seal, 20 years
§ 9-3-23&24

13.19 (c) Written notice of the broker
Written notice of the broker would not terminate the agency relationship, because the broker cannot unilaterally end the relationship. In addition to those listed in the question, a date of expiration agreed upon by the parties in the engagement or in an amendment to the engagement could also terminate the relationship. § 10-6A-9(a)

13.20 (b) All advertising must be under the direct supervision of the broker and in the name of the firm.
"All advertising by associate brokers, salespersons, and community association managers must be under the direct supervision of their broker and in the name of their firm." Rule 520-1-.09(2.1)

13.21 (c) The licensee must present all offers to and from the seller, even when the property is subject to a contract.
The seller's agent must promote the interests of the seller by "….timely presenting all offers to and from the seller, even when the property is subject to a contract of sale;" § 10-6A-5(a)(2)

13.22 (d) Disclosure of information between the broker and an affiliated licensee representing the client is not a breach of confidentiality.
"Disclosures between a broker and any of the broker's affiliated licensees assisting the broker in representing the seller shall not be deemed to breach the duty of confidentiality…." § 10-6A-5(a)(5)

13.23 (c) that the dual agent is prohibited from disclosing adverse material facts to either party in a dual agency relationship.
BRRETA clearly defines a duty of an agent, regardless who the agent is representing, is to disclose to all parties any adverse material facts of the property or the immediate neighborhood. § 10-6A

13.24 (c) the broker is not considered to have fiduciary relationship or owe fiduciary obligations to the client but is responsible for exercising reasonable care in discharge of duties.
"A broker who performs brokerage services for a client or customer shall owe the client or customer only

the duties and obligations set forth in this chapter, unless the parties expressly agree otherwise in a writing signed by the parties. A broker shall not be deemed to have a fiduciary relationship with any party or fiduciary obligations to any party but shall only be responsible for exercising reasonable care in the discharge of its specified duties as provided in this chapter and, in the case of a client, as specified in the brokerage engagement." § 10-6A-4(a)

13.25 (c) in a timely manner, but no later than when any party first makes an offer.
"A licensee shall make or cause to be made a written disclosure to both buyer and seller or to both lessor and lessee, as the case may be, revealing the party or parties for whom that licensee's firm is acting as agent or dual agent and from whom that licensee's firm will receive any valuable consideration for its efforts as agent in the transaction … The written disclosures required by this paragraph must be made in a timely manner, but in any event not later than the time that any party first makes an offer to purchase, to sell, to lease, or to exchange real property." Rule 520-1-.06(4)(b)

13.26 (d) Prospective tenants have an obligation to inspect and familiarize themselves with potentially adverse physical conditions of the property and neighborhood.
"Nothing in this subsection shall limit any obligation …of prospective tenants to inspect and to familiarize themselves with potentially adverse conditions in the physical condition of the property, any improvements located on the property, and the surrounding neighborhood." § 10-6A-6(b)(2)

13.27 (c) advising the client on legal issues and matters beyond the expertise of the broker.
For each client (buyer, seller, landlord, tenant), BRRETA states that the agent owes to that client to obtain expert advice in areas beyond the expertise of the broker. That would including accounting advice, legal advice, structural engineering advice, and any other area beyond the expertise of the licensee. § 10-6A-7(a)(d)

13.28 (b) are ministerial acts performed for a customer.
BRRETA lists among the ministerial duties that can be performed to a customer "Providing pre-printed real estate form contracts, leases, and related exhibits and addenda; acting as a scribe in the preparation of real estate form contracts, leases, and related exhibits and addenda;" Because they are ministerial acts, they do not create an agency relationship. These duties can also be performed by a designated agent for his/her client. § 10-6A-14(a)

13.29 (d) an attorney.
Closings must be conducted by an attorney. A broker performing a closing is considered the unauthorized practice of law.
https://www.grec.state.ga.us/infobase/tableofcontents/chapter47.html

13.30 (b) $601.50
The tax for recording the note is at the rate of $1.50 for each $500.00 or fractional part of the face amount of the note. The maximum amount of recording tax on any single note is $25,000. Failure to pay the tax will incur a 50 percent penalty of the tax amount and 1 percent interest per month from the time the tax was due. Solution: Mortgage amount of $200,250 ÷ 500 = 400.5. Round to 401 because .5 is a fractional part of 500. 401 x $1.50 = $601.50. https://dor.georgia.gov/intangible-recording-tax

13.31 (a) Seven days
Any covered contract shall be voidable by the buyer until at least seven days after the seller has furnished to the prospective buyer the documents specified in this subsection. The copy of any such document which must be executed in order to be effective shall be a copy of the executed document. § 44-3-111(b)

13.32 (c) a broker who provides assistance to consumers by performing ministerial acts.
"Transaction broker" means a broker who has not entered into a client relationship with any of the parties to a particular real estate transaction and who performs only ministerial acts on behalf of one or more of the parties, but who is paid valuable consideration by one or more parties to the transaction pursuant to a verbal or written agreement for performing brokerage services." § 10-6A-3(14)

13.33 (d) Obeying all lawful directions of the customer
Obeying all lawful directions is a duty owed to a client represented a licensee, not to a customer. Other duties listed in answers a, b and c are required by the transaction broker. § 10-6A-14(b)

13.34 (a) 60 days from the landlord or 30 days from the tenant.
"Tenancy at will notice required for termination is 60 days' notice from the landlord or 30 days' notice from the tenant is necessary to terminate a tenancy at will." § 44-7-7

13.35 (d) If the tenant refuses to sign the damages list, he/she should not list in writing the items to which the tenant dissents.
"Prior to tendering a security deposit, the tenant shall be presented with a comprehensive list of any existing damage to the premises, which list shall be for the tenant's permanent retention. The tenant shall have the right to inspect the premises to ascertain the accuracy of the list prior to taking occupancy. The landlord and the tenant shall sign the list and this shall be conclusive evidence of the accuracy of the list but shall not be conclusive as to latent defects. If the tenant refuses to sign the list, the tenant shall state specifically in writing the items on the list to which he dissents and shall sign such statement of dissent." § 44-7-33

13.36 (c) security deed.
A security deed is the most common form of securing a real estate financing instrument in Georgia, preferred by Lenders over mortgages because a mortgage creates only a lien on the property, but the security deed transfers title to the lender to secure the debt.
https://www.grec.state.ga.us/infobase/table%20of%20contents%20pdf/Chapter%2039.pdf

13.37 (b) Timely presentation of any offer, even if the subject property is under contract
" A broker engaged by a buyer shall …promote the interests of the buyer by…
timely presenting all offers to and from the buyer, even when the buyer is a party to a contract to purchase property;" § 10-6A-7(a)(2)(B)

13.38 (c) If the broker appoints designated agents, broker and brokerage will be deemed to be dual agents.
"If a broker appoints different designated agents in accordance with subsection (a) of this Code section, neither the broker, the broker's licensees, nor the real estate brokerage firm shall be deemed to be dual agents." § 10-6A-13(b)

13.39 (a) 40
§ 48-5-7.

13.40 (c) A relationship in which the broker acts on behalf of a client with the client's authority
""Agency" means every relationship in which a real estate broker acts for or represents another by the latter's express authority in a real property transaction;" Rule 520-1-.02(2)(a)

13.41 (c) Escrow agreement.
" "Brokerage engagement" means a written contract wherein the seller, buyer, landlord, or tenant becomes the client of the broker and promises to pay the broker a valuable consideration or agrees that the real estate broker may receive a valuable consideration from another in consideration of the broker's producing a seller, buyer, tenant, or landlord ready, able, and willing to sell, buy, or rent the property or in consideration of the broker's performing property management services or performing community association management services. Such contracts or agreements as an exclusive listing contract, an open listing contract, a buyer broker agreement, a property management agreement, a community association management agreement, and an exclusive tenant representation contract are examples of brokerage engagements;" Rule 520-1-.02(2)(d)

13.42 (b) their employing/sponsoring broker
Included in "Unfair Trade Practices" is "Accepting a commission or other valuable consideration by a licensee from anyone other than the broker holding that licensee's license without the consent of that broker;" § 43-40-25(b)(8)

13.43 (d) Retake the licensing exam but not the prelicense course.
Any licensee seeking to activate a license which has been on inactive status must have satisfactorily completed the continuing education requirements which would have been required if on active status or in lieu thereof, requalifying as an original applicant. This requirement does not apply to an inactive licensee who can furnish to the Commission evidence that he or she has met the continuing education requirement for each renewal period that his or her license has been on inactive status. Rule 520-1-.05(2)&(6)

13.44 (c) Imprisonment

" The commission shall have the full power to regulate the issuance of licenses, to revoke or suspend licenses issued under this chapter, and to censure licensees." § 43-40-14

13.45 (b) 25

"In order to qualify to become an applicant for a community association manager's license, an individual shall:...Furnish evidence of completion of at least 25 instructional hours in a community association manager's course of study approved by the commission;" § 43-40-8

13.46 (a) issuance of a cease and desist order and a fine of up to $1,000/day.

"... the commission may issue a cease and desist order prohibiting any person from violating the provisions of this chapter by engaging in the practice of a real estate broker without a license... The violation of any cease and desist order of the commission... shall subject the person violating the order to further proceedings before the commission, and the commission shall be authorized to impose a fine not to exceed $1,000.00 for each transaction constituting a violation of such order. Each day that a person practices in violation of this chapter shall constitute a separate violation." § 43-40-3.

13.47 (d) anyone.

"The commission may, upon its own motion, and shall, upon the sworn written request of any person, investigate the actions of any applicant for licensure, licensee, or real estate courses and instructors approved by the commission." § 43-40-27(a)

SAMPLE TEST: Georgia License Examination Sample Test

S 1. (b) Trade fixtures that are personal property.

Trade fixtures are items of a tenant's personal property that the tenant has temporarily affixed to a landlord's real property in order to conduct business. Trade fixtures may be detached and removed before or upon surrender of the leased premises. Should the tenant fail to remove a trade fixture, it may become the property of the landlord through accession. Thereafter, the fixture is considered real property.

S 2. (c) Severance and affixing.

Severance is the conversion of real property to personal property by detaching it from the real estate; affixing, or attachment, is the act of converting personal property to real property by attaching it to the real estate, such as by assembling a pile of bricks into a barbecue pit, or constructing a boat dock from wood planks.

S 3. (d) absolute fee simple estate.

The fee simple freehold estate is the highest form of ownership interest one can acquire in real estate. It includes the complete bundle of rights, and the tenancy is unlimited, with certain exceptions. The fee simple absolute estate is a perpetual estate that is not conditioned by stipulated or restricted uses.

S 4. (c) the estate may revert to a grantor or heirs if the prescribed use changes.

The defeasible fee estate is perpetual, provided the usage conforms to stated conditions. Essential characteristics are: the property must be used for a certain purpose or under certain conditions; and, if the use changes or if prohibited conditions are present, the estate reverts to the previous grantor of the estate.

S 5. (a) conventional life estate.

A conventional life estate is a freehold estate that is limited in duration to the life of the owner or other named person. Upon the death of the owner or other named individual, the estate passes to the original owner or another named party. A legal life estate is created by law as opposed to a property owner's choice.

S 6. (a) a condominium owner owns a unit of air space whereas the co-op owner owns a proprietary lease.

The owner of a condominium has a fee-simple ownership interest in his/her unit and its air space. Whereas, a co-op owner has a leasehold, not fee-simple, interest with the property's corporation. Since the corporation owns an undivided interest in the cooperative property, debts and financial obligations apply to the property as a whole, not to individual units as in a condominium.

S 7. (d) Trustor, trustee and beneficiary.
In an estate in trust, a fee owner-- the grantor or trustor-- transfers legal title to a fiduciary-- the trustee-- who holds and manages the estate for the benefit of another party, the beneficiary.

S 8. (c) fee simple ownership of the airspace in a unit and an undivided share of the entire property's common areas.
A condominium is a hybrid form of ownership of multi-unit residential or commercial properties. It combines ownership of a fee simple interest in the airspace within a unit with ownership of an undivided share, as a tenant in common, of the entire property's common elements, such as lobbies, swimming pools, and hallways.

S 9. (a) the date of recordation.
Among junior liens, date of recording determines priority. The rule is: the earlier the recording date of the lien, the higher its priority. For example, if a judgment lien is recorded against a property on Friday, and a mortgage lien is recorded on the following Tuesday, the judgment lien has priority and must be satisfied in a foreclosure ahead of the mortgage lien.

S 10. (b) A state in which a mortgagor retains title to the property when a mortgage lien is created.
In lien-theory states, laws give a lender on a mortgaged property equitable title rather than legal title. The mortgagor in a lien theory state retains legal title.

S 11. (b) transfers with the property.
The term appurtenant means "attaching to." An easement appurtenant attaches to the estate and transfers with it unless specifically stated otherwise in the transaction documents.

S 12. (c) Giving constructive notice of one's rights and interests in the property.
Recorded instruments may include deeds, mortgages, liens, easements, sale contracts, and marriage, probate and tax records. The primary purpose of recording and maintaining records of these instruments is to provide constructive notice of the conditions of a property's title-- who owns it, who maintains claims against it.

S 13. (c) A chronology of successive owners of record of a parcel of real estate.
Chain of title refers to the succession of owners of record dating back to the original grant of title from the state to a private party. It is thus more than a mere list; it is a chronological list as reflected in title records.

S 14. (c) Title insurance.
A title insurance policy indemnifies the policy holder against losses arising from defects in the title and is thus generally accepted as the best evidence of marketability after a Torrens certificate, which is not available in every jurisdiction. A signed deed is no evidence of marketability, only of an intent to convey title. An attorney's opinion and a title certificate, while forms of evidence of marketability, do not guarantee clear title or offer any protection against a defective title.

S 15. (c) percentage lease
A percentage lease allows the landlord to share in the income generated from the use of the property. A tenant pays percentage rent, or an amount of rent equal to a percentage of the tenant's periodic gross sales.

S 16. (d) net lease.
A net lease requires a tenant to pay for utilities, internal repairs, and a proportionate share of taxes, insurance, and operating expenses in addition to rent.

S 17. (b) The leased property is foreclosed.
A foreclosure extinguishes all prior interests in a property, including a leasehold.

S 18. (c) the construction conforms with applicable building codes.
Building inspectors inspect a new development or improvement for code compliance. If the work complies, the municipality or county issues a certificate of occupancy which officially clears the property for occupation and use.

S 19. (b) takes title subject to the same restriction.
Deed restrictions attach to the title of the property. Therefore, the restriction passes to the new buyer.

S 20. (a) She has the right to re-possess the property because the grantee has violated the condition.
A deed condition may restrict certain uses of a property, much like a deed restriction. However, violation of a deed condition gives the grantor the right to re-take possession of the property and file suit for legal title.

S 21. (a) To create a consistent, unchanging standard for identifying a property's unique location.
A legal description of real property is one which accurately locates and identifies the boundaries of the subject parcel to a degree acceptable by courts of law in the state where the property is located. The general criterion for a legal description is that it alone provides sufficient data for a surveyor to locate the parcel. A legal description identifies the property as unique and distinct from all other properties.

S 22. (b) They identify an enclosed area, beginning and ending at the same point.
The metes and bounds description always identifies an enclosed area by starting at an origination point, called point of beginning, or POB, and returning to the POB at the end of the description.

S 23. (a) is void.
By changing any of the terms of an offer, the offeree creates a counteroffer, and the original offer is void. At this point, the offeree becomes the offeror, and the new offeree gains the right of acceptance. If accepted, the counteroffer becomes a valid contract provided all other requirements are met.

S 24. (a) may be assigned.
A real estate contract that is not a personal contract for services can be assigned to another party unless the terms of the agreement specifically prohibit assignment. Listing agreements, for example, are not assignable, since they are personal service agreements between agent and principal. Sales contracts, however, are assignable, because they involve the purchase of real property rather than a personal service.

S 25. (c) A two-year lease.
A contract may be in writing or it may be an oral, or parol, contract. Certain oral contracts are valid and enforceable, others are not enforceable, even if valid. For example, most states require listing agreements, sales contracts, and leases exceeding one year to be in writing to be enforceable.

S 26. (b) a dual agent.
Dual agency occurs whenever a single broker represents both principal parties to a transaction. Here, since Bob and Sue work for Bill, Bill is the dual agent.

S 27. (a) upon first substantive communication.
The agent must provide written notice to all parties or their agents as soon as substantive communication occurs, which can include initial face-to-face contact.

S 28. (d) neither seller nor buyer.
In recent years, the brokerage industry has striven to clear up the question of who works for whom, and who owes fiduciary duties to whom. One solution allows a broker to represent no one in a transaction. That is, the broker acts as a transaction broker, or facilitator, and has no allegiance to buyer or seller.

S 29. (b) the principal has proposed an illegal act, which should not be obeyed.
An agent must comply with the client's directions and instructions, provided they are legal. If the directive is illegal, the agent must also immediately withdraw.

S 30. (b) negotiated with clients.
The amount of a broker's commission is whatever amount the client and broker have agreed to.

S 31. (b) the client may be liable for a commission and marketing expenses.
With an exclusive right-to-sell listing, if the property sells during the term of the revoked listing, the client is liable for the commission. If the property does not sell, the client is liable for the broker's actual costs.

S 32. (b) the agent has a claim to a commission if the owner sells or leases to a party within a certain time following the listing's expiration.

Many listings include a protection clause stating that, for a certain period after expiration, the owner is liable for the commission if the property sells to a party that the broker procured, unless the seller has since listed the property with another broker.

S 33. (c) the advertising must not be deceptive.

Advertising may not be misleading or deceptive in promoting the brokerage or listed properties. Blind ads are also prohibited without exception. Salespersons, moreover, must identify their employer.

S 34. (a) collusion.

Collusion is the illegal practice of two or more businesses joining forces or making joint decisions which have the effect of putting another business at a competitive disadvantage.

S 35. (b) The brokers have illegally fixed prices.

Price fixing is the practice of two or more brokers agreeing to charge certain commission rates or fees for their services, regardless of market conditions or competitors.

S 36. (a) The seller may cancel the contract, since it can be ruled invalid.

A contingency that is too broad, vague, or excessive in duration may invalidate the entire contract on the grounds of insufficiency of mutual agreement. To avoid problems, the statement of a contingency should be explicit and clear, have an expiration date, and expressly require diligence in the effort to fulfill the requirement.

S 37. (d) claim the deposit as compensated damages for the buyer's failure to perform.

If a buyer fails to perform under the terms of a sale contract, the breach entitles the seller to legal recourse for damages. The usual remedy is forfeiture of the buyer's deposit as liquidated damages, provided the deposit is not grossly in excess of the seller's actual damages.

S 38. (b) The optionor must perform if the optionee takes the option, but the optionee is under no obligation to do so.

An option-to-buy places the optionee under no obligation to purchase the property. However, the seller must perform under the terms of the contract if the buyer exercises the option. An option is thus a unilateral agreement. Exercise of the option creates a bilateral sale contract where both parties are bound to perform.

S 39. (b) a decline in demand for all types of real estate in the real estate market.

Businesses that support the departing company will lay off or fire new employees, causing some to leave town in search of work. Some of these businesses may also have to cease operations. Hence the demand for residential real estate, as well as for commercial and industrial, will decline, and new construction will probably also halt until some other factor increases demand again.

S 40. (b). rental prices in that market will rise

An undersupply of commercial properties in relation to demand will most likely increase prices, as renters have fewer choices and less bargaining power.

S 41. (b) absorption.

Absorption is the amount of available property that becomes occupied over a period of time, usually measured in square feet.

S 42. (b) $17,000.

First derive the annual depreciation, which is the cost divided by the economic life. Then multiply annual depreciation times the number of years to identify total depreciation. Remember to subtract depreciation from the original cost if the question asks for the ending value. Thus, ($20,000 ÷ 20 years x 3 years) = $3,000 total depreciation. The ending value is $20,000 – 3,000, or $17,000.

S 43. (b) Apartment buildings.

The income capitalization approach, or income approach, is used for income properties and sometimes for other properties in a rental market where the appraiser can find rental data. The approach is based on the principle of anticipation: the expected future income stream of a property underlies what an investor will pay for the property.

S 44. (c) estimates net income and applies a capitalization rate to it.
The steps are: estimate potential gross income; estimate effective gross income (potential minus vacancy and credit losses); estimate net operating income (effective minus total operating expenses); select a capitalization rate; and apply the capitalization rate. Use the formula: income ÷ cap rate = value.

S 45. (c) potential gross income minus vacancy and credit loss minus expenses.
Net operating income, or NOI, is always income after vacancy, credit loss and expenses. It does not, however, include debt service.

S 46. (b) $400,000.
Value = Income ÷ Cap rate. Thus, V= $40,000 ÷ .10 = $400,000.

S 47. (a) the interest rate may vary.
Adjustable rate mortgages (ARMs) allow the lender to change the interest rate at specified intervals and by a specified amount. Federal regulations place limits on incremental interest rate increases and on the total amount by which the rate may be increased over the loan term.

S 48. (b) A wraparound lender can profit when the interest rate of the wraparound exceeds that of the underlying mortgage.
In a wraparound loan arrangement, the seller receives a junior mortgage from the buyer, and uses the buyer's payments to make the payments on the original first mortgage. This potentially enables the seller to profit from any difference between a lower interest rate on the senior loan and a higher rate on the wraparound loan.

S 49. (b) a blanket mortgage loan.
A blanket mortgage is secured by more than one property, such as multiple parcels of real estate in a development.

S 50. (b) Payments are not sufficient to retire the loan.
Negative amortization causes the loan balance to increase over the term. This occurs if the borrower's periodic payment is insufficient to cover the interest owed for the period. The lender adds the amount of unpaid interest to the borrower's loan balance.

S 51. (b) the loan amount needs to be less than the property's value.
Lenders must have a margin of borrower equity to protect against falling real estate values which increase the risk of the loan. Without this margin, a lender can incur a loan loss in a foreclosure sale since the proceeds may be less than the loan amount.

S 52. (b) Truth-in-Lending laws
Truth-in-Lending Laws, implemented by the Federal Reserve's Regulation Z, regulate the disclosure of costs, the right to rescind the credit transaction, advertising credit offers, and penalties for non-compliance with the act.

S 53. (d) Participants sell mortgage-backed securities in order to buy pools of loans.
Secondary mortgage market organizations buy pools of mortgages from primary lenders and sell securities backed by these pooled mortgages to investors. By selling securities, the secondary market brings investor money into the mortgage market. By purchasing loans from primary lenders, the secondary market returns funds to the primary lenders, thereby enabling the primary lender to originate more mortgage loans.

S 54. (a) cost recovery expense.
Cash flow is the difference between the amount of actual cash flowing into the investment as revenue and out of the investment for expenses, debt service, and all other items. Cash flow concerns cash items only, and therefore excludes depreciation (cost recovery), which is not a cash expense.

S 55. (c) dividing net income by the price paid for the property.
The investment return measure known as return on investment (ROI) is calculated by dividing net income by the value of the investment. This yields a rate of return on investment.

S 56. (a) Installing a higher capacity air conditioning and purifying system.
Basis is increased by the cost of capital improvements made to the property. Examples of capital improvements are: putting on an addition, paving a driveway, replacing a roof, adding central air conditioning, and rewiring the home. Repairs, maintenance, and redecorating are not generally considered capital improvements.

S 57. (c) There are no federal ad valorem taxes on real property.
There are no federal taxes on real property. The Constitution of the United States specifically prohibits such taxes. The federal government does, however, tax income derived from real property and gains realized on the sale of real property.

S 58. (b) the assessed value of property.
General property taxes are levied on an ad valorem basis, meaning that they are based on the assessed value of the property. Assessed value is determined according to state law, usually by a county or township assessor or appraiser.

S 59. (d) The prohibition may be legal if performed correctly.
The condominium association may be exempt from fair housing prohibitions against age discrimination if it is established as a retirement community in which 80 % of the dwellings have one person who is 55 years of age or older and it has amenities for elderly residents.

S 60. (c) The agent and the owner.
The owner has illegally discriminated, and the agent, by going along with the owner, is equally guilty of violating fair housing laws.

S 61. (b) Inspection fees.
Prorated items are expenses that both parties must share. Non-prorated items are one-time individual charges such as sale commissions, recording fees, and title insurance.

S 62. (d) A lender paying a fee to a broker for referring a borrower to the lender.
RESPA prohibits the payment of fees as part of a real estate settlement when no services are actually rendered. This prohibition includes referral fees for such services as title searches, title insurance, mortgage loans, appraisals, credit reports, inspections, surveys, and legal services.

S 63. (b) Copies of required communications to principals.
Some communications with transaction parties are good and necessary for business. Others are required by law, and records of them must be maintained for a statutory period. Required records typically include listing agreements, offers, contracts, closing statements, agency agreements, disclosure documents, correspondence and other communication records, notes and any other relevant information.

S 64. (a) refuse to use terms that refer to or describe any of the classes of persons protected by the laws.
Before entering into a listing agreement, a licensee should explain that it is necessary to comply with fair housing laws and obtain the potential client's acknowledgment and agreement. The agent should make it clear that the agent will reject the use of terms indicating race, religion, creed, color, national origin, sex, handicap, age or familial status to describe prospective buyers. Such terms should be avoided in conversation as well as in advertising.

S 65. (a) Alterations to a rental space made to fit a particular tenant
Alterations made specifically for certain tenants are called build-outs or tenant improvements. The work may involve merely painting and re-carpeting a rental space, or erecting new walls and installing special electrical or other systems.

S 66. (c) maintain a special trust account in a qualified financial depository.
State laws and real estate commission rules specify how a property manager is to manage trust funds. In general, the agent is to maintain a separate bank account for these funds, with special accounting, in a qualified depository institution. The rules for how long an agent may hold trust funds before depositing them, and how the funds are to be disbursed, are spelled out. The fundamental requirements are that the owners of all funds must be identified, and there must be no commingling or conversion of client funds and agent funds.

S 67. (c) 3
The total area of the living room is (8' x 14' + 8' x 18' + 8' x 16' + 8' x 18') = 528 SF. They will therefore need 528 / 200 SF, or 3 whole gallons.

S 68. (d) 218'
Since the investor paid $100,000 total, and that equals $250 per frontage foot, there are 400 frontage feet (100,000 / 250). If the property is two acres, it totals 87,120 SF. Dividing this by 400 produces a lot depth of 217.8'.

S 69. (c) Yes with $360 left over.
The loan she can get amounts to ($240,000 x 80%), or $192,000. The points charge is ($192,000 x .02), or $3,840. Total closing costs are then $3,840 + 800, or $4640. Thus she has $360 to spare.

S 70. (c) $90,000
First, the sale price is 115% of the appraised value, so the appraised value is $230,000 / 115%, or $200,000. The lender will lend $140,000 (70% of appraised value), so the investor will have to come up with $90,000 ($230,000 – 140,000).

S 71. (c) $96,000.
Since the comparable has an extra half-bath, it is adjusted downward to equalize with the subject. Conversely, since it has no patio, the appraiser adds value to the comparable. Thus, $100,000 minus $5,000 plus $1,000 equals $96,000.

S 72. (c) $508
The total assessed value is ($84,550 + 235,000), or $319,550. The annual tax is based on ($319,550 / 100) = 3195.5 100's. Round up to 3196. To derive the annual tax, multiply 3,196 x 1.91, or $6,104.36. Divide this by 12 for the monthly escrow: ($6,104 / 12) = $508.

S 73. (d) $92,000
The formula for equity is (current value – indebtedness). The current value is ($180,000 + 25% x 180,000), or ($180,000 x 125%), or $225,000. The current debt is ($180,000 x 80%) - $11,000, or $133,000. Their equity is therefore $92,000.

S 74. (b) $166,150
Use the formula: Gain = (Net selling price – adjusted basis) where adjusted basis = (beginning cost – depreciation). The selling price is $240,000 x 5% annual appreciation x 10 years, or ($240,000 + 50% x 240,000), or $360,000. Since land cannot be depreciated, the depreciable basis is ($240,000 total cost – 60,000 land value), or $180,000 (land = 25% total value). Annual depreciation = ($180,000 / 39 years), or $4,615. Thus total depreciation is ($4,615 x 10 years), or $46,150. The adjusted basis is therefore ($240,000 – 46,150), or $193,850. The total gain is therefore ($360,000 – 193,850), or $166,150.

S 75. (c) $80,000
Applying the formula (percent of insurable property value carried / 80% replacement cost) x claim = recovery), divide the amount of coverage carried ($160,000) by 80% of the insurable property value ($250,000) to get the percent of the claim the company will pay (80%). Multiply this percentage by the claim amount to get $80,000, what the company will pay.

S 76. (b) Indicating that a property is not available for sale or rent when it is available
Refusing to rent or sell to someone who does not qualify financially or rent to someone who is a threat to other tenants is not a violation. Also, fair housing laws state that licensees should market the features of the property to avoid fair housing violations. "No licensee or employee or agent of any licensee shall represent to a person that any housing accommodation is not available for inspection, sale, purchase, rental, or lease when in fact it is so available, or to refuse to permit a person to inspect any housing accommodations, because of such person's race, color, religion, sex, handicap, familial status, or national origin." Rule 520-1-.13(2)(e)

S 77. (b) A licensee discovering a client has used misleading advertising must immediately take steps to stop the advertising until in compliance.

"Whenever a licensee becomes aware that a principal with whom the licensee's firm has a brokerage engagement is advertising to sell, buy, rent, lease, or exchange real estate in such a manner that is inconsistent with this rule, the licensee must immediately take steps to stop the advertising until it complies with this rule." Rule 520-1-.09(2)

S 78. (c) 10 days

Owners must abide by many of the fair housing laws, with few exemptions. Any discriminatory ad is illegal whether property is listed or not. Licensees cannot be disciplined by the Commission without being afforded a hearing. The brokerage name must be in all ads. Listed as a violation is " (11) Placing a sign on any property offering it for sale or rent without the written consent of the owner or the owner's authorized agent and failing to remove such sign within ten days after the expiration of listing;" § 43-40-25(b)(11)

S 79. (a) Transfer tax is based on the sale price, and the intangible recording tax is based on the loan amount.

Transfer tax is paid at closing; the intangible recording tax is paid during the loan process and is usually charged to the buyer. Real estate taxes must be paid prior to recording the transaction documents. https://dor.georgia.gov/real-estate-transfer-tax; https://dor.georgia.gov/intangible-recording-tax

S 80. (d) An individual actively licensed with one firm may not work as support personnel for a different firm.

The brokerage firm and the affiliated licensee must have agreements with support personnel. Unlicensed personnel are prohibited from performing any licensing activity. "An individual actively licensed with one firm may work as support personnel for a different firm or for a licensee(s) of a different firm with the written consent of the broker of each firm. An individual whose license is on inactive status may work as support personnel for a firm or any affiliated licensee." § Rule 520-1-.07(6)(c)

S 81. (b) Review all client contracts within 30 days for compliance with rules and regulations

Affiliated licensees may be independent contractors or employees. Designated agency is an option available to brokerages. The Commission does not dictate what is included in the broker-licensee agreement. "Reviewing for compliance with this chapter and its rules and regulations all listing contracts, leases, sales contracts, management agreements, and offers to buy, sell, lease, or exchange real property secured or negotiated by the firm's associates. This review shall take place within 30 days of the date of the offer or contract;" § 43-40-18(c)(3)

S 82. (c) deposit the earnest money into his personal account.

Because John is a principal in the transaction, he does not represent the seller. He is required to disclose that he is a licensee and include that disclosure in the purchase contract. He is also required to advise his broker in writing that he is purchasing the property. "Failure of a licensee to deposit into a trust account trust funds received in connection with a transaction in which a licensee is a principal" is a violation. Rule 520-1-.14(3)(y)

S 83. (d) must disclose environmental issues of which they are aware.

Environmental issues of which the licensee is aware must be disclosed, but the licensee has no duty to discover potential environmental issues. "All adverse material facts pertaining to the physical condition of the property and improvements located on such property including but not limited to material defects in the property, environmental contamination, and facts required by statute or regulation to be disclosed which are actually known by the broker which could not be discovered by a reasonably diligent inspection of the property by the buyer." § 10-6A-5

S 84. (a) A broker engaged by a client does not violate the brokerage engagement by providing assistance to the other party in the transaction by performing ministerial acts.

Ministerial acts are not licensing activity and may be performed by support personnel or by licensees. They are not tasks that require an agency relationship. A broker engaged by any client may perform ministerial acts for the other party in the transaction. § 10-6A-5

S 85. (c) Jane must obtain Donna's written permission for the referral and disclose the fact that Jane will receive a referral fee.
Broker may refer potential buyers or sellers to brokers in another state. Brokers are not required to disclose the amount of the referral fee. "Failing to obtain a person's written agreement to refer that person to another licensed broker for brokerage or relocation services and to inform such person being referred whether or not the licensee will receive a valuable consideration for such referral" is a violation. § 43-40-25(b)(36)

S 86. (c) An auctioneer selling real estate
Administrators, executors, and attorney-in fact under a power of attorney legally represent another person and can perform real estate activities on behalf of the person(s) they represent. Listed as a licensing activity under the definition of broker is "Auctions or offers or attempts or agrees to auction real estate". § 43-40-1(2)(f)

S 87. (d) had reasonable procedures in place for supervising affiliates' actions and did not participate in or ratify the violation.
"A real estate broker or qualifying broker shall be held responsible for any licensee whose license is affiliated with such broker's firm should such licensee violate any of the provisions of this chapter and its attendant rules and regulations unless the broker is able to demonstrate that such broker: (1) Had reasonable procedures in place for supervising the affiliate's actions; (2) Did not participate in the violation; and (3) Did not ratify the violation." § 43-40-18(b)

S 88. (d) A homicide or suicide on the property, if asked by a potential buyer
There is no cause of action for failure to disclose the property was the site of a homicide, other felony, suicide or death by accidental or natural causes; however, an owner, real estate broker, or affiliated licensee of the broker must answer truthfully if asked. § 44-1-16(a)(1)(A)&(B)

S 89. (b) Representing or attempting to represent a broker, other than broker holding license, without knowledge and consent of broker holding license
Listed as an unfair trade practice is "Representing or attempting to represent a real estate broker, other than the broker holding the licensee's license, without the express knowledge and consent of the broker holding the licensee's license." § 43-40-25(b)(7)

S 90. (a) requesting judicial review in the county of the Commission's domicile.
"Any person who has exhausted all administrative remedies available within this chapter and who is aggrieved by a final decision in a contested case is entitled to judicial review …. Notwithstanding any provision of subsection (b) of Code Section 50-13-19 to the contrary, initial judicial review of a final decision of the commission shall be available solely in the superior court of the county of domicile of the commission." § 43-40-26(c)

S 91. (b) acts on behalf of and performs brokerage activity on behalf of the broker.
"Associate broker" means a person who acts on behalf of a real estate broker in performing any act authorized by this chapter to be performed by the broker." § 43-40-1(1)

S 92. (d) under no circumstances.
Commission disputes between brokers or between brokers and associated licensees are not covered in license law. Commission disputes may be taken to court.

S 93. (d) revoking a license.
Citations are an option the Commission may use for minor infractions. The Commission may "issue a citation to the licensee in lieu of initiating the process for the imposition of sanctions. A citation issued by the Commission may include an order to complete a course of study in real estate brokerage or instruction; to file periodic reports by an independent accountant on a real estate broker's designated trust account; and/or to pay a fine not to exceed $1,000.00 for each violation, with fines for multiple violations limited to $5,000.00 in any one citation." Rule 520-1-.14(1)

S 94. (a) two
"No action for a judgment which subsequently results in an order for collection from the real estate education, research, and recovery fund shall be started later than two years from the accrual of the cause of

action thereon." However, the Commission may investigate for three years, or longer for certain alleged violations.

S 95. (c) If the tenant does not give up possession as required in the lease, a dispossessory affidavit can be filed in court.

Tenants' right to the security deposit and the landlord's duty to make repairs may not be waived. A tenancy at will requires 60 days' notice from the landlord, or 30 days' notice from the tenant. § 44-7-50, § 44-7-7, https://www.grec.state.ga.us/infobase/tableofcontents/chapter29.html

S 96. (b) title theory state

Georgia is a title theory state because the lender (mortgagee) holds title until the loan is paid in full. The borrower (mortgagor) retains equitable title.

S 97. (c) limited warranty deed

https://www.grec.state.ga.us/infobase/table%20of%20contents%20pdf/Chapter%2016.pdf

S 98. (b) Covenant of further assurance

https://www.grec.state.ga.us/infobase/table%20of%20contents%20pdf/Chapter%2016.pdf .

S 99. (a) 50 years

 https://www.grec.state.ga.us/infobase/table%20of%20contents%20pdf/Chapter%2016.pdf

S 100. (c)   State Certified General Appraiser

https://www.grec.state.ga.us/greab/types.html

Appendix: Real Estate Licensing-Related Websites

Georgia Real Estate Candidate Handbook
This contains crucial information regarding the AMP/PSI Georgia Real Estate Exam. Make sure to download and read this participant booklet to fully understand the entire test taking process.
https://documents.goamp.com/Publications/candidateHandbooks/GAREP-handbook.pdf

<u>Key Georgia Contacts</u>

Georgia Real Estate Commission
229 Peachtree Street, N.E.
International Tower, Suite 1000
Atlanta, Georgia 30303
404-656-3916
grecmail@grec.state.ga.us
http://www.grec.state.ga.us/

AMP Testing Service
(Applied Measurement Professionals, Inc.)
Note: AMP has been acquired by PSI
18000 W. 105th Street
Olathe, KS 66061-7543
800-345-6559
info-amp@goamp.com
www.goamp.com

Georgia Association of REALTORS®
3200 Presidential Dr.
Atlanta, GA 30340
770-451-1831
http://www.garealtor.com/

Atlanta Association of REALTORS®
5784 Lake Forrest Dr. NW
Atlanta, GA 30328
404.250.0051
realtors@abr.org
http://www.abr.org/

If you liked Georgia Real Estate License Exam Prep, check out the other titles of Performance Programs Company!

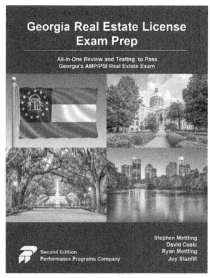

Cramming for your real estate exam? You need Georgia Real Estate License Exam Prep!

Where can you buy Georgia Real Estate License Exam Prep?
Georgia Real Estate License Exam Prep (GA-RELEP) is available as a printed book or e-book through nearly all online retailers.

Looking for a real estate principles textbook? Get what all the students love -- Principles of Real Estate Practice in Georgia!

Principles of Real Estate Practice in Georgia is invaluable reference material for Georgia real estate professionals. Its 580-pages contain the essentials of real estate law, principles, and practices taught in real estate schools and colleges across Georgia.

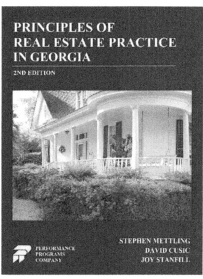

Where can you buy Principles of Real Estate Practice in Georgia?
Principles Real Estate Practice in Georgia is available as a printed book or e-book through nearly all online retailers.

Struggling with real estate math? The solution to that equation is Real Estate Math Express!

Real Estate Math Express is a concise, easy-to-study test preparation guide to help real estate students improve their real estate math scores to pass the state licensing test. The primary feature of Real Estate Math Express is that it contains all necessary formulas and practice questions in 70+ pages.

Where can you buy Real Estate Math Express?
Real Estate Math Express is available as a printed book or e-book through nearly all online retailers.

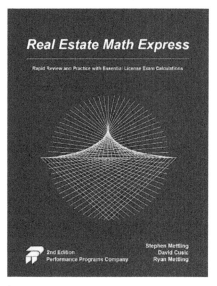

Publisher Contact
Ryan Mettling
Performance Programs Company
502 S. Fremont Ave., Ste. 724,Tampa, FL 33606
ryan@performanceprogramscompany.com
www.performanceprogramscompany.com

294